Thomas Cadell

Of the origin and progress of language

Volume 6

Thomas Cadell

Of the origin and progress of language
Volume 6

ISBN/EAN: 9783742844880

Manufactured in Europe, USA, Canada, Australia, Japa

Cover: Foto ©Andreas Hilbeck / pixelio.de

Manufactured and distributed by brebook publishing software (www.brebook.com)

Thomas Cadell

Of the origin and progress of language

OF THE
ORIGIN AND PROGRESS
OF
LANGUAGE.

*Graiis ingenium, Graiis dedit ore rotundo
Musa loqui, præter laudem nullius avaris.*
                                    HORAT.

VOL. VI.

EDINBURGH:

PRINTED FOR BELL & BRADFUTE, EDINBURGH.

AND

T. CADELL, IN THE STRAND, LONDON.

M DCC XCII.

CONTENTS.

BOOK I.

Of the Matter and Subject of Rhetoric.

         Pag.

Introduction,   - -   1

Ch.
1. *The common definition of Rhetoric not compleat.—What is wanting to it, added.—Observations upon the nature and use of rhetoric.—Of absolute necessity in popular governments—may be*

Ch. Page

either abused, or used to good purposes, like other arts, - - 7

2. *Of the importance of Rhetoric—it persuades not by words only, but by arguments.—These arguments of three kinds, viz. arguments from the person of the speaker, from the persons to whom he speaks, and, lastly, from the subject itself.—This last kind admits of a subdivision; for the arguments may be only applicable to that subject, or they may be applicable to many others.—These of the dialectical kind, and may prove both ways.—Of the division of Rhetoric, according to its subject, into the Deliberative, Judicial, and Epideitic,* - - 21

3. *Of Rhetorical arguments taken from the subject itself.—Difference in this respect betwixt Rhetoric and Science.—In what respects Rhetoric is different from Sophistry—different also from other arts, in this respect, that*

the *subject* of other art is limited.—The *subject* of Rhetoric, things that every body is supposed to know more or less.—Rhetorical arguments all general, and applicable to many different cases.—Rhetoric applicable to arts and sciences; but they must be treated in a Rhetorical manner.—The wonderful extent of the Dialectic art.—No man, but one of so great genius and learning as Aristotle, could think of reducing it to rule and method.—Some other things, he had studied, prepared him for such a work—particularly what he has written upon Rhetoric.—Difference betwixt Rhetoric and Dialectic.—General division by Aristotle into four heads—This a most comprehensive division, including all the topics of argument upon every subject.—Some instances of the topics, as arranged under these several heads.—The invention of the art of Dialectic does more honour to the genius of Aristotle, being intirely his own, than

Ch.	Pag.

any other of his works.—The philosopher and grammarian may both find matter of instruction in this work.—Cicero's judgment of the stile of it.—Of Alexander Aprodisienses's commentary upon the Dialectic of Aristotle—The greatest use of this work is to correct the text of Aristotle—It is a wonder that there are not many more errors in Aristotle's text, considering how providentially his works were perserved—If they had not been preserved, we should have had no complete system of philosophy, such as is to be found in Aristotle's writings.—Of Cicero's topics—addressed to Trebatius the lawyer—illustrated by examples from the law.—Cicero's skill in the law.—The ignorance, not only of Trebatius, but of almost all the philosophers of that age, in the philosophy of Aristotle. — That philosophy would have been lost, if it had not been preserved in the Alexandrian school. 30

| Ch. | Pag. |

4. *All the arguments belonging to the subject are taken from the Dialectic art; and the Topics from which they are to be deduced are to be found there.—Those arguments are only in the cause.—The others from the person of the speaker or hearer out of the cause.—Yet these only insisted on by the writers on rhetoric before Aristotle.—The arguments from the subject are all Enthymemas, that is, imperfect syllogisms.—All reasoning of every kind reducible to syllogism.—The Enthymema called a Dialectical Syllogism, but used in all kinds of reasoning.—The complete syllogism very seldom used by any writer;—but thrice by Aristotle.—No inference from thence of the inutility of the doctrine of the syllogism.—Aristotle's observation concerning the invention of Dialectic and Rhetoric, applies to all arts,—and likewise to all sciences,* - - - 58

Ch.	Pag.

5. *Of the arguments taken from the persons of the speaker or hearers.—In all causes that are argued of every kind, the hearers must judge or form an opinion.—That must depend, in a great measure, upon what they think of the speaker, and upon their own affections and passions.—The judgment they form of the speaker, reducible to three heads.—What influences the minds of the hearers is of four kinds, their passions, their habits, their ages, and their fortune.—Of the passions, and particularly of Anger.—Of the appeasing of Anger.—Of Love—Hatred—Fear—Shame—Want of shame—Gratitude—Pity—Indignation—Envy—Emulation.—What Aristotle has written here upon the passions the most valuable thing of the kind to be found.—He quotes Homer very much to the purpose upon this subject.—In this Rhetorical work he shows not only the greatest knowledge of human nature, but of*

| Ch. | Pag. |

the world, and the affairs of life, much more than could be expected from a man so much engaged in philosophy.—Of sententious sayings and Enthymemas with respect to the passions. - - - 64

6. Of the division of Rhetoric into Deliberative, Judicial, and Epideictic. —This division was first made by Aristotle, and arises from the nature of speech, in which there must be a speaker, hearer, and subject.—Aristotle first made a science of Rhetoric, as well as of other things.—The subject of the three kinds of Rhetoric explained.—A threefold division of Rhetoric, taken from the end which it proposes.—Rhetoric addressed not only to many, but to one:—Therefore of universal use in human life.—Of the subjects of which deliberative Rhetoric treats, and the things necessary to be known by an orator of that kind.—Under the head of Deli-

berative Eloquence, he treats of happiness, which is the end of all deliberation.—Every advantage of mind or body to be wished for, there enumerated.—Of the idea of good, without which there can be no happiness.—That belongs to the intellectual part of our mind.—The subject of the Epideictic is the το καλον.—Two definitions of that given;—but they are only popular descriptions.—Under that head, and in the chapter upon Happiness, every thing is enumerated that is beautiful and praise-worthy in human life.—Of the Judicial kind of Rhetoric.—The subject of it Injury and Injustice.—Here every thing that is bad in human nature is set before us.—His threefold division upon the subject of Injury and Injustice.—This division most accurate and complete.—Of the motives to Injury.—What is pleasant is the chief motive.—Definition of Pleasure.—Of the pleasures of sense.—Imagination a

Ch.		Pag.
	weaker kind of sense.—It makes things both past and future give us pleasure, as if they were present;—even things disagreeable that are past.—The pleasure in grief and hope accounted for in that way.—Selflove, and the pleasure we take in ourselves, in that way accounted for.—The second thing to be considered with regard to Injury, is the character and dispositions of the person who injures.—Here a complete character of a villain is given.—The third and last thing belonging to Injury is an account of the persons most liable to be injured.—And thus is completed his account both of the villain and of villainy.—Conclusion of this book, and of what is to be said upon the matter *of Rhetoric.*	73

BOOK II.

Of the *Stile* of Rhetoric.

Ch. Pag.
1. *The ornaments of Stile necessary for an orator who speaks to the people.—If the audience are wise men, they will mind nothing but the matter; and all they will require, will be to understand the matter.—The Stile of the orators at first poetical;—but this corrected in later times.*—Stile consists of words and the composition of words.—*The last of these most difficult.—This illustrated from other arts.—Words divided into* proper *and* tropical.—*The proper signification must be well understood, otherwise we cannot know whether it be properly transferred to another signification.—*

Ch.		Pag.

Of proper words—there should be a variety of them, signifying the same thing;—but not too great a variety, as in Arabic.—Of Homer's language;—more rich in synonymous words, only diversified a little by some change in the sound, than any other language in Greek. — Homer's language not composed of different Dialects, but the different Dialects made out of it.—An account how it comes to be so rich a language.—It is a dialect of the Shanscrit which was the antient language of Egypt, that went both to India and Greece.—More variety of derivation, composition, and flection, in Homer, than in the other Greek Dialects;—but more variety still in the Shanscrit.—The definition of a Trope.—Philosophical account of Tropes given by Aristotle.—Of the Metaphor.—This word used in a large sense by Aristotle;—but is only used in Rhetoric in the common sense of the word, to denote a similitude

Ch.	Pag.

betwixt two things.—It is a Simile in one word.—Of the proper use of Metaphor, and of the abuse of it   91

2. *Of* Composition—*it gives a variety and beauty to Stile, which no choice of words can do;—is of greater difficulty than the choice of words—therefore neglected in modern times, and in later times among the antients.—All Stiles now of the same kind, affecting what is called* fine *language.—In Composition a progress as in other arts.—The steps of this progress, from the shortest sentence to a period of several members.—There must have been a time for this progress—and the first composition must have been in short sentences.—This progress proved by facts, as well as by reasoning.—The writings of Moses an example of short composition.—This kind of Stile imitated in later times by Salust and Tacitus among the Romans, and by some French and En-*

glish writers.—A very bad Stile, especially when it affects obscurity.—Of the pleasure that some have in decyphering such a Stile.   104

3. *Composition in short sentences does not deserve the name of composition.—Of Composition in longer sentences.—The figures belonging to that composition of three kinds;—figures of the Syntax—of the Sense—and of the Sound.—The difference of the arrangement of words in the learned languages and in the modern.—Words at a distance from one another connected together, in the learned languages, by genders, numbers, and cases.—This produces a great effect in composition.—Milton has availed himself of the few cases we have in English, to compose some fine periods.—The artificial composition in the learned languages not introduced at once.—A simpler composition used at first.—Our language is so crouded with consonants and monysyl-*

lables, that no composition could make it so pleasant as the Greek and Latin.—Objection to the artificial composition, that it makes the sense obscure.—This answered, and shewn that it has the contrary effect.—This artificial composition, so very various, has its bounds.—A bad art in this matter, as well as in other things.—Of the Figures of Syntax.—Some of these only proper for poetry.—Three of them may be used in oratory.—Elipsis, Parenthesis, and Repetition.—The Elipsis much used by Domesthenes, and other Attic writers;—it gives a terseness and neatness to the style.—Parenthesis, a beautiful figure—much used by Demosthenes;—in speaking it has a wonderful good effect.—Repetition, moderately used, has likewise a good effect.—Of the figures of the sense.—These divided into three kinds, such as are Pathetic, Ethic, and, lastly, such as only vary the form of the stile, so as to make it different from common speech.—Of the Pathetic kind are Exclamation, Hyperbole, Epithets, Profopopoea, and painting the subject.—Of the different use of these by Cicero and Demosthenes.—Of the Ethic kind, as many figures as there are manners and characters to be imitated.—Difference betwixt Poetry and Oratory with respect to these figures.—Of the Figures of Sense of the third kind, without passion or characters.—These without number.—An example given of the variety of this figure - 115

4. *Of the third class of the figures of language which affect the sound, viz. the Melody and the Rhythm.—The measured Rhythm or versification of the antient languages, to be treated of in the book upon Poetry;—but of the Rhythm of their prose, something to be said in this book.—Of the melody of speech.—The difference betwixt that melody and the melody of music.*

| Ch. | Pag. |

—It has a greater resemblance to the Recitativo of the Italian opera, than any other music we know;—but differs from that also.—The Melody therefore of Language, a musical tone flowing through the whole speech, not rising too often nor too high.—No language perfect without it.—Origin of the Melody of Language.—Singing more natural to man than speech. —This the most difficult of all human inventions.—Men therefore sung before they spoke.—Language, as well as the race of men, came from the south and east.—People of these countries more musical than the people of the north and west.—When men began to speak, they joined music with their articulation.—Of the melody of the Chinese language.—This a most wonderful language.—Particular information which the author had concerning that language.—The Chinese first used musical tones, before they learnt to articulate.—This they learned from

Ch.		Pag.
	Egypt.—Progress of the art there.—Answer to those who deny that ever a language existed with melody.—This proved from facts.—The melody of language lost in all degenerate languages.—Of the variety of melody in the Greek language.—Not the same variety in the Latin.—Melody, therefore, not so much studied in the Latin composition.	131
5.	*Of Rhythm.—This a word taken from the Greek—not used by Cicero, but by Quintilian.—Not well expressed by* numerus *in Latin, or* quantity *in English.—A definition of Rhythm.—We have no practice of it, any more than of the melody of language.—Difference betwixt music and language.—Music cannot be without melody and rhythm, but a language may be without either.—Of the rhythm in prose—Of this we have no perception; but it was an essential part of the antient oratorial com-*	

position.—*Reason why the antients must have practised rhythm in their prose.*—*The orations of Demosthenes, pronounced by him with all the variety of rhythm, must have given the greatest pleasure to the learned ears of the Athenians.*—*The composition of Demosthenes altogether different from common speech.*—*There must have been a beauty in it, as pronounced by him, of which we can hardly form an idea.*—*This would have been the case of other arts, if monuments of them had not come down to us.*—*We should not by this be discourged from the study of the antient arts.*—*By that study not only the beauty of Arts is to be learned, but the beauty of Manners and Characters.*—*A perfect character not otherwise to be formed.*—*Of* Periods.—*Both the sense and the sound of them better than of short sentences.*—*Without Periods our Rhetorical Stile must be nothing but vulgar speech.*—*A Period makes the*

Ch.	Pag.
	found more beautiful, as well as conveys the sense better.—This expressed in Aristotle's definition of a Period.—Periods must not be too long; nor must all be periodised - 155

6. *A taste for writing, as well as for other fine arts, to be formed only by the imitation of the antients.—Reason for this.—The Romans learned to write in that way, therefore we ought not to be ashamed to do so.—We cannot learn properly at second hand from the Romans.—They did not excel in any of the fine arts, though they learned them all from the Greeks;—could not even write their own history properly.—Reasons why the Romans did not excel in the fine arts.—*First, *want of genius for them;—In this the Greeks excelled all the world, as the Egyptians excelled in sciences and philosophy:—*Next, *their manners and occupations;—great economy and penurious living, absolutely neces-*

sary for them in the first ages of their state;—That in process of time produced the love of money, and the accumulation of it by the Patricians.—The consequence of which was a division in their state.—Description of their antient study by Horace.—They did not apply to the arts till after the Punic wars were ended, when they had got money and could live at their ease;—began then by translating.—Soon after that the wealth of Asia came among them, with luxury and the love of money.—Their youth bred to count money.—The consequence of this was, that no arts could flourish among them.—The pleasures of the Romans, as well as their occupations, were such, that arts could not flourish among them.—Of their Circus and Amphitheatre.—Comparison of the occupation and manners of the Athenians with those of the Romans.—War and arms the only occupation of the Athenians.—Their Theatre *the finest entertainment that ever was. —No Amphitheatre among them.— Such being the case, impossible that the Romans could equal the Athenians in arts.—The Athenians,* praeter laudem, nullius avari.—*Horace could not have been so great a poet, if he had not studied in Athens.—He there learned Philosophy, and to write Lyric Poetry and Dialogue better than any other Roman. — Degeneracy of the Roman taste after the days of Augustus, by their forsaking the imitation of the Greek models.—The Romans, therefore, Horace only excepted, models for no kind of writing—least of of all for the oratorial.—Their taste in it entirely spoiled by the schools of declamation, which were unknown in the better times of Greece. — The Greek writings, therefore, are the models for stile.—There, both the ornaments of speech, and the proper use of them, are to be learned.—The imitation of the Greek authors should be-*

gin with translation.—This more pleasant from Greek to English than from Latin to English.—Of the Ridiculous Character of Stile.—The nature of the Ridiculous, and why Laughter is peculiar to man.—Not common among men who have a high sense of the beautiful in sentiments and manners.—This exemplified by the Indians of North America.—An account of the behaviour of those Indians, both in their public assemblies and in their private conversations.—The true objects of Ridicule are the vain of our own species.—Men addicted to laughter should consider how they look when they laugh, and what a noise they make.—This Character of Stile should be very little used in oratory—is not consistent with gravity and dignity.—Both Cicero and Quintilian say a great deal too much of it. —But the orator may be pleasant and facetious though not ridiculous.— That does not make men laugh, which

Ch.	Pag
is a pitiful ambition.—Wit, if rightly understood, may be used in oratory; but there must not be too much of it.—Humour altogether improper.—Young orators apt to exceed in the ornaments of speech.—The cure for this is the practice of business; but of real business, not fictitious.—The great art of an orator is to conceal art.—The attention of the hearers must not be drawn to words from things	173

BOOK III.

Of *Action* or *Pronunciation*.

1. *Of* Pronunciation, or Action, *as the antients called it.*—Three things comprehended under Action.—One of them the most important of all, viz. the management of the voice.—The say-

Ch.	Pag.

ings of Demosthenes, and Antonius the Roman orator, upon the subject of Action.—To excel in Oratory both nature and art must concur.—Of the requisites from nature.—These divide into qualities of the mind and of the body;—and first, of the qualities of the body. — Rhetoric distinguished from all the other fine arts by requiring these qualities.—The first bodily quality of a speaker, size and figure.—Quotation from Milton on this subject.—A voice sweet and expressive of feeling; or if not, strong and commanding.—A good speaker ought also to be well winded.—Of the qualities of the mind which the orator requires;—And first, a sense of the Pulchrum and Honestum.—This peculiar to human nature.—A quotation from Cicero on this subject.—The extent of this sense—it goes to every word and every action.—Quotation from Milton and Tibullus on this subject.—The taste of the French very

Ch.	Pag.

elegant in this matter.—If not bestowed by nature, no teaching can give it.—The Grave and Dignified also belong to the orator.—This likewise from nature.—Also genius and natural parts.—A perfect orator ought to be superior to his audience.—This was the case of Pericles.—Recapitulation of the natural qualities of mind required to make an orator.—What Art bestows, next to be considered. - - - 205

2. *Education, absolutely necessary for making a speaker.—Should begin early, even with the nurse and the mother.—Examples of the advantage of a mother speaking well.—All those that are about children should have nothing faulty in their pronunciation.—After the child is come to be a boy, his pronunciation must be formed with great care.—Our schools defective in that article.—The consequence of that is, that men speak ill, who would*

Ch.	Pag.
otherwise have spoken well.—To speak well in private conversation, a necessary prelude to public speaking.—This, in boys, should be carefully attended to.—Natural defects by that attention may be corrected.—An affected tone and manner of speaking to be carefully avoided	218

3. *Of the* Education *necessary to make a speaker.—Of action in speaking, and what is comprehended under it.—Of the tone of Public Speaking.—The difference betwixt* Speaking, Talking, Prating, *and* Pratling.—*A voice and ear for Speaking as well as for Music.——The difference betwixt* Speaking *and* Talking *is in the tone of the voice.—What that difference is.—The young scholar to be exercised in speaking, talking, and prating the same thing.—Of the tones of passion and sentiment.—Without these there is a Monotony in speaking.— Even where there is no variety o*

passion or sentiment, difference of matter *requires different times—especially in composition in periods with parentheses.—Of Periods.—The sense conveyed more forcibly by being suspended, till it comes out at the end of the Period.—This Suspense must be marked by the voice.—Practice of composing and speaking Periods to be acquired by reading antient orations.—The student of oratory should know the difference betwixt languages, and their excellencies and defects.—Our language superior to the French, by having accents.—Those accents too strong in common use, so as to obscure the following syllables.—They should therefore be softened by the speaker.— Of* Emphasis.—*Use of it too common in public speaking—it hurts both the sense and sound of a Period;—if very loud and frequent, it makes* barking *of speaking.—Oratory should not study too much the pleasure of the ear by the use of the figure* Parisosis.—

Ch.   **Pag.**

The nature of this figure.—Intemperately used by Cicero.—Of the look, mein, and action of the features of the face in speaking.—Art may do something in that matter, but nature more.—Of the gesture of the body;—this from nature—but may be governed by art.—The orator must not be a pantomine, nor even a player.—Of the use of gesture among the French and Italians.—Among us not so much of it.—But there must be some.—It should not be insignificant nor too violent.—Of the appearance of Ulysses in Homer, when he began his speeches;—This not an idea formed by Homer of a great speaker, but a portrait of Ulysses.—Such an appearance not to be recommended to an orator.—The arts of Action and Pronunciation ought not to be neglected even in speaking upon subjects of science to men who understand the science.   227

BOOK IV.

Of those who have excelled in the *Rhetorical Art.*

Ch.   Pag.

1. *Subject of this Book.—Examples of those who have excelled in this art, taken chiefly from the Greeks.—The first example from Homer.—The eulogiums upon Homer by the Halicarnassian, Hermogenes, and Quintilian.—Of the speeches in the Iliad—more in number than in any other poem.—Examples of them;—and first, Agamemnon's speech to the army, in the second book:—That a most artfull speech:—The speeches of Ulysses and Nestor upon the same occasion—different, but well suited to their characters:—In the ninth book, containing the embassy by the Greeks to Achilles,*

Ch.	Pag.
there is the finest speaking to be found in the Iliad;—the speeches of Ulysses, Phoenix, Ajax, very different from one another—but wonderfully suited to their characters and the occasion:—The composition in the speech of Achilles, remarkably distinguished from any other composition in Homer.—The character of Diomede very well marked by his speaking on two important occasions:—The different effects of his speaking, upon the Greeks, compared with the effect which the speaking of Nestor and Ulysses had upon them:—Diomede's character also marked by his not speaking.	251

2. Of the Orators of later times in Greece and Rome.—Of the difficulty of excelling in that art, greater than in any other art;—therefore so few eminent orators either in Greece or Rome.—Yet it was an art very much practised, not only in peace but in

war.—*Pericles the greatest orator that ever was in Greece.—Nothing of him come down to us.—Demosthenes the next greatest in Greece, and Cicero the greatest in Rome.—These two compared together.—Quintilian's judgment of Cicero.—The high eulogium bestowed upon him by that critic.—Not much regard to be paid to the stile of the writers in Quintilian's age, nor to their taste and judgment.—Cicero had not that magnanimity and elevation of mind which is necessary to form a great orator;—Therefore he spoke with fear and trembling before a people whom he despised as the* dregs of Romulus.—*The* vanity *of Cicero another reason why he could not excel in his art.—Examples of this vanity,—Besides the vanity of the individual, he had a* national *vanity, which made him speak of the Greeks with contempt.—Of the poetry of Cicero.—Connected with his* vanity, *was his taste for*

Ch.		Pag.
	the ridiculous.—This taste he has considered as necessary for an orator, and has given precepts for it at great length.— Quintilian has collected many of the jests in his orations.—Difference betwixt Cicero and Demosthenes or even the best comic writers.—Of the qualities of body possessed by Cicero.—By nature weak and infirm.—That increased by his too great vehemence in speaking.—A very bad account given of his action and pronunciation by himself.—To correct this manner he travelled to Athens and to Asia.—Returned very much improved.—He learned therefore not only to write from Greek masters, but also to speak and pronounce.—One defect in the pronunciation of Cicero that he does not appear to have studied the melody, but only the rhythm of his language.—In this respect his pronunciation very different from that of Demosthenes.—The way, that Cicero learned the art of speaking, such,	

that he could not have been an orator like Demosthenes.—It was by practising declamation that he learned.—Of the nature of that kind of speaking.—Of the difference betwixt the Greek and Latin rhetoricians.—Of the figures of composition relating to the sound.—These ought not to be much studied in speeches of business.—But one thing relating to the sound much studied by the antient orators, viz. the rhythm.— Of the rhythm of their prose.—The nature of it.—Some denied the existence of it.—Of the melody of the Greek language, and the variety of that melody.—Cicero says nothing of the melody of the Latin language.—His oratory therefore defective in that respect.— Of the music of Demosthenes's composition—not such an ornament as could draw the attention of the hearer from the matter. Cicero appears to have had no idea of the melody of oratorial composition.— He has adorned his stile by other

| Ch. | Pag. |

figures of the sound, which are of the poetical kind.—An account given of these figures:—Also with figures of the sense that are poetical, such as Exclamation *and* Prosopopoea.—*The Halicarnassian's opinion of Demosthenes.—The Author's opinion of Cicero, the reverse of that of Quintilian.—Cicero's critical works very much better than his Orations.—Praise of his dialogue* De Oratore.—*His stile extremely copious.—Very well imitated by some late Italian writers in Latin.* - - - 270

3. *Julius Caesar a greater orator than Cicero.—His eloquence is praised by Cicero under the characters of Brutus and Pomponius Atticus.——Natural advantages which Caesar had, and which contributed much to make him excel as an orator:—first his birth—then his military genius—the beauty of his person—a fine voice, and a graceful dignified action.—To all these*

advantages Cæsar joined great application to the art.—Studied at Mitylene under a great master, Cratippus, and practised daily rhetorical exercises.—His speaking the most elegant of all the Latin orators.—This not owing so much to his domestic education as to his deep learning.—He wrote a book upon the Latin language, addressed to Cicero.—Pure Latinity the ground work of oratory.—This formerly learned by imitation of those who spoke well.—But the language, now corrupted by the conflux of strangers, to be restored only by art and science.—These Cæsar, applied, and in that way he became so great an orator, joining the ornaments of eloquence with the purity of language.—Conclusion of the eulogium of Cæsar's eloquence from the mouth of Atticus.—Cæsar was the Pericles of Rome.—He comes up to the idea of a perfect orator.—And he was likewise the greatest and most

Ch. Pag.

amiable man of whom we read in history. - - - 310

BOOK V.

Of the *Oratory* of Demosthenes, containing Observations on his *Matter* and *Stile.*

1. *Demosthenes the greatest orator in antient times, and greater than any that can be in modern.—Reasons why it is impossible that any thing can be composed to be spoken, so perfect as the composition of Demosthenes.—The greatest part of Demosthenes lost, as he is only read, not heard.—Praise of him by his rival Eschines.—Of the natural defects of the bodily qualifications of Demosthenes;—his ha-*

bit infirm;—his voice weak;—and his articulation imperfect.—Of the wonderful industry and application by which he supplied those natural defects;—such as shutting himself up for months together in a habitation under ground—and speaking with pebbles in his mouth.—By these means he overcame nature, and transformed himself into another man.—He could not have done so, if he had not had a genius which led him to the study of Rhetoric in preference to all other studies.—The occasion upon which he shewed this natural propensity.—Of the education he had as an orator.—He may be said to have been self-taught.—He began the practice of the art, not in the school of declamation, but with real business:—Did not attend Isocrates but Isaeus; and studied Thucydides.—The best lesson of all, he got from a player.—To practice what he had learned from him, he shut himself up in a subter-

Ch.	Pag.

raneous habitation,—studied there the melody and rhythm of speech,—and to compose in periods. - 320

2. *The* Matter *most valuable in every good writing.*—*This holds particularly of the orations of Demosthenes.*—*We cannot judge rightly of these orations, without knowing the political conduct of Demosthenes, and the state of Athens at that time.*—*Of the original government of Athens;*—*first monarchical, then aristocratical, and at last entirely popular.*—*The council there did not controul the people, any more than the Senate in Rome.*—*Of the character of the Athenians:*—*A noble, magnanimous, disinterested people;*—*in later times the deliverer of Greece from the Persians;*—*shewed their great temper and moderation, as well as heroic bravery*—*The people of Athens corrupted by wealth and luxury:*—*They desired to live an easy and indolent*

| Ch. | Pag. |

life at the public expence.—This indulgence first given them by Pericles, who introduced the theatrical money, which every citizen received.—After that, under different pretences, the whole money of their treasury was given to the people; and, in the time of Demosthenes, the whole expence of the state was defrayed by the richer citizens.—The consequence of this misuse of public money, was to make the people effeminate and indolent;— did not fight themselves, but employed mercenaries, whom they did not pay.—These, therefore, did no good; for which they blamed their commanders:—But still they were a very intelligent and clever people.—Of the state of affairs in Greece,—particularly of the Lacedemonians, Thebans, and Athenians.—In the distracted state of Greece, Philip of Macedon appeared.—A history of his family,—of himself, and his education under Epaminondas.—Of the progress of his arms,—*first in Thrace,—then in Thessaly,—then in the wars with the Phocians, whom he utterly destroyed,—then with the Locrians; and, last of all, with the Athenians and Thebans, and their allies, whom he utterly defeated in the great battle of Chaeronaea.—He was assisted in those operations by Persons whom he had in his pay in the several states of Greece.—In the beginning of these conquests of Philip, Demosthenes appeared.——The distracted state of Greece then, there being no people among them who were leaders.—In this state of Greece, Demosthenes acted the greatest part that ever was acted in the political line.—The wonderful influence of his councils, and his eloquence upon the Thebans, when he persuaded them to join the Athenians against Philip, which put him to a stand.—In the decisive battle of Chaeronaea, his behaviour, as a soldier, not so bad as represented by some authors.—Steady and firm in opposing the Macedonian power.—Never took money from the Macedonians, as other demagogues did;—formed a great confederacy and great army against Philip;—In forming this confederacy, he had more difficulties to struggle with at home than abroad. —He had thrte paſſions of the Athenians to combat with; theer love of pleaſure and eaſe, their love of money, and their vanity.—Their vanity much flattered by their demagogues. —Demoſthenes rather abuſed them than flattered them:—His Philippics rather an invective againſt the people of Athens than againſt Philip, whom he praiſes for his bravery and contempt of danger.—Nothing but a noble manly ſpirit, as well as great eloquence, could have perſuaded the people of Athens to engage in ſuch a war againſt Philip.—He encourages the Athenians, by telling them, that if they will yet do what is right, all* will be well;—also by shewing them that Philip was not invincible.— What distinguishes chiefly the matter of Demosthenes from that of any other orator, is his insisting so much upon the topic of the pulchrum and honestum: —Examples of this.—Learned this in the school of Plato,—and by imitating Pericles, who had been the scholar of Anaxagoras.—There can be nothing perfect in the arts without philosophy.—Of Demosthenes's skill in mixing together the topic of the possible, the profitable, and the honourable.—The difference betwixt the rhetorical and the didactic stile in that respect.—One great difference betwixt Demosthenes and Cicero as to the matter.—Demosthenes never speaks of himself in his orations, except when it is absolutely necessary, as in the case of the oration De Corona.—Cicero introduces himself very often into his orations, even in private causes.—Modesty affected by Ci-

CONTENTS. xlv

Ch.   Pag.

cero, *a sure sign of the greatest vanity.—A great artist, such as Demosthenes, can never be satisfied with his own performance.*   -   340

3. Stile *divided into the words and the composition of the words.—The words ornamented by* Tropes, *composition by* Figures. *The stile of Demosthenes simple with respect to the words ; but the composition artificial.—He excelled in two stiles diametrically opposite to one another, the plain and simple, the artificial and elaborate.—Of his excellence in the first, his speech against Olympiodorus is a proof.—The difficulty of excelling in that composition.—The stile of his public orations perfectly different.—This artificial stile not the stile of conversation, nor of the decrees of the senate and people.—It is made by figures of composition, not by metaphorical or poetical words.—These* Figures *of three kinds, the Figures of the syntax, of the sense, and of the*

sound.—The Figures of syntax very few in Demosthenes.—His Figures of the sense not such as Cicero uses.—Not so immoderate in his use of Figures of the sound as Isocrates is.—Figures of sound are produced by a certain similarity of sound, which strikes the ear. —The Halicarnassian mentions several of them, among others Antithesis, *a figure also of the sense.—Of the peculiarities of Demosthenes's stile:— First, the arrangement of the words. —That in his public orations very different from the stile of Lysias, or his own stile in private causes.—Examples of the inversion of the natural order.—Shewn that this may be done in some degree in English.—This artificial composition makes the stile of Demosthenes obscure to one who is not a good Greek scholar.—Dr Johnson's judgment of the stile of Demosthenes. —It could not be obscure to the people of Athens.—Wherein the artifice of this composition consists. — Example*

*of it, with a correction of the text.—
The use of accustoming one's self to
such a composition.—Another peculiarity of Demosthenes's stile is Hyperbatons and Parentheses.—This makes
the δεινοτης or density of his stile.—
Another peculiarity of his stile is the
roundness or compactness of his periods.—A period must have a beginning and an end, of which the connection must be perceptible, and marked by the voice in reading or speaking.—Of that figure of the sound
which consists of like endings.—This
an ornament of the prose stile among
the antients, as well as of modern
poetry.—Several examples of it from
Isocrates.—The difference betwixt it
and what is called the παρονομασια.
Of the similarity of the composition
or structure of periods.—This figure
of sound also much too frequent in I-
socrates.—Isocrates concludes his periods too frequently with a verb.—
This a general practice among the*

Ch.	Pag.

Latin writers.—Some apology to be made for both.—Comparison of the stile of Plato with that of Demosthenes.—Isocrates also avoided studiously the concourse of vowels gaping upon one another.—Plutarch's account of his stile.—Such a stile was very suitable to the genius and spirit of the writer.—Demosthenes studied the music of his language, and made of it a noble melody and dignified rhythm, with suitable variety.—The variety of Demosthenes's stile, the most distinguishing characteristic of it.—In this he excells all other authors.—Demosthenes to be considered not as a writer only of orations, but as a speaker.—He studied action and pronunciation very much, and excelled in it more than in any other art.—The beauty of his orations pronounced by himself not to be conceived by us.—What is come down to us of Demosthenes, only the lifeless carcass of his orations.—Those only orators, who

Ch.	Pag.
	speak their orations.—It does not appear that Cicero excelled in action.— As to the composition of Cicero, it does not deserve the character which Quintilian gives of Demosthenes's. composition — He imitated Isocrates more than Demosthenes, particularly in the figures of the sound.—Examples of that—Quintilian prefers him to Demosthenes.—It became a piece of national vanity among the Romans, to prefer their own writers to the Greeks.—But this was not the case in the days of Cicero.—The critics of that time disapproved of his stile	391
4.	*Lord Mansfield's oration pronounced at Oxford upon the subject of Demosthenes's speech,* De Corona.*--The greater part of it lost by the fire which burnt his house some years ago.—The whole of what remains not translated from the Latin, but only some observations made upon it.—First observation is, That Demosthenes insists*	

CONTENTS.

Ch. Pag.

4 more upon the topic of the Pulchrum and Honeſtum, than any other orator.—This obſervation made alſo by Panetius the philoſopher—Demoſthenes learned this in the groves of the academy.—It was particularly neceſſary that he ſhould inſiſt upon it in this oration, and it was the only way he could reconcile the Athenians to the meaſures he had adviſed.—He ſwears, that they did not err, that famous oath, by the manes of thoſe that fell at Marathon, Salamis and Plataeae.—The people to be admired who liſtened to ſuch a topic of perſuaſion, as well as the orator who uſed it.—The character of the people of Athens at that time, compared with their character in later times.—What Livy ſays of them then.—2d Obſervation of Lord Mansfield, that Demoſthenes has neceſſarily introduced the praiſe of himſelf, and with it connected the praiſe of the Athenians, ſo that he could not have made a de-

*fence, that must have been better received by the people.—*3d *Obſervation of Lord Mansfield, That Demoſthenes has concealed the orator under the form of a history, in which he has given us an account of the loſs of the liberties of Greece, by the corruption of the Daemagogues, ſuch as Æſchines, in the ſeveral ſtates of Greece.—This hiſtory otherwiſe very curious and inſtructive.—Lord Mansfield's obſervation upon the ſtile of Demoſthenes.—That it is as excellent as the matter, but appears not at all elaborate, and draws the attention of the reader, not to the words, but to the matter.—This the greateſt praiſe of ſtile.—He excels in concealing the art which he beſtows upon his words. —This art, as he practiſed it, was wonderful.—But the generality of readers ſo carried away by the importance of the matter, as not to perceive it;—but it is perceived by the learned critic.—Æſchines acknowledged his excellence in compoſition.—He a-*

bounds with Parentheses, which are a great beauty in a stile that is to be spoken:—But the pronunciation of Parentheses must be good;—If so, they convey the meaning more forcibly than if they were connected with the rest of the sentence.—Lord Mansfield prefers the stile of Demosthenes to Cicero's.—If his discourse had been continued, he would have given examples of the puerilis fucus of the stile of Cicero.—One given by the author, where two passages from Demosthenes and Cicero, containing the same thought, are compared.—The words both of Cicero and Demosthenes given. —Of the use my Lord Mansfield has made of his eloquence, formed upon the model of Demosthenes;—has made one use of it very suitable to the office of a judge.—Conclusion of the volume, with an address to my Lord Mansfield, exhorting him to bear with patience the infirmities of old age, comforting himself with the thoughts of a life so well spent.   456

ERRATA.

Pag. 9. line 4 in the note, for *ineps* read *inops*
68. 4. in the note, *for* αλιιβομινοιο *read* κατ-αλιιβομινοιο
84. 1. in the note, *after* γαρ, *insert* τι
153. 20. *for* they were distinct syllables, *read* it was one long syllable
159. 12. *after* than *insert* of
160. 3. in the note, *for* by Demosthenes, *read* from Demosthenes
188. 20. *for* Adjicere *read* Adjecere
195. 8. *for* and *read* nor
245. 20. in the note, *for* exerted, *read* exserted.
272. 14. *for* is *read* was
323. 7. for *Morialists*, read *Moralists*.

INTRODUCTION.

THIS great work, which I have undertaken, and which is now drawing towards a conclusion, I should have thought very imperfect, if, after giving an account of the origin of language, and explaining the nature of it, with respect both to its matter and form, and compared together different languages, shewing in what they severally excelled or were defective, I had said nothing of stile and composition, by which language produces its effect, and answers the purposes intended by it. I have, therefore, in my third volume, treated of stile in general; and explained some general characters of it, such as the the *austere*, the *florid*, the *sublime*, the *witty*, and the *humorous*. In my fourth volume I have been more particular, and divided ſtile, according to the ſubjects of which it treats, into ſix different kinds; the epiſtolary, the dialogue, the hiſtorical ſtile, the didactic, the rhetorical, and, laſtly, the poetical*. In that volume, and the fifth, I have treated of the firſt four kinds of ſtile, and I am now come to ſpeak of the two laſt, namely, the rhetorical and poetical, in which the beauty of ſtile is moſt conſpicuous, and produces the greateſt effect.

In treating of theſe arts, I ſhall follow the ſame method that I have followed in treating of the grammatical part of language, and of the other kinds of ſtile of which I have ſpoken. As I have not written a formal treatiſe upon thoſe other ſtiles, ſo I do not propoſe to write one upon rhetoric; but only to give the philoſophical principles upon which it is founded: For I cannot ſeparate philoſophy from any art or ſcience, as I think the principles of none of them

* Vol. 4. book 2. cap. 6. in the beginning.

can be perfectly understood without philosophy; nor without philosophy can they ever be brought to any great degree of perfection; and, among other arts, Horace has told us, that the writing art is founded upon philosophy—

> Scribendi recté sapere est et principium et fons.
> Rem tibi Socraticæ poterunt oftendere chartæ.

It is in this way that Aristotle has treated of these arts; and in this respect, his three books of rhetoric, and his single book of poetry, mutilated as it is, and little better than a fragment, are of very great value*. Following, therefore, his footsteps, and making the best use I can of the lights he has thrown upon the subject, I will endeavour to explain the nature, and shew the proper use of rhetoric and poetry.

I begin with rhetoric, the most ancient art of the two, and of the greatest utility. It is coeval with civil society and government; for, in the first ages of society, go-

---

* See upon his rhetoric and poetry, vol. 5. p. 402. and 403.

vernment was carried on by public speaking, as governments of single men, by arbitrary will, were not then known: For though, in the first ages of society, there were men of superior abilities, both of mind and body, and who therefore were destined by God and nature to govern their fellow-creatures, it was by council and persuasion that they governed; nor indeed could they govern otherwise in those early ages. Accordingly we find, that among all the barbarous nations, which have any kind of established government, public speaking is very much practised, and is really an art. This is the case of the Indians of North America, among whom a chief, though he may be very eminent in war, is not regarded, if he cannot speak: And among the New Zealanders, though not near so far advanced in the arts of life as the Indians of North America, rhetoric is practised; for I was informed, by a man of very good sense and observation, who accompanied Captain Cook in the voyage to New Zealand, that when we first landed in the island, there came a body of the

INTRODUCTION. v

natives to us, among whom there was an orator, who made a speech to us of considerable length, in which, he said, there was more expression by the voice, the look, and the gestures of the speaker, than ever he had seen or heard of; so that it was evident that this orator was a practised speaker, and who had made a study of the art. And it was so among the Greeks, at the time of the Trojan war, when, as Homer tells us*, the two arts that distinguished man most, were war and eloquence. Poetry, on the other hand, though it may be applied to useful purposes, is more an art of pleasure than of utility. It was therefore of later invention, even later than music, which I hold to have been practised by men, though no doubt very rudely, before they learned to articulate; and accordingly those Indians

---

* Homer, speaking of public assemblies, says,

—— 'ινα τ' ανδρες αριπρεπεις τελιθουσι.

Iliad. 9. v. 441.

And Phoenix taught Achilles

Μυθων τε ρητηρ' εμεναι, πρηκτηρα τε εργων.

Iliad. 9. v. 443.

of North America, though they have both mufic and eloquence, have not any thing that deferves the name of poetry.

In this introduction, it is proper to let the reader know, that, as I have learned my philofophy from Plato and Ariftotle, fo I have alfo learned any thing I know of the fine arts from the fame authors; and rhetoric particularly I have learned from Ariftotle's three books upon the fubject. Whoever, therefore, thinks that thofe arts are fufficiently taught in the many modern books written upon the fubject,—or who thinks, that, by his own genius and natural parts, he can difcover every thing that is neceffary to be known in them, needs not take the trouble to read this work; but may reft fatisfied with his own difcoveries, or with what he has learned from modern writers.

OF THE
ORIGIN AND PROGRESS
OF
LANGUAGE.

VOL. VI. BOOK I.

Of the Matter and Subject of Rhetoric.

CHAP. I.

The common definition of Rhetoric not compleat.—What is wanting to it, added.—Observations upon the nature and use of rhetoric.—Of absolute necessity in popular governments—may be either abused, or used to good purposes, like other arts.

THE word *rhetoric* we have taken from the Latins, as the Latins took it from the Greeks: For the Latins having no arts, I mean liberal arts, of their own, before they became acquainted with the Greeks, and having learned them from the Greeks, they took their names from the Greek language: and among others they took the name of Eloquence, and called it Rhetoric. And it was the same with respect to the sciences, which they denominated by Greek words, such as *mathesis, mathematica, astronomia, geographia,* and even *grammatica*; and at last they adopted the word *philosophia*, which before they were in use to express by a word of their own growth, viz. *sapientia* * ; so that, though Cicero

---

* In the time of Cato the censor, the word *philosophia* was not used in Rome, but in place of it *sapientia*.

boasts so much of the copiousness of the Latin language*, yet there was not a word in it to denote even the art he practised himself, and which, in a country of liberty, must be an art of general use.

Therefore Cato said, that *agricultura est proxima sapientiae*. Nor do I think that it was used in Latin earlier than the days of Cicero; and even after his time, Horace uses the old word *sapere*, to denote the study of philosophy, as in the lines above quoted. And here we may observe in passing, a remarkable difference between the Latin and the Gothic, which is commonly believed to be a barbarous language; for the Goths formed all the terms of art and science from their own language, by derivation and composition. This, as I have observed elsewhere, (vol. 4. p. 171.) is evident from the Gothic translation of the Gospels, still extant: And I am well informed, that in Iceland, where the Gothic is still preserved in the greatest purity, the terms of art and science are at this day all of their own growth.

* *De Natura Deorum*, lib. 1. cap. 4. *De Oratore*, lib. 2. cap. 4. And in his Tusculan Questions, book 2. cap. 14. he has an exclamation upon the subject, *O verborum ineps interdum, quibus abundare te semper putas, Graecia!*—so great was his national vanity. What was his personal vanity is well known.

Rhetoric is commonly defined the art of persuasion; and no doubt it is an art of persuasion. But something more must be added to the definition to make it complete, and to distinguish rhetoric from other arts, which likewise persuade; for a geometer persuades, and in the most forcible way too, so that it is impossible you can withhold your assent, yet he is not a rhetorician or orator.

It should seem, then, that as both the mathematician and orator persuade, it must be in a different manner. And if we attend, we shall find this difference betwixt the two, that the geometer, at the same time that he persuades, teaches and instructs; for he defines and divides, lays down principles that are certain and clear, and from those principles deduces consequences as certain; in short, he *demonstrates*, and not only persuades the person to whom he speaks, but gives him science, by shewing him both that the thing is, and why it is, and how it cannot be otherwise. On the other hand, the orator persuades,

Chap. I. Progress of Language 11

but he does not teach, nor communicate any science; or, if he does so, he goes out of the province of rhetoric. And indeed it would be impossible to communicate science in a harrangue, which lasts only for a few hours, and is generally addressed to people, a great part of whom may be supposed not capable of science, if they had time and leisure to apply to it. Besides, the subject of an oration is commonly matters relating to civil or political life, incapable, by their nature, of being reduced to art or science, and depending often upon future events, concerning which we can only guess or conjecture. It appears, therefore, that we must add to the common definition, and say, that rhetoric is the art of persuasion, without demonstrating or teaching any art or science *; and that men may be so persuaded, and are most commonly so, is

---

* This is agreeable to Plato's notion of the art, see his Gorgias, p. 310, *et seq.* editio Ficin. His words are, ἡ ῥητορικὴ ἄρα, ὡς ἔοικε, πειθοῦς δημιουργός ἐστι, πιστευτικῆς ἀλλ' οὐ διδασκαλικῆς; that is, "The rhetor or orator "is an artificer of persuasion, which convinces, or " makes believe, but does not teach."

a fact of daily experience. An orator, therefore, is not obliged to be learned in any one art or science, as his business is to perfuade, without teaching or demonstrating any thing. Nor must it be thought that this definition implies any contradiction, as if rhetoric were an art, and yet without art; for it is only without art, in so far as it may not know the particular art, if there be any, to which the subject it treats belongs; but it is an art, in so far as it knows how to perfuade, without the knowledge of that particular art.

Another difference between teaching and rhetoric is, with respect to the stile or manner: For an art or science may be taught by way of dialogue, or question and answer, and is best taught in that way; whereas rhetoric always uses continued discourse, or what we call an oration or harrangue, of which the stile and composition is very different from that of dialogue, or even of a continued discourse in which science is delivered. We must therefore add still further to the definition of rhetoric, and say, That it is the art of persuasion, without demonstrating or teaching, and in continued discourse, of which the stile is different from common speech.

From this definition, several observations arise: And, in the first place, it appears to be true what Aristotle says*, that rhetoric, like dialectic, (a kindred art, of which I shall speak more hereafter), has no determinate subject, but may be practised indifferently upon all subjects, though, as I have observed, the common subject of it be the affairs of life. But there is nothing to hinder any matter of art or science to be made the subject of an oration: But then it must be treated not scientifically, or as an art, but rhetorically; so that it is the manner of treating the subject, not the subject itself, which constitutes the nature of this art.

2do, Though the subject be a matter of art or science, it is not necessary, as I have observed, that the orator should understand

---

* Rhetor, lib. 1. cap. 1.

that art or science. And this was the great boast of the sophists of old, that they possessed an art of such universal use, that it applied to all subjects, and enabled them to talk more plausibly, upon any matter of art, than the artist himself, and to convince whom the artist could not convince*.

But, 3*tio*, This can only be when the hearers do not understand the art or science; for, if they understand it, it is impossible that any arguments, used by a person who does not understand it, should convince them. But if, on the contrary, they do not understand it, they will be more readily convinced by this artificer of persuasion, than by any thing the man who understands that art or science, but not the rhetorical art, can say to them. What, therefore, Plato says of rhetoric in general, will certainly apply to this case;— That the orator not understanding, among those who likewise do not understand, will

* Plato, ibid. p. 313.

speak more persuasively than he who understands *.

4*to*, It follows from what is said, that as rhetoric does not require any scientific knowledge of the subject of which it treats, and speaks to people who have not that knowledge neither, it may persuade what is false as well as what is true; so that truth and falsehood appear to be indifferent to this art, as well as the subject of which it treats. The profession, therefore, of Gorgias the sophist, that he could make the worse reason appear the better, though it was thought a very impudent profession, was nothing more than professing that he understood the rhetorical art, and could make that use of it if he would.

And, lastly, from all that has been said, it is evident that it is a most dangerous art, of which the worst use may be made;

* Plato's words, speaking of the orator, are, ὁ ἐκ
'ειδὼς ἄρα τῷ εἰδότος ἐν ἐκ εἰδόσι πιθανώτερος 'ἐσται. p. 313.
ibid.

and it was therefore no wonder that Gorgias, by letting the full extent of his art be known, brought difgrace upon himfelf in the opinion of the people, and upon all his brother fophifts, and which Ariftophanes, in his comedies, endeavoured to turn againft philofophy itfelf. But I think it is true, what the fame Gorgias in Plato fays in defence of his art, that it holds of all other arts as well as of rhetoric, that an ill ufe may be made of them: And he mentions the art of boxing *, or fighting of any kind, of which the worft ufe has been made, and is daily made. But, fays he, a good ufe may likewife be made of it; and the fame ufe may be made of the rhetorical art. And he gives an inftance of patients, whom he himfelf perfuaded to take medicines, or to fuffer any operation to be performed upon them, when his brother, who was a phyfician, could not perfuade them. And the people may be confidered as fick or difeafed perfons, that

---

* Plato, ibid. p. 312.

Chap. I. Progress of Language. 17

cannot be directed by art or science, but must be led by good words and fine speeches; and therefore, in all cases where the people are to be persuaded, the rhetorical art appears to be very useful. And in the ancient states, particularly those of Athens and Rome, where not only the fate of the nation, but the life and fortune of every private man *, depended upon the resolutions of the people, it was of absolute necessity; so that we are not to wonder that it was so much cultivated among them. And in the modern popular governments, it must likewise be of great influence, and the greater, the less corrupt these governments are: For of a popular

---

* This was the consequence of their courts of justice being so popular, as to consist sometimes of a thousand persons, which was the case of one of the courts of Athens, and these draughted out of the body of the people by lot. It may be observed in passing, that all the courts in this country, and in all the other feudal kingdoms of Europe, were, in antient times, likewise popular, consisting of all the *pares curiae*, or vassals of the king or lord.

assembly, there are only two things which can determine the resolutions, eloquence, and faction or corruption. It is in vain, therefore to inveigh against eloquence, as Plato does, representing it not as an art, but rather as a thing of experience and observation, whose object is what is pleasant, not what is good, being with respect to the mind what cookery is with respect to the body; for it was of necessary use in his time, and still is in all free governments: And though no doubt a bad use may be made of it as well as a good, that is what it has in common with all other arts. In the hands of a wicked man, it is indeed the most dangerous of all instruments; and accordingly it is a certain fact, that almost all the republican states of Greece were ruined by the corruption and venality of their demagogues; but in the hands of a wise and good man *, it may be,

---

* It may be observed, that Gorgias in Plato runs himself into a contradiction, and is silenced, by admitting two things, neither of which he ought to have admitted; 1*st*, That an orator should know what justice is, which, if he did not know before, Gorgias

Chap. I. PROGRESS OF LANGUAGE.

and often has been, productive of the greatest good. Nor should it disparage the art so much, as at first sight it may seem, that by its nature it may be employed to maintain falsehood as well as truth; for even that may not be a bad use of it, because it is sometimes as necessary to deceive

professes to teach. 2*dly*, That he who knows justice is just, that is, practices justice. For by these two admissions he contradicts what he had said before, that an orator might make a bad use of his art, for which he that taught him the art is not answerable. Ibid. p. 312, and 314. The first of these, erroneous admissions is observed by Polus, the friend of Gorgias, who says, that Gorgias made it through shame, because he would not admit that a man, possessed of his art, did not know what justice was; or that he did not teach it at the same time that he taught rhetoric. Ibid, p. 315. But the other, which is as much a paralogism, is not observed. It is with this attention that we ought to examine many of the reasonings which Plato puts into the mouth even of Socrates, and to distinguish betwixt such as he uses for the instruction of his followers, like those in the books De Republica and De Legibus, and such as he uses against the Sophists, as in this case against Gorgias, which are often not conclusive, but serve the purpose of confuting the Sophist.

the people for their good, as to deceive children, fick perfons, or thofe that are difordered in their fenfes. Ariftotle therefore, I think, did nothing unworthy of a philofopher, when he wrote a fyftem of rhetoric; for as it is an inftrument that will certainly be ufed by the bad, the good muft be armed in the fame way, otherwife the match will not be equal. And though it may be faid, as it was by fome of the antient philofophers, that it was no art or fcience, but a thing only of obfervation and experience, and that an orator was no better than a mere empyric; yet it cannot be denied that it will be better practifed by certain rules and obfervations, collected and digefted, than without rule: For even cookery, to ufe Plato's comparifon, is better practifed by a book of receipts, than at random and by mere guefs and conjecture.

CHAP. II.

Of the importance of Rhetoric—it persuades not by words only, but by arguments.—These arguments of three kinds, viz. arguments from the person of the speaker, from the persons to whom he speaks, and, lastly, from the subject itself.—This last kind admits of a subdivision; for the arguments may be only applicable to that subject, or they may be applicable to many others.—These of the dialectical kind, and may prove both ways.—Of the division of Rhetoric, according to its subject, into the Deliberative, Judicial, and Epideitic.

FROM what has been said in the preceding chapter, it appears, that the ancient Sophists did not much exaggerate the importance of their art, when they represented it to be of such extent, as to comprehend, in some sort, every other art, and the orator to triumph over all other artists, at least in the opinion of the people; nor do I think it undeserving of the magnificent title which Cicero gives it, of *Queen of Arts*. It remains now to be inquired, by what means it performs such wonders.

And, in the first place, it must be obvious, that it is not by sounds only, or by mere words, that it produces such effects; for though these no doubt have a great influence upon the people, yet they must necessarily, for that purpose, have some meaning; because it is true what Cicero says, even in the judgment of the people, *Nihil tam furiosum est quam verborum, vel optimorum, inanis sonitus, nulla subjecta sententia aut scientia.* It is therefore not stile and composition only, that will convince even the people; but it is argument chiefly, of one kind or another: And for that reason I begin, following the example of Aristotle, with the arguments belonging to rhetoric, as being the principal part of the art; after which I will speak of the stile.

As there is no author more accurate in his divisions than Aristotle, I will adopt the division he has given of rhetorical arguments into three heads. They are all, says he, drawn either from the person of the speaker, from the persons of the hearers, or from the subject itself; for no argument can be conceived that is not from one or other of these topics. The arguments of the two first kind are clearly rhetorical, not belonging to any particular art or science. But with respect to the arguments of the third kind we must make a distinction: For some of them may be drawn immediately and directly from the subject, being of such a nature as to be applicable only to that subject; and if the subject be a matter of art or science, such arguments will not be rhetorical, but belonging to that art or science: And in some cases they may be demonstrative; nor is there any thing to hinder the orator to use arguments of that kind, if they be suited to the capacities of the people, which some things in morals and politics are when well explained. The other kinds are general, and belonging to many other subjects; and such arguments are all of the rhetorical or dialectic kind. For with respect to such arguments, there is no difference in substance betwixt rhetoric and dialectic, but only in the stile and manner, as shall be afterwards more fully explained. And this sort of argumentation is particularly to be attended to, because it explains what hitherto must have appeared inexplicable to many readers—How the rhetorical art can enable a man to argue upon a subject, even though it be a matter of art or science, which he has never learned, and of which, consequently, he can have no particular knowledge, and this too more plausibly, if he speak to the people, than even the artist or man of science himself, who has not studied or practised the rhetorical art. What makes this thing the more surprising is, that all reasonings, as well as the dialectical and rhetorical, must be from general propositions. But what makes the difference is, that the arguments used in particular arts and sciences are drawn from general propositions indeed, but which apply only to that particular art or science; whereas the propofitions, from which dialectic and rhetoric argue, apply to many different fubjects. And another difference is, that the propofitions, from which we infer the conclufions in particular arts and fciences, muft be felf-evident truths, or truths demonftrated: Whereas the principles, from which the rhetorician argues, are neither felf-evident nor demonftrated propofitions, but fuch as are generally admitted to be true, by thofe to whom the orator addreffes himfelf. Arguments of this kind are the only arguments that can be properly ufed with men who are not fuppofed to underftand any art or fcience; and therefore it was in this way, chiefly, that the Sophifts of old, and the orators, argued. But, though the practice was univerfal, it was not reduced to any art or method, till Ariftotle, to whom arts, as well as philofophy, has been fo much obliged, compofed his books of Topics, which contain thofe general propofitions, applicable to fo many fubjects, from which the Sophifts and orators drew their arguments: And the name of Topics was given to the work, because it was the place or seat of arguments, *sedes argumentorum*, as Cicero has explained the word. But although the Sophists of old, and many of the orators, made a very bad use of those topics, we are not to suppose that Aristotle, when he wrote this book, meant to form an art of sophistry or deceit, which would have been unworthy of a philosopher: But he insists, that from the propositions laid down in the Topics, those who use them should argue fairly, and not infer conclusions which the premises do not warrant. Upon this subject I have said a good deal more in the first volume of Ancient Metaphysics *, and have illustrated what I have said by examples, in one of which Aristotle shews, that an argument, drawn from a certain topic, was so far from being conclusive, that the contrary might be inferred from it.

* Book 5. chap. 4. p. 405.

Having thus shewn what the end proposed by rhetoric is, of what kind the arguments it uses are, and from what sources those arguments are drawn, it remains only, in order to give a general view of the nature of this art, that I should give some account of the subjects upon which it is employed. And first, it is employed in matters of deliberation to persuade those, to whom it is addressed, to act in the business, about which they deliberate, in one way rather than in another; and this is called deliberative eloquence. The second is employed in determining controversies among men about their lives and fortunes, before judges, who are to decide upon the speeches of the orators: And here we may observe, from what Aristotle has told us, that the subject of this kind of rhetoric was not questions of private property among the citizens, but public trials, in the form of accusation and defence; for questions of the other kind do not appear to have been at all debated by orators or lawyers in Greece, nor in Rome, till the Romans had done what no other nation of antiquity did; I mean, had formed a syftem of the law of private property, which though they did not get from the Greeks, they got the principles of philofophy, upon which they founded it. And this is eloquence of the judicial kind. The third and laft ufe of it is to praife or difpraife, fo that it is either panegyric or invective. It is faid, in Greek, to be of the Epideictic kind; becaufe it is for fhow and oftentation, and not for bufinefs. This name is, I think, very improperly tranflated by the word *demonſtrative*, by which one fhould have thought, that the tranflator had underftood, that the Greek word Epideictic, meant the fame thing as Apodeictic. And yet I obferve that not only Quintilian, but alfo Cicero, ufes this improper tranflation, for want, I fuppofe, of a more proper word in Latin: But they had better, I think, have ufed the Greek word, as they have taken many other terms of art from the Greek, and even the word *rhetoric* itfelf, as I have obferved in the beginning of this volume.

From what is said in this and the preceding chapter, the definition of rhetoric may be collected to be, ' An art of per-
' suasion without science or demonstration,
' upon subjects of deliberation, of judicial
' decision, or of praise or dispraise, by
' arguments taken either from the nature
' of the subject, from the person of the
' speaker, or the persons of the hearers.'

CHAP. III.

Of Rhetorical arguments taken from the subject itself.—Difference in this respect betwixt Rhetoric and Science.—In what respect Rhetoric is different from Sophistry—different also from other arts, in this respect, that the subject of other arts is limited.—The subject of Rhetoric, things that every body is supposed to know more or less.—Rhetorical arguments all general, and applicable to many different cases.—Rhetoric applicable to arts and sciences; but they must be treated in a Rhetorical manner.—The wonderful extent of the Dialectic art.—No man, but one of so great genius and learning as Aristotle, could think of reducing it to rule and method.—Some other things, he had studied, prepared him for such a work—particularly what he has written upon Rhetoric.—Difference betwixt Rhetoric and Dialectic.—General division by Aristotle into four heads—This a most comprehen-

five division, including all the topics of argument upon every subject.—Some instances of the topics, as arranged under these several heads.—*The invention of the art of Dialectic does more honour to the genius of Aristotle, being intirely his own, than any other of his works.*—The philosopher and grammarian may both find matter of instruction in this work.—Cicero's judgment of the stile of it.—*Of Alexander Aprodisienses's commentary upon the Dialectic of Aristotle*—The greatest use of this work is to correct the text of Aristotle—It is a wonder that there are not many more errors in Aristotle's text, considering how providentially his works were preserved—If they had not been preserved, we should have had no complete system of philosophy, such as is to be found in Aristotle's writings.—*Of Cicero's topics—addressed to Trebatius the lawyer—illustrated by examples from the law.*—Cicero's skill in the law.—The ignorance, not only of Trebatius, but of almost all the philosophers of that age, in the philosophy of Aristotle.—*That phi-*

losophy would have been *lost, if it had not been preserved in the Alexandrian school.*

BEFORE I come to speak of the three kinds of eloquence I have mentioned, the Deliberative, the Judicial, and the Epideictic, I will say something of the arguments which rhetoric uses upon all the several subjects of which it treats. These also I have reduced to three classes, viz. arguments drawn from the subject of which the orator treats; from the person of the speaker; and, lastly, from the persons of the hearers: And I will begin with the first, which ought certainly to be the principal in every oration.

From what has been said in the former chapter, a distinction must be evident betwixt rhetoric and science of any kind; for all sciences are founded upon axioms, or self-evident propositions, from which all their conclusions are deduced by demonstrative reasoning. On the other hand, the rhetorical art is founded in opinion,

Chap. III. Progress of Language. 33

and all its arguments are drawn from what is generally believed to be true, the το ενδοξον, as Ariſtotle calls it, or what is admitted to be true by your adverſary. If from theſe opinions, concluſions are by fair argumentation drawn, then it is not ſophiſtry, but truly rhetoric; for the rhetorician does not differ from the ſophiſt ſo much in the principles he lays down, as in his manner of arguing from them.

There may be alſo a difference obſerved betwixt rhetoric and other arts and ſciences in this reſpect, that the ſubjects of other arts are limited and determined, ſuch as the ſubjects of phyſic, geometry, arithmetic, &c.*; whereas rhetoric has for its ſubject every thing that can be deliberated upon, can be tried in a court of juſtice, or can be praiſed or diſpraiſed;—in ſhort, rhetoric comprehends all the affairs of men, and the whole buſineſs of human life. This Ariſtotle has obſerved, in the firſt chapter

---

* Ariſtot. lib. 1. Rhet. cap. 2. in initio.

of his rhetoric, where he has told us, that the subject of rhetoric is things which every body is supposed to know, more or less, without having studied any particular art or science; and therefore, says he, every body accuses or defends, praises or blames, and reasons about what is right or wrong, profitable or unprofitable, in actions.

And here we may see the reason why the arguments I am now speaking of, that is, arguments from the subject, cannot be confined to that particular subject, but must be general, and applicable to many other subjects. There may, indeed, be arguments used by the orator, that are applicable only to that subject; but these, I say, are not rhetorical arguments, nor is it of these that Aristotle treats: And indeed it would be impossible to make any thing like a system of them, or to reduce them to rule, all particular cases being so different one from another; and accordingly Aristotle tells us, that neither rhetoric nor dialectic are conversant about particular things, but only about generals, nor has it, like other arts, a definite subject *. Rhetorical arguments, therefore, are all deducible from general propositions, applicable to many particular cases, quite different from one another. These propositions Aristotle has reduced to certain heads, which he calls Topics, as I have observed, that is, *places* where arguments are to be found †.

And rhetoric not only may be applied to all the affairs of human life, but to philosophy, arts, and sciences. These, however, must not be treated as matter of science, but matter of opinion: And the arguments used must not be deduced from the principles of that art or science, but from the common apprehensions of men; in short, they must be rhetorical arguments. To the definition, therefore, which I have given of rhetoric ‡, it may be added, ' It is an art of persuasion, not only in mat-
' ters of deliberation, of judicial decision,
' and of praise or dispraise; but upon the

---

* Lib. 1. Rhet. cap. 2.
† See p. 26.
‡ See p. 29.

' subject of any art or science, though not
' by arguments from the principles of those
' arts and sciences, but from the common
' opinions of men.'

From what has been said, the reader may perceive the wonderful extent of the subject, which Aristotle has reduced to art and method in his books of *topics*, and given it the name of *Dialectic*; a word, before his time, of very indeterminate use, and applied by Plato to logic, metaphysics, and all kinds of reasoning. The subject, as we have seen, comprehends not only all the affairs of life, but every question of philosophy, arts, or sciences. Accordingly, Aristotle, in his books of topics, has mentioned several questions of philosophy, such as the famous dispute betwixt him and his master concerning ideas, and also concerning virtue, whether it was nothing else but science, as Plato makes it to be. To form a system of reasoning upon so many various subjects, and to reduce to certain heads all the variety of arguments that may be used upon these subjects, must appear at first sight so amazing a work, that we can hardly believe that any man should have so much as thought of reducing it to any form or order; so that we need not wonder that no man before Aristotle performed it. Some sophists, indeed, mentioned by Aristotle, had particular topics that they were very fond of, and drew many arguments from them; but none of them ever thought of reducing all this kind of reasoning into a system, and dividing it into certain heads. This was reserved for a man of the genius and learning of Aristotle; nor could even he have executed it, if he had not before studied logic so much, and formed a system of it, where he has shewn what rules are necessary to make reasoning demonstrative. In this way he laid the foundation of all sciences, and indeed shewed us what science was: And this I think may naturally have led him to think whether reasoning, not demonstrative, might not likewise be formed into a system, such as would facilitate the use of it: For that this reasoning is of much more general use than demonstrative reasoning, such as we employ in sciences, is evident; and therefore Aristotle, by reducing it to order and method, and so facilitating the use of it, has certainly performed a very useful work, such as no man could have executed, but one who had studied reasoning so much as he had done, and who, besides, had acquired a more extensive knowledge of all arts and sciences than any other man ever was possessed of. Moreover, the study of eloquence, which, it appears, from his *Rhetorica ad Alexandrum*, that he studied and wrote upon at the desire of his pupil, would naturally lead him to study dialectic, which is so nearly connected with rhetoric, that it furnishes to us all the arguments of the kind I am now speaking of, that is, arguments drawn from the subject of the oration; and very many arguments also upon the other two branches of the art I mentioned may be drawn from the topics. Aristotle, in the beginning of his Rhetoric, has very properly observed the similarity betwixt rhetoric and dialectic; and indeed, the great difference betwixt the two arts, is more in the ſtile and manner than in the matter: For rhetoric goes on in a continued diſcourſe, and in a ſtile different from common ſpeech; whereas the dialectic went on in the way of converſation, as the name imports; and the reaſoning was conducted in the Socratic method, by queſtion and anſwer; and it was from the propoſitions granted by the perſon who anſwered the queſtion, that the other party formed his arguments, not from propoſitions that he aſſumed himſelf, or borrowed from any art or ſcience; and accordingly Ariſtotle employs his eighth and laſt book of topics in giving directions how the queſtion ſhould be put and anſwered. And, laſtly, the ſtile of dialectic being no other than the ſtile of common ſpeech, is quite different from the ſtile of rhetoric.

As order and method were abſolutely neceſſary in treating an art of ſo great extent, Ariſtotle has begun his treatiſe upon it, by dividing it into four different heads, more general than the topics, which are to be conſidered as only the ſubdiviſions of those general heads; for as accurate division is the great organ of philosophy, and of all arts and sciences, no man has employed that organ more successfully than Aristotle. The four general heads are, 1*mo*, The definition of the thing which is the subject of the inquiry;—2*do*, The genus, under which Aristotle, in this division, includes the species and the difference; and they are certainly both virtually included in the genus;—3*tio*, What is proper or peculiar to the subject;—And, *lastly*, What is only accidental, that is, may or may not be a quality of the subject. And that every proposition or problem of dialectic falls under one or other of these classes, he has proved both by induction and syllogism*. And he begins his work with the topics relating to *accident*, being more general and comprehensive than any of the other heads, because, with regard to it, there is nothing to be proved, but that it exists in the subject,

---

* Lib. 1. *Topicorum*, cap. 8.

without confidering whether it makes any part of the effence of the fubject, which is the cafe of the other three.

In order to give the reader a general idea of the method that Ariftotle has followed in the execution of this great plan, I have, in the firft volume of my Ancient Metaphyfics *, given fome examples of thefe Topics, and of Ariftotle's manner of arguing from them, from which, and particularly the laft example there mentioned, it appears how cautious Ariftotle was that there fhould be no deception in the arguments drawn from thefe general topics. How little he was difpofed to teach an art of fophiftry, is apparent from a work which he has fubjoined to his Topics, intitled, *De Sophifticis Elenchis*. In this work he has fhewn all the art which the Sophifts made ufe of, to deceive men into an opinion of their great learning and abilities, by endeavouring to

---

* Lib. 5. chap. 4.

convince men of the greateſt paradoxes, of which it appears that they made a very profitable trade. In this work he has ſhewn, not only the art of the Sophiſts in making uſe of thoſe topics to deceive men, but he has taught how we are to guard againſt that deception, and refute ſuch ſophiſtical arguments.

This work of Ariſtotle upon the Topics is ſuch as to give me a greater idea of the extent of his genius and learning than any one other work that he has executed. That he got a great part of his philoſophy from the philoſophers before his time, I have no doubt; and I think I have made it very probable that he owed that great diſcovery of the analyſis of the operations of the human intellect in reaſoning, contained in his books of Analytics, to the Pythagorean ſchool*. But if his Logic was not his own, I think there is not the leaſt reaſon to doubt that his Dialectic was his

---

* Preface to vol. 3d of Ant. Metaph. p. liii. and following.

own; and if so, I think I have shewn that it was a most wonderful discovery, and which I think may be made very useful: For, as Cicero has observed in the beginning of his treatise upon the Topics, the invention of arguments is the first and most necessary thing in speaking. Now I think I can venture to affirm, that there is not an argument of the rhetorical kind, upon any subject, which may not be found in one or other of those *places*, or seats of argument, with which Aristotle has furnished us. Now, let a man's genius be ever so great, and his knowledge as comprehensive as any man's can be, yet, when he comes to invent arguments upon any subject, he would, I should think, be much the better for having an index, such as Aristotle has given us, directing him to the place where they are to be found, so that he has nothing more to do, but to apply them to the case he is studying.

Besides the copiousness of argument which this work furnishes to the rhetorician, the philosopher and the grammarian must be much pleased with the accurate distinction of things and of words, which he finds there; and though we have in it the elegant Attic brevity in perfection, yet there is no obscurity for want of words; and his stile, upon the whole, deserves the commendation which Cicero gives it in the beginning of his Topics, where he says, that a judicious reader ought to be allured not only by the matter of this work, *sed dicendi quoque incredibili quadam cum copia tum etiam suavitate.*

We have upon this work a commentary of Alexander Aphrodisiensis, the first commentator upon Aristotle of the Alexandrian School. It is very full and accurate, and shews that the author perfectly understood the meaning of Aristotle. But he has explained his meaning so well himself, and illustrated it by examples so much, that I think he does not need a commentator; and the best use that can be made of the Aphrodisian's commentary, is to correct some errors in the manuscript, of which, however, there are not many in

Chap. III. PROGRESS OF LANGUAGE. 45

this work. And indeed I wonder that there are not many more in this, and every other work of Ariftotle, as many as are in his book upon Poetry, confidering the fate of Ariftotle's writings, which lay fo long under ground, but were at laft difcovered and brought to light*,

Haud equidem fine mente, reor, fine numine Divum ;

for if it be true what Plato fays, that philofophy is the greateft gift of the gods to mortal men, we muft think this a remarkable inftance of a good providence, by which fo complete a fyftem of philofophy was reftored to the world.

And here I think it may not be improper to give the reader a general view of this great fyftem of philofophy, which Ariftotle has left us, and which may be faid

---

* See an account of this given in the preface to vol. 3. of Ant. Metaph. p. xxxviii. See alfo the Life of Ariftotle by Diogenes Laertius, with a quotation from Strabo, and another from Plutarch, concerning his writings, prefixed to Du Vall's edition of his works

to have been miraculously preserved to us. What we have first in the editions of his works, and which is very justly so placed, being a proper introduction to all philosophy, and indeed to all science, is his Logical works, of which the first may be called the Doctrine of Ideas, without which there can be no philosophy or science of any kind. Of these he has given a most comprehensive system in his book of Categories, so grand and comprehensive, that those among us, who think proper to philosophise without the assistance of the antients, cannot have so much as an idea of it. Nor is it possible it could have been produced in any other school than that of Pythagoras, who had learned in Egypt that wisdom of the Egyptians in which Moses was instructed: For it is a system that takes in the whole of things existing in the universe; and therefore the work of Archytas upon the subject, is very properly intitled, περι του παντος, that is, *Of the whole of things:* And the work is as useful as it is grand and comprehensive; for, as I have shewn elsewhere *, without it there could be nothing perfect in philosophy or science of any kind, because there could be no perfect definition.

But ideas are no more than the materials of reasoning, the first step of which is Propositions. Upon these Aristotle has very properly bestowed a whole book, which he has intitled, περι ἑρμηνειας, or, *De Interpretatione*, and indeed they required nothing less, considering the wonderful variety of them, and all the several speciefes of them, according to the difference of the subject, the praedicate, the matter, and the manner of the proposition; the number of them all together amounting to no less than 3024, a number which must appear incredible to those who have not made a study of logic †.

Of propositions, some, but very few, are self-evident; and if we were to go

---

* Origin and Prog. of Lang. p. 72 and following of the 2d edition of vol. 1st.
† See preface to vol. 3. of Ant. Metaph. p. 49.

no farther in reasoning, than to perceive the connection betwixt the subject and praedicate of such propositions, no art or science ever could have been invented. At the same time, it was of absolute necessity that there should be some self-evident propositions; for if every thing was to be proved, nothing could be proved: And therefore we ought to admire the goodness of God, who has enabled us by nature, without any art or teaching, to perceive the truth of such propositions, upon which all science is founded, and without which, in this our fallen state, we never could have brought our intellectual part to any degree of perfection.

And here begins the great process of reasoning, and which only is *reasoning* in the English sense of the word. It is performed by that discursive faculty of the mind, in Greek called διανοια. By it, from certain propositions, we deduce others, and from these others; and so we go on, till we arrive at the conclusion we desire: And if the propositions with which we begin are self-evident propositions, or propositions that have been demonstrated, and the deductions from them properly made, then is the reasoning Demonstrative. And this is the reasoning which Aristotle has explained with such wonderful accuracy in his *first* and *last* Analytics. Every reasoning of this kind, and indeed of every kind, must be in syllogisms. The subject, therefore, of these books of Analytics is the syllogism, which he has annalysed into three propositions, and three terms; by which these propositions are so syllogised or brought together, as to infer the conclusion. But of this I have spoken at more length elsewhere*, where I have shewn, that Aristotle, in order to explain perfectly the nature of the syllogism, has divided it into three figures, and these again he has subdivided into fourteen modes. All this intricate work I know those of this age,

---

* See the preface to Ant. Metaph. p. 49 and 50.

who think themselves philosophers, will despise: But I can assure them, that without the study of this logic of Aristotle, they can only reason as vulgar men do, without knowing what truth or science is: And they will reason as illiterate men speak, who can, by mere practice and habit, put their words together so as to express their meaning; but not having learned the grammatical art, they cannot tell by what rule that is done. Our philosophers, therefore, of this age, though they inquire much about truth and science, do not so much as know what science is: Nor do they appear to have the curiosity which Pontius Pilate, the Roman governour of Judea had, who asked of our Saviour what truth was; which proves to me, that although the Aristotelian philosophy was very little known in Rome, as I shall afterwards show, Pilate had got some idea of this work of Aristotle, as much, at least, as to excite his curiosity to know what truth and science was, which to discover, is the professed intention of Aristotle's works *.

* See the beginning of his First Analytics.

In these books of analytics, Aristotle has explained most accurately the nature of demonstrative reasoning, and enabled us to argue with men of science upon subjects of science. But by far the greater part of mankind have no science, yet they have opinions, and form propositions upon different subjects, and from these propositions they argue; for otherwise they would not be rational creatures. With such men our chief intercourse in life is; and if we were not taught to argue with them in their own way, I should think the reasoning art imperfect and defective. To collect all the opinions of the vulgar upon the subject of every art and science, or of every occurrence in human life, would have been an endless work and of little or no use, if it could have been accomplished. But to digest these opinions in order, and to rank them under certain heads, so as to make them of ready use, was a most useful work, and does the greatest honour to the author of it. Now this Aristotle has done in his Dialectical works or Topics, and in his Rhetoric. In the first of these he has given us topics, which apply chiefly to arts and sciences: In the second we have the topics, from which we argue in political matters, or in the common affairs of life. And he has not only given us the topics upon these subjects, but he has shewn how we are to argue from them; and has taught us that most important lesson in logic, to know *what is consequent, what is repugnant, and from what being given what follows*. And to these two he has subjoined his treatise *De Sophisticis Elenchis*, in which he has detected the arts of the sophists, and shewn how we are to guard against them. All these works I have mentioned, viz. his Categories, his book upon Propositions, his *First* and *Last* Analytics, his Dialectic or Topics, and his work against the Sophists, are all of the logical kind, and make all together a most wonderful system of the operations of the discursive faculty of the human mind; for in them are contained all the forms of argumentation that can be imagined; and there is a variety of knowledge shewn, not only in arts and

Chap. III. PROGRESS OF LANGUAGE. 53

sciences, but in the business of human life, such as one can hardly believe could have fallen to the share of any one man. And thus Aristotle has had the honour to complete the last part of the philosophy of Egypt, which came to Greece from the School of Pythagoras; for before Aristotle wrote, it appears that a considerable part of the moral philosophy, the natural, metaphysical, and theological, belonging to this school, was known in Greece. But he first taught the Greeks to know what science was, about which we see so much disputation in the *Theætetus* of Plato, but nothing decided *.

If Aristotle had never written any thing else except this great logical work, I should have thought that he had employed his time very well, and that philosophy was very much indebted to him. But besides his logical works, he has given us a sys-

* Who desires to know more upon this subject, may read what I have written in the *fifth* volume of this work, p. 356, and following.

tem of morals, the beſt extant, and alſo of politics, which, ſo far as it has gone, I think excellent: Then he has given us the Philoſophy of Nature, the only philoſophy of that kind which I know: And he has concluded with that philoſophy which goes beyond nature and the material world, and is therefore called Metaphyſics. And not content with all this, he has given us a work upon Poetry, of which only *one* book is come down to us, of *three* which he is ſaid to have written. And thus mutilated and imperfect, yet I think it a moſt valuable work, as it gives us the philoſophy not only of poetry, but of all the fine arts. And I am not aſhamed to own, that without ſtudying it, I ſhould not have known what poetry was; but ſhould have thought, as many others do, that verſification and fine diction make poetry *. Beſides theſe great works, there are ſeveral detached pieces preſerved

---

* Who would deſire to know more of the writings of Ariſtotle, may read what I have ſaid in the third chap. of the 2d book of vol. 5.

Chap. III. Progress of Language. 55

to us, such as his Problems, a work of great curiosity; his *Quaestiones Mechanicae*, and his book upon Physiognomy, and others: For he wrote altogether, as Diogenes Laertius informs us, four hundred books, of which only about one hundred and thirty are preserved to us*. But even in these we have a complete system of philosophy such as is not to be found in the writings of any other ancient author. What appears to me more extraordinary than any thing I have yet mentioned of this philosopher, is, that he lived no more than sixty-three years, eight of which he employed in educating the Conqueror of the World; and yet he found time, not only to write so many books, but to establish the best school of philosophy in Greece, which he taught walking in the Lyceaum.——But to return to the Topics from this degression, which though long, I hope the reader will not think foreign to the purpose.

There is a book of Topics written by

---

* See Du Vall's edition of Aristotle, in the introduction, p. 7.

Cicero, and addreſſed to Trebatius the lawyer. It was written, as he tells us, aboard a ſhip, in his return from Greece, without the uſe of any books; and allowances being made for that, I think the work has a good deal of merit, as it ſhews that he had ſtudied Ariſtotle's Topics very diligently. As he addreſſed it to a lawyer, he has taken his illuſtrations and examples chiefly from the civil law of the Romans, which I ſuppoſe Trebatius would underſtand much better than if he had taken his examples, as Ariſtotle has done, from philoſophy. And it appears from theſe examples, that Cicero underſtood the civil law very well; ſo that we need not wonder of his boaſting, that if he was provoked by the lawyers, he would profeſs himſelf a lawyer in three days. Cicero tells us, in the beginning of this treatiſe, that he put Ariſtotle's work into the hands of Trebatius, but he did not underſtand it: And what is more extraordinary, a very learned rhetorician, into whoſe hands Trebatius put the book, did not underſtand it neither. Cicero adds, what I think ſtill more extraordinary, that the philosophers themselves, at that time were, a very few excepted, quite ignorant of Ariſtotle's works. And I am perſuaded, that if his philoſophy had not been revived in the Alexandrian School, it would have been again loſt; or if the manuſcripts had been preſerved, a great part of them would not have been intelligible to us without the aſſiſtance of the commentators of that ſchool.

CHAP. IV.

All the arguments belonging to the subject are taken from the Dialectic art; and the Topics from which they are to be deduced are to be found there.—Those arguments are only in the cause.—The others from the person of the speaker or hearer out of the cause.—Yet these only insisted on by the writers on rhetoric before Aristotle.—The arguments from the subject are all Enthymemas, that is, imperfect syllogisms.—All reasoning of every kind reducible to syllogism.—The Enthymema called a Dialectical Syllogism, but used in all kinds of reasoning.—The complete syllogism very seldom used by any writer;—but thrice by Aristotle.—No inference from thence of the inutility of the doctrine of the syllogism.—Aristotle's observation concerning the invention of Dialectic and Rhetoric, applies to all arts,—and likewise to all sciences.

IN the preceding chapter I enlarged so much upon the dialectic art, because it is from it that we get all those arguments of the kind of which I am now speaking, that is, arguments which arise from the subject itself; for whether they be taken from the case as stated, or whether they arise from the testimony of witnesses, evidence of writings, the authority of authors, or from examples of what has happened in former times, they are all to be found in the dialectic art. The other two kinds of arguments, which are taken either from the persons of the hearers or speakers, are all, as Aristotle has observed, out of the cause: And therefore in the courts of justice in some states, and particularly in the Areopagus in Athens, the pleaders were forbid to use any arguments of that kind, as being foreign to the subject in dispute *. And yet, says he, those, that have written upon the art before me, have

---

* Aup. Rhetoric, cap. 1.

said very little upon the arguments of the first kind, which only can be said to belong to the cause; but insist very much upon the other kinds of arguments, which are foreign to the cause.

In this chapter he observes, that the arguments which arise from the subject itself, and are properly in the cause, are all *Enthymemas*, that is, imperfect syllogisms, or syllogisms in which one or other of the two propositions, from which the conclusion is drawn, is not mentioned, as being well known to the hearer, and being supposed to be in his mind, from which supposition the name is given to the syllogism. It is commonly called the Dialectical Syllogism; but it is used in all kinds of reasoning: For there can be no reasoning without syllogism; and even the demonstrations in mathematics consist all of this imperfect kind of syllogism. The complete syllogism, consisting of three propositions, the major, minor, and conclusion, is very seldom to be found in any writing or speaking. I have heard of a doctor in

England, who had the curiosity to go through Aristotle's writings, in order to find there complete syllogisms; and I was told he could find but three. And indeed my wonder is, that in a writer, who has so little superfluity of words, he should have found so many. From thence the Doctor would no doubt infer the inutility of the doctrine of the syllogism, which Aristotle has laboured so much in his books of Analytics. He might have as well argued, that because in speaking or writing we do not mention the distinction of letters and syllables, therefore the analysis of speech into these component parts was quite useless. There is another observation made by Aristotle in this chapter, which applies equally to dialectic and rhetoric, and is worthy of being taken notice of, as it accounts for the origin not only of these arts, but of every other. Rhetoric, says he, and dialectic belong to no particular art, and therefore they are practised more or less by those who have learned no art; for all men prove or disprove, praise or blame, accuse or defend. But the greater part of men do this from mere custom and habit, without rule or method; and when it is so done, says he, we observe that some do it well, and others not well. And when we observe for what reason some do it well, while others do it ill, this is the beginning of the art; and I will add, that it is the beginning of all arts: For the first essays in them all have been from nature; and by observing what is well or ill done in them, the art has been begun, and, by degrees, very slow degrees at first, has been perfected; so that Aristotle has here given us the progress of the human mind in the formation of all arts, and, I think I may add, of all sciences. For the first attempts of the mind in science, as well as in art, must have been rude extempore essays of our intellectual faculty, upon subjects of science, without order or method, definition or division, the necessity of which would only be discovered in process of time, when we begin to discover what rude and imperfect work we make without these.

CHAP. V.

Of the arguments taken from the persons of the speaker or hearers.—In all causes that are argued of every kind, the hearers must judge or form an opinion.—That must depend, in a great measure, upon what they think of the speaker, and upon their own affections and passions.—The judgment they form of the speaker, reducible to three heads.—What influences the minds of the hearers is of four kinds, their passions, their habits, their ages, and their fortune.—Of the passions, and particularly of Anger.—Of the appeasing of Anger.—Of Love—Hatred—Fear—Shame—Want of shame—Gratitude—Pity—Indignation—Envy—Emulation.—What Aristotle has written here upon the passions the most valuable thing of the kind to be found.—He quotes Homer very much to the purpose upon this subject.—In this Rhetorical work he shows not only the greatest knowledge of human nature, but of the world, and the affairs of life, much more than could be expected from a man so much engaged in philosophy.—Of sententious sayings and Enthymemas with respect to the passions.

I COME now to speak of the last kind of arguments I mentioned, those which arise from the persons of the speakers or of the hearers, and which must have their weight in all the three kinds of Rhetoric I have mentioned; for in all the three, as Aristotle has observed*, the hearers judge: When they deliberate, they judge; when they hear causes tried, they judge; and when any person or thing is praised or dispraised, they also form a judgment one way or another. Now these judgments must depend very much, not only upon their opinion of the subject which the orator treats, and from which those intrinsic arguments I have spoken of

* Lib. 2. Rhetoric. cap. 1.

are derived; but alſo upon the characters, manners, and diſpoſitions of the hearers; and likewiſe upon the opinion they may have of the ſpeaker. Their opinion of the ſpeaker muſt depend upon the judgment that they form of three things concerning him; firſt, his wiſdom and his underſtanding of the ſubject; next, his virtue and good diſpoſitions; and, laſtly, his good will and affection towards the hearers. If he want the firſt of theſe, he cannot argue the cauſe properly; if the ſecond, he may miſlead the hearers deſignedly; and although he want neither of theſe, but have not good will to the hearers, he may not be at ſufficient pains to inform them. For the moral character of the ſpeaker or hearers, and their prudence and underſtanding, Ariſtotle refers us to what he has ſaid in his books of Morals. But, as to their affections and paſſions, he has treated of them very fully in his ſecond book upon Rhetoric.

Ariſtotle, in the 12th chapter of this ſecond book, mentions four things which influence the judgment of men; 1*mo*, their παθη, or Paſſions; 2*do*, their ἑξεις, or Habits; 3*tio*, their Age; and, laſtly, their Fortune or Condition in life: And he has told us what he means by each of theſe. The Paſſions, he ſays, are ſuch as anger, indignation, envy, and ſuch like. By Habits, he ſays, he means diſpoſitions virtuous or vitious, and which are called in Greek th τα ηθη, as diſtinguiſhed from the τα παθη. By Age he means youth, manhood, or old age: And by Fortune he means birth, wealth, and power, or the oppoſite of theſe; and in general, good or bad fortune. The paſſions he has explained at great length, beginning with Anger, on which he has beſtowed a pretty long chapter, explaining the diſpoſitions of men who are liable to anger, with whom they are angry, and for what reaſon [*]. In the next chapter he explains what he calls πραϋσις, that is, the appeaſing and quieting

---

[*] Lib. 2. De Rhetor. cap. 2.

Chap. V. Progress of Language. 67

of anger. In the next chapter he proceeds to tell us what Love and Hatred is, and to explain the difference betwixt anger and hatred. In the fifth chapter he lets us know what Fear is, what things are frightful, and how those who are afraid are affected. In like manner he, in the next chapter, explains what Shame is, and also what the want of it is. And in the two next chapters he explains what Gratitude is, and then what Pity is. After this he lets us know what Indignation is; what Envy, and what Emulation, in so many different chapters. All these seveveral passions he has explained and defined with philosophical accuracy: Nor indeed do I think that all that has been written upon the passions in antient or modern times will give so much pleasure and instruction to the philosopher, as these few chapters of Aristotle* And I think it

---

* He has observed in our passions that wonderful mixture of things so opposite as pain and pleasure; and I am much pleased with his quotations from Homer, which prove that he knew this mixture as well

may be said in general of these books of Rhetoric, that there is no work extant from which we can learn so much of human nature, and even of what is called the knowledge of the world: For Aristotle appears to me to have studied with wonderful attention the affairs of men, and the business of human life, much more than could be expected from a man engaged in such philosophical speculations, and who has formed the most compre-

as Aristotle; particularly with respect to anger, which is certainly a very uneasy passion; yet he says at the same time it has a sweetness like that of honey.

'Ος τι πολυ γλυκιων μελιτος καταλειβομενοιο
Ανδρων εν στηθεσσι αεξεται;

for which Aristotle has accounted very well, lib. 2. cap. 2. and lib. 1. cap. 11. And even as to grief and lamentation, in which one should think there was nothing but pain and affliction, Homer, he observes, (ibid. lib. 1. cap. 11.) has found out that there is a certain pleasure in the indulgence of grief,

'Ως φατο, τοισι δε πασιν υφ' 'ιμερον ωρσε γοοιο.'

So that it appears Homer was acquainted with all the movements of the human mind, even those the most removed from common apprehension.

henfive fyftem of philofophy that I believe ever was formed by any one man. Thefe books I would alfo recommend to the ftudy not only of the philofopher, but of the fcholar and grammarian, who will there learn the propriety of all the Greek words that are ufed upon the fubject of the characters, fentiments, affections, and paffions of men, a fubject of very great extent, comprehending what is moft pleafing and interefting in human life. And, if he is a man of tafte, he will be extremely pleafed with the ftile, which well deferves the character that Cicero has given of it*, and is, I think, a perfect model of the Didactic.

In the fecond chapter Ariftotle has given us a great many γνωμαι, or fententious fayings, applicable to the paffions and characters of men: And he obferves very juftly, that the ufe of thefe makes the ftile what the Greeks call *ethical*, that is, expreffive of the manners of men†. He

---

* P. 44. of this vol.
† Rhetor. lib. 2. cap. 21.

gives us alfo a great number of Enthymemas, or arguments upon this fubject: But they are all included in thofe general topics mentioned in the dialectic; fo that here in his Rhetoric he does no more than apply them to the fentiments and paffions of men.

CHAP. VI.

Of the division of Rhetoric into Deliberative, Judicial, and Epideictic.—This division was first made by Aristotle, and arises from the nature of speech, in which there must be a speaker, hearer, and subject.—Aristotle first made a science of Rhetoric, as well as of other things. —The subject of the three kinds of Rhetoric explained.—A threefold division of Rhetoric, taken from the end which it proposes.—Rhetoric addressed not only to many, but to one.—Therefore of universal use in human life.—Of the subjects of which deliberative Rhetoric treats, and the things necessary to be known by an orator of that kind.—Under the head of Deliberative Eloquence, he treats of happiness, which is the end of all deliberation.—Every advantage of mind or body to be wished for, there enumerated.—Of the idea of good, without which there can be no happiness.—That belongs to the intellectual part of our mind.—*The subject of the Epideictic is the* τo χαλον.—*Two definitions of that given;—but they are only popular descriptions.*—*Under that head, and in the chapter upon Happiness, every thing is enumerated that is beautiful and praise-worthy in human life.*—*Of the Judicial kind of Rhetoric.*—*The subject of it Injury and Injustice.*—*Here every thing that is bad in human nature is set before us.*—*His threefold division upon the subject of Injury and Injustice.*—*This division most accurate and complete.*—*Of the motives to Injury.*—What is pleasant *is the chief motive.*—*Definition of* Pleasure.—*Of the pleasures of sense.*—*Imagination a weaker kind of sense.*—*It makes things both past and future give us pleasure, as if they were present;—even things disagreeable that are past*—*The pleasure in grief and hope accounted for in that way.*—*Self-love, and the pleasure we take in ourselves, in that way accounted for.*—*The second thing to be considered with regard to Injury, is the character and dispositions of the person who injures.—Here a complete character of a villain is given.—The third and last thing belonging to Injury is an account of the persons most liable to be injured.—And thus is completed his account both of the villain and of villainy.—Conclusion of this book, and of what is to be said upon the* matter *of Rhetoric.*

I COME now to speak of the three kinds of Rhetoric I mentioned in the beginning of this book, the Deliberative, the Judicial, and the Epideictic; a division taken from the subject of Rhetoric, and first made by Aristotle, as well as the division of the arguments used upon these subjects. And indeed it appears to me, that Aristotle first made a science of rhetoric, as well as of dialectic; and I believe I may add of morals, natural philosophy, and metaphysics. This division of the subjects of rhetoric he has explained most accurately and philosophically in the third chapter of his first book of Rhetoric, where he tells us that there are three things to be considered in all speech, namely, the speaker, the person to whom he speaks, and the subject upon which he speaks; and all the three are of absolute necessity, so that no speech can be conceived without them. Besides, there is the end or purpose of speaking: And this necessarily refers to the hearer, who is either only to form an opinion of what he hears, and is simply what Aristotle calls θεωρος; or he is to determine and act, and him Aristotle calls Κριτης. And it is either upon things past or things to come that he is to determine. If it is upon things past, he is what we call a judge; if upon things to come, he is a senator, or a member of any assembly that deliberates upon such things. If again he does no more than speculate, and only forms opinions, it must be upon the subject of qualities, powers, and faculties; all which Aristotle has expressed by the single word of Δυναμεις. And thus, says he, we have of necessity three kinds of rhetorical speech, the deliberative, the judicial, and the epideictic or demonstrative, as it is improperly called *. Then he goes on, still dividing with his usual accuracy, and tells us that the deliberative consists either of Exhortation or Dehortation, προτροπη or αποτροπη, as he expresses it, that is, *advising* or *disuading*. The judicial consists of Accusation or Defence, that is, κατηγορια or απολογια ; for, as I have observed †, it was not the custom in Athens to plead upon matters of civil right, or points of law, as we call them. And, lastly, the subject of the epideictic is either praise or blame.

Rhetoric, as well as every other art, must propose some end. The general end of Rhetoric, as I have said ‡, is to persuade. This is divided according to the three different kinds of rhetoric. The end of the deliberative is to persuade what is useful, and disuade what is hurtful: And to inforce this, it insists up-

* See p. 28. of this vol.
† P. 27.   ‡ P. 20.

on what is juſt or unjuſt, what is honourable and praiſe worthy, or otherwiſe. The end of the Judicial Rhetoric is the juſt or the unjuſt; and to inforce this, it aſſumes the other things I have juſt now mentioned. In praiſing or diſpraiſing, our object is the beautiful and honourable, or the contrary, and whatever has any reference to theſe *.

Having thus accurately divided and ſubdivided the ſubjects of rhetoric, he proceeds to explain the firſt kind of rhetoric, namely, the *Deliberative*. But, before I ſay any thing particular of it, it is proper to obſerve, that all the three kinds of rhetoric may not only be addreſſed to many hearers, but to one; though commonly in Greece, where the governments were popular, they were addreſſed to the many. But, that they may be addreſſed alſo to one, he has expreſsly told us in the eighteenth chapter of his ſecond book. With reſpect to judicial proceedings, they are often, a-

* Lib. 1. cap. 3.

Chap. VI. Progress of Language. 77

mong us, before one judge; and as we plead before one single person, so we may also advise a single person, and likewise appeal to his judgment when we praise or dispraise any person. And thus it appears, that the rhetoric of Aristotle is of universal use in human life.

Our author, in his first book, has given us several chapters upon deliberative rhetoric; and, as that which deliberates upon public affairs is of the greatest importance, he mentions the several subjects of public deliberation, which, with his usual accuracy, he divides into five classes *, and shortly mentions what it is necessary that a speaker should know with respect to each of these articles, in order to be able to give good advice concerning them. But he tells us what is very true, that the knowledge of these things belongs to the political science, and not to rhetoric.

The next chapter treats of a great sub-

* Lib. 1. cap. 4.

ject—Happiness; which, he says, is the end of all deliberation and consultation about what we are to do or not to do. And here we have a most full enumeration of all the things that make a life happy and prosperous, belonging either to mind or body, and every thing most accurately defined and explained. And particularly with respect to the body, we have explained, better than any where else that I know, what a παλαιστικος is, what a πυκτικος, what a παγκρατιαστικος and what a πενταθλος. All these exercises were very much practised by the Greeks, and gave a strength and vigour to their bodies which is unknown in modern times.

With the subject of this chapter is much connected the subject of the next, which is the το αγαθον, or *what is good;* without which there can be no happiness. It is a more determined and more philosophical idea than that of Happiness; for, as Aristotle has explained it, it belongs entirely to the intellectual part of our nature, and to that governing principle in us which directs the conduct of our lives, and provides for every thing that is conducive to the welfare of mind or body. And as we often debate about what is the greater good, which muſt always be the caſe when two things both good are preſented to us, he has given us a long chapter upon the ſubject of the compariſon of good things, where he has furniſhed a great number of topics to enable us to determine what is the greater, and what is the leſſer good *.

The next kind of rhetoric, he conſiders, is the Epideictic, the ſubject of which is praiſe or diſpraiſe. And here we have a very long and fine chapter †, wherein we have all the Virtues enumerated, and ſhortly, but very accurately defined and explained. As Virtue belongs to the το καλον, or the beautiful, and is inſeparable from it, according to the notions of the ancients, he ſpeaks a great deal of it, and has given us two definitions of it. The firſt is,

---

* Lib. 1. cap. 7.
† Lib. 1. cap. 9.

That, which being eligible for its own sake, is praise-worthy. The other is, *That, which being good, is pleasant because it is good.* The last I like the best, because it mentions a quality of the το καλον, which distinguishes it from every thing else belonging to man, namely, that it gives pleasure, not pleasure of every kind, but a pleasure arising from what is good. They are both, however, rather descriptions than definitions properly so called: For they only tell us certain qualities and effects of the thing, not what it is itself, or what constitutes its essence*; but they are sufficient for the purpose of this work, of which the subject, as he has more than once told us, is not any particular science, such as that of morals. There is, however, in this chapter, what may be called an abridgment of his work upon morals. And in it, and the other chapters of this

---

* See what I have said on this subject, in vol. 2d. of Ant. Metaph. p. 105, and following; where, I think, I have mentioned that which is of the essence of the *Beautiful*, and without which it cannot be conceived to exist.

book upon the subject of happiness, and the το αγαθον, you have every thing enumerated and described that is beautiful, praise-worthy, pleasant, and agreeable in human nature or in human life, more accurately, though shortly, than is any where else to be found: Nor is there any thing that I read with more pleasure or more instruction.

The last kind of rhetoric is the Judicial, the subjects of which, among the Greeks, was only, as I observed, accusation and defence. Injury, therefore, and Injustice, were in this kind of rhetoric the topics of argument. And here we have displayed to us, by our author, all the crimes and vices of men, as in the former part of the work we had exhibited to us all their virtues and good qualities; so that in this work of Aristotle we have the whole of human nature, what is good and what is bad in it, set before us.

The subject of Injury and Injustice he

has divided as accurately as any other subject which he treats: For having told us what injustice is, he inquires, first, from what motives men commit injustice; secondly, in what situation, in what circumstances, and how disposed they are when they do so; and, thirdly, Who are the persons that are most liable to be injured? And this is a division which undoubtedly exhausts the subject *. In his inquiry into the motives of injuries, he has enumerated all the causes of the actions of men; and he tells us, that every thing, we do voluntarily, proceeds from our apprehension of its being either good or pleasant. What is Good he had already explained, in what he had said upon deliberative rhetoric; and he now explains, in one of the longest chapters of the whole work, what Pleasure is.

Pleasure he defines to be ' a certain mo-
' tion of the mind;' but as all our motions, both of mind and body, must be in con-

---

* Lib. 1. cap. 10.

formity to our nature, he adds, ' That it is a
' conſtituting or placing of our mind, by a
' movement quick and ſenſible, into a na-
' tural ſtate,' that is, a ſtate ſuch as the
nature and diſpoſition of our mind at the
time requires: ' And the oppoſite of this is
' Pain*.' As all pleaſure, therefore, is according to nature, and as cuſtom is, according to a common ſaying, a ſecond nature,
it follows from thence, that what we are
accuſtomed to is pleaſant. But he tells us
at the ſame time, that change is alſo pleaſant: For always the ſame becomes at laſt
an exceſs of the habit or diſpoſition of the
mind, from which a change relieves it.

* Ariſtotle's words are, 'Υποκεισθω δ' 'ημιν, ειναι την 'ηδονην, κινησιν τινα της ψυχης, και καταστασιν, αθροαν και αισθητην, εις την 'υπαρχουσαν φυσιν· λυπην δε, τουναντιον. *Rhetoricor.* lib. 1. cap. 11. Here the reader will obſerve the expreſſion 'υπαρχουσαν φυσιν, where according to the propriety of the Greek language, the word 'υπαρχουσαν denotes, as I have tranſlated it, the ſtate of the mind at the time the pleaſure is felt. So that this definition will comprehend what we would call the moſt unnatural pleaſures, if, at the time, they be deſired by the mind.

The pleasures of sense he just mentions, being well known to every body: But he adds what is not commonly known, that the Phantasia, or imagination, is a kind of weaker sense; and therefore what our imagination presents to us, whether it be past or to come, if it be a pleasant object, gives us pleasure. And even things which were not agreeable, when they were present, after they are past, give us pleasure in remembering them, such as dangers that we have escaped, especially if we have escaped them by prudence and resolution; and here, as upon other occasions, he very properly quotes two lines of Homer*. It is imagination, too, that makes the pleasure of grief above mentioned, as he has very well explained it: For, says he, a man, that grieves for the loss of a friend, has that friend so represented to him by his imagination, that he seems to see him, and enjoys, in some sort, the

---

* ——Μετα γαρ, και αλγεσι τερπεται ανηρ,
Μνημενος, 'οστις πολλα παθη, και πολλα εοργη.

Chap. VI. Progress of Language. 85

pleasure that he enjoyed in his company, conversation, and actions. From the imagination of things to come, he accounts for the pleasure of anger, above mentioned; and in general, of all things which we desire and hope for: For, says he, if we hope for a thing, we see it as present. In short, he gives a philosophical account of all our pleasures, and even of the pleasure we have in ourselves, or what is commonly called self-love: For, says he, all animals love and delight in what is congenial to them, thus a man has pleasure in a man, a horse in a horse, and so on with respect to other animals. Now nothing can be more congenial to a man than himself: Therefore he loves himself, and every thing belonging to himself; such as his works and his productions of every kind, and among others, his children.

The next chapter presents to us the worst face of human nature; for it de-

* Lib. 1. cap. 12.

scribes those dispositions of the mind which form the character of an unjust and wicked man. This was the second thing he proposed to speak to, upon the subject of injury and injustice. And here he has given us a most accurate portrait of the character of a villain, so full and complete, that I think it is impossible to add any thing to it*.

In the same chapter he describes the persons who are most liable to be injured, which was the third thing he proposed upon this subject. And on this head, as in every part of this work, he has shewn a wonderful knowledge of the world, and of the ways of men. When we join with what he has said upon this head, the description of a villain under the former head, we have a full and most accurate picture of villainy, as well as of a villain.

To enter into all the particulars under

---

* Lib. 1. cap. 12.

those two heads, would carry me much farther than is neceſſary or proper in a work, of which the intention is, as I have said, not to give a complete treatiſe of Rhetoric, but only a general plan of this fine work of Ariſtotle, and to direct the attention of the reader to the ſeveral parts of it, which I think are of the greateſt importance. And indeed my chief deſign, in all that I have written upon the philoſophy or the learning of the antients, is to revive, if poſſible, the ſtudy of antient arts and ſciences, *veteres revocare artes*, as Horace expreſſes it, and to ſhew the reader that he cannot perfectly underſtand any art or ſcience without the ſtudy of thoſe unfaſhionable books to which I refer. Without that ſtudy, I think I have ſhewn, in my books of metaphyſics, that no man can be a philoſopher; and, in the ſecond volume of this work, I think I have alſo ſhewn, that no man can be a complete grammarian, nor perfectly comprehend in what the art of language conſiſts; and from what I have ſaid, and will further ſay in this volume, I hope to make it appear, that he cannot underſtand the principles of any of the fine arts; and in ſhort, that without the ſtudy of theſe antient books, he cannot be a ſcholar, a critic, or a man of true taſte, any more than a philoſopher.

And here I conclude this book, and all that I think it is proper to ſay upon the *matter* of Rhetoric. The ſubject of the next book will be the *ſtile* of Rhetoric.

BOOK II.

Of the Stile *of* Rhetoric.

CHAP. I.

The ornaments of Stile neceſſary for an orator who ſpeaks to the people.—If the audience are wiſe men, they will mind nothing but the matter; and all they will require, will be to underſtand the matter.—The Stile of the orators at firſt poetical;—but this corrected in later times.—Stile conſiſts of words and the compoſition of words.—The laſt of theſe moſt difficult.—This illuſtrated from other arts.—Words divided into proper and tropical.—The proper ſignification muſt be well underſtood, otherwiſe we cannot know whether it be properly transferred to another signification.—Of proper words—there should be a variety of them, signifying the same thing;—but not too great a variety, as in Arabic.—Of Homer's language;—more rich in synonymous words, only diversified a little by some change in the sound, than any other language in Greek.—Homer's language not composed of different Dialects, but the different Dialects made out of it.—An account how it comes to be so rich a language.—It is a dialect of the Shanscrit which was the antient language of Egypt, that went both to India and Greece.—More variety of derivation, composition, and flection, in Homer, than in the other Greek Dialects;—but more variety still in the Shanscrit.—The definition of a Trope.—*Philosophical account of Tropes given by Aristotle.—Of the* Metaphor.—*This word used in a large sense by Aristotle;—but is only used in Rhetoric in the common sense of the word, to denote a similitude betwixt two things.—It is a Simile in one word.—*

Of the proper use of Metaphor, and of the abuse of it.

THE Stile of Rhetoric, which is the subject of this second book of mine, is the subject of Aristotle's third book, which he begins with observing, That if the hearers of rhetorical speeches were such as they ought to be, there would be no need of ornaments of speech: They would require no more of the orator, than that he should make himself understood, and not offend their ears; for it would be the matter they would mind, and not the words. But the hearers are such, that they are not to be convinced by reason and argument only, without the blandishment of fine language. And if Demosthenes and the other orators of Greece had spoken in the same way that Socrates did in his trial, who, as Plato and Xenophon inform us, disdained to use any ornament of words, they would have been as unsuccessful as he was. We must therefore add, to the definition I have given of Rhetoric*, 'That the ſtile of it ſhould be different from common ſpeech.'

Ariſtotle, in the firſt chapter of this third book, tells us that the poets, by their diction, as well as by their numbers, pleaſed the people very much, and were much admired, though there was often very little ſenſe or matter in their works. In imitation of them, he ſays, the ſtile of the orators was at firſt very poetical; and he mentions Gorgias as ſpeaking in that ſtile. And, ſays he, there are many who ſtill admire this poetical ſtile of eloquence: But among the learned the diſtinction is clearly eſtabliſhed. And even the tragic poets, he ſays, write in a ſtile much more familiar, and liker to common ſpeech; ſo that it would be ridiculous to imitate thoſe who, themſelves, do not now compoſe in that ſtile.

Stile neceſſarily conſiſts of two things;

---

* P. 35 and 36.

Words, and the Composition of these words into sentences or periods *. Of these two the last is the most difficult: And it is so in all arts, as well as in the writing or speaking art. In painting, for example, it is more difficult to put together figures properly in a piece, than to paint the single figures. In poetry, it is much more difficult to put together properly the several parts of a drama, or of an epic poem, than to invent particular incidents, and to adorn them with characters and manners. And every composer as well as performer in music, knows how much more difficult it is to put together properly the notes, so as to make a good piece of music, than to use the finest notes. But, as single words are the materials of which all writing or speaking is composed, we must begin with explaining the nature of them.

Words, with respect to stile and composition, are divided into proper, and tro-

---

* Vol. 3d. of this work, chap. 1.

pical, or figurative, as they are commonly, but improperly called. These I have defined and distinguished from one another, in the beginning of the third chapter of the third volume of this work: And from the definition there given, it is evident they are so connected, that the one cannot be understood without the other: For, if I do not know what the proper word signifies, it is impossible I can apply it justly in a tropical signification, by which it is transferred from its proper sense to another which has a connection with that sense. It is therefore a capital defect in Dr. Johnson's English Dictionary, as I have elsewhere observed*, that he has not distinguished the proper signification of words from the tropical use of them. This is an error which the French Academy has carefully avoided, and which makes their dictionary one of the most valuable dictionaries that we have in any language.

As there can be no beauty in any work,

---

* Vol. 5th. of this work, p. 274.

whether of nature or of art, without variety in a certain degree, so there can be no real beauty in language without a variety of words, and not of tropical words only, but of proper. For a language is much more agreeable and pleasant to the ear, when it is not obliged to express the same thing even by the same proper word, but can diversify the speech by some variety even of these words. At the same time this variety may be carried too far. For I have heard it observed of the Arabic, if my memory does not fail me, that it has very often six or seven words expressing the very same thing, without trope or figure. This, I think, makes the language too bulky and cumbersome. But the Greek, in this respect, as well as in every other, is more perfect than any language that I know: For it has a very considerable number of synonymes, but not too many.

The language of Homer is in this respect, as well as in every other, the most perfect that is to be found in Greek, or in any other language that I understand: For he has not only many synonymes; but, by various terminations and flections, by adding, taking away, and inserting letters, he has made the same word different from itself, without any change of the sense; yet not so different, but that it is easily known to be the same by those who have studied the art of his language. Now we are not to suppose, as many do, that this variety of words was taken from the several dialects of the Greek, such as the Doric, Ionic, Attic, &c.; for, in the first place, there is no evidence that those dialects existed at the time that Homer wrote; or, if they did exist, they must have been formed out of the same language in which Homer wrote, not that language out of them. And, secondly, supposing those dialects to have existed at the time Homer wrote, we cannot believe that any author, much less such an author as Homer, would have written a mongrel Babylonish dialect, made out of the different dialects, then spoken in Greece, and which would not have been intelligible to any of the nations that spoke any one of those dialects.

Chap. I. Progress of Language. 97

The fact, therefore, appears to be, that the language, in which Homer wrote, was the learned language of Greece, and the language of their poetry, the firſt writing among them*. Nor are we to wonder at its being ſo rich and copious, that it ſeems not to be one, but many languages; for there is a language ſtill exiſting, and preſerved among the Bramins of India, which is a richer, and in every reſpect a finer language than even the Greek of Homer. All the other languages of India have a great reſemblance to this language, which is called the Shanſcrit: But thoſe languages are dialects of it, and formed from it, not the Shanſcrit from them. Of this, and other particulars concerning this language, I have got ſuch certain information from India, that if I live to finiſh my hiſtory of man, which I have begun in my third volume of Antient Metaphyſics, I ſhall be able clearly to prove, that the Greek is

---

* It is upon record, that Phercydes was the firſt writer of proſe in Greek.

derived from the Shanscrit, which was the ancient language of Egypt, and was carried by the Egyptians into India, with their other arts, and into Greece by the colonies which they settled there. This is a most curious and important fact in the history of man; but for our present purpose it is sufficient to observe, that it is a great beauty of a language, to have such a variety in the sound of the same words, if that introduces no confusion, and is agreeable to the rules by which the language is formed.

But though the Greek of later times has not that variety of sound of the same word without any change of the signification, yet it has a great number of words which are similar both in their sound and signification, though not exactly denoting the same thing. These are words formed by derivation, composition, and flection, the three great arts of language, without which it would have been impossible to have connected together millions of words, so that they could be comprehended in the

Chap. I. Progress of Language. 99

memory and readily used*. All these words, however different in their sound and signification, come all under the denomination of words *proper*; for there is nothing in them that can be called trope or figure. But even in these the language of Homer is more rich than any other language in Greek, but not so rich as the original language, the Shanscrit, in any of the three articles I mentioned, derivation, composition, or flection: And particularly it has in it words of wonderful composition, some of which I have been shewn.—And so much for proper words.

As to *tropical* words, it is not the difference of sound merely that makes a trope, but there must be a change of the word from its native and genuine signification, to another that is different. In this way I have defined a trope, in the third volume of this work†, where I have

---

* Vol. 5. p. 434.
† Book 4. chap. 3. p. 24. and chap. 4. p. 32.

explained, at great length, the feveral kinds of tropes, very various and different one from another. But Ariftotle has reduced them all to rule, and made philofophy of them as well as of every thing elfe of which he has treated. See his definition of them, and his divifion of them into four different kinds, which I have given in the laft chapter quoted of the third volume *.

In poetry all the different tropes are ufed, and particularly by Homer, as I have fhewn in the fourth chapter above quoted; but in the rhetorical ftile there is hardly any other trope ufed except what is commonly called Metaphor, a word ufed by Ariftotle to comprehend all tropes; and that, no doubt, is the true etymological fenfe of the word. But we ufe it to denote only one of the four kinds of trope mentioned by Ariftotle, and which he calls κατα το αναλογον, being taken from the refemblance, fimilitude, or

---

* Book 4. chap. 3. p. 37.

Chap. I. PROGRESS OF LANGUAGE. 101

analogy that one thing has to another*. It is a trope not only much used in poetry and rhetoric, but in common speech; and the reason is, that it both adorns the stile, and expresses the thing in a more lively and forcible manner; for a metaphor is a simile in one word. And, if it be taken from any great subject, it magnifies the thing spoken of: But, on the other hand, if it be taken from a low subject, it lessens and vilifies the thing. And as extolling or depreciating is used in all the three different kinds of rhetoric, it is of very general use in the art; and Aristotle speaks of it as the only trope proper to be used in prose composition †.

I have said a good deal about the proper use of this trope, in the fourth chapter above referred to, where I have inculcated what I have before observed, in this chapter ‡, that we must perfectly understand

---

* Ibid. p. 37 and 38.
† Lib. 3. Rhet. cap. 2.
‡ P. 94.

the meaning of the proper word, and also the meaning of the tropical word which we use in place of it. The knowledge, therefore, of both, is absolutely necessary, and they must be carefully distinguished one from another: So that, as I have observed *, a dictionary of any language, which does not accurately distinguish the two, beginning with the proper, and from thence deducing the metaphorical use of the word, is very imperfect of its kind. I have also shewn the abuse of metaphors, by making them too frequent, and so making either a riddle of the composition, if the metaphors be not clear; or though they be clear, too many of them make a stile of similes. And so much for single words, which are the materials of composition.

* Vol. 3. p. 41 and 42.

CHAP. II.

Of Compofition—*it gives a variety and beauty to Stile, which no choice of words can do;—is of greater difficulty than the choice of words—therefore neglected in modern times, and in later times among the antients.—All Stiles now of the fame kind, affecting what is called* fine language.—*In Compofition a progrefs as in other arts.—The fteps of this progrefs, from the fhorteft fentence to a period of feveral members.—There muft have been a time for this progrefs—and the firft compofition muft have been in fhort fentences.—This progrefs proved by facts, as well as by reafoning.—The writings of Mofes an example of fhort compofition.—This kind of Stile imitated in later times by Saluft and Tacitus among the Romans, and by fome French and Englifh writers.—A very bad Stile, efpecially when it affects obfcurity.—Of the pleasure that some have in decyphering such a Stile.*

I COME now to speak of the second part of Stile, namely, Composition; it is of so much greater power and influence than single words, that the whole stile, as I have observed elsewhere *, is in English not improperly, I think, denominated from it: It is of so great variety as to make different stiles of the same words: And in the same stile it gives a variety which it is impossible any choice of words can give. It gives such beauty to the stile, too, as well as variety, that in a passage that I have quoted from the Halicarnasian †, he compares it to the rod of Minerva in Homer, which could transform a beggar into a king or hero, or, *vice versa:* By which he means, that, of the most common words, good composition will make fine poetry or prose; and con—

---

* Vol. 3. chap. 5. in the beginning.
† Ibid. p. 46.

trary ways, bad compofition will difgrace the beft words: And he gives examples of both.

As compofition, therefore, is of fuch power and influence, and of fuch beauty and variety, it is no wonder that it is of fuch difficulty,—of much more difficulty than the choice of the words, which are only the elements of compofition. This it has in common, as I have obferved*, with compofition in all arts. And this difficulty of the practice is the reafon why not only in our times, but in the times of the Halicarnafian, compofition was fo much neglected, and nothing ftudied but the choice of words; and, as we all at prefent affect to write fine language, and think we cannot make it fine otherwife than by poetical words, metaphors, and figures of different kinds, the confequence is, that we have no difference of ftile fuited to the different fubjects, but all

* P. 93. of this volume.

write a language that is, as I have observed elsewhere, a motley mixture of the froth of rhetoric and the flowers of poetry.*.

There must have been a progress in this art so various and so difficult; and it is a matter of some curiosity to trace this progress, which, I think, we can do from monuments yet existing. But before we do that, we must recollect that there is no composition, properly so called, but of words, more or fewer, making some sense by themselves: For if any number of words be collected together, but make no sense of any kind, it is not composition, any more than a disorderly collection of the materials of any other art. Composition, therefore, necessarily consists of a certain number of words, having a certain meaning; and this is what we call, in English, a *Sentence*. Now this composition may consist of more or fewer words.

* See what I have said further upon this subject, in the third dissertation which I have annexed to the 2d. vol. of this work.

It cannot be of fewer than two: But it may be of many more. When the words are few, it is a ſhort ſentence; when they are many, it is a long ſentence: And when that long ſentence is divided into what we call members, which make by themſelves ſome kind of ſenſe, but an imperfect one, and dependent upon the ſenſe of the whole ſentence, then there begins to be beauty and variety, if theſe members be well compoſed, and fitly put together; and if there be in the whole ſentence a certain roundneſs and circumduction, making what we call a period, then is the compoſition complete, and truly rhetorical.

But was this perfection of compoſition attained at once? Or was there not a progreſs in it, as in other arts? And I think there was, as well as in every thing elſe belonging to language; unleſs we are to ſuppoſe that a language, ſuch as the Shanſcrit or the Greek, and fine ſpeaking and writing, came down to us from Heaven directly: But my opinion is, that, whatever aſſiſtance we may have got at firſt from superior intelligencies to enable us to invent the first elements of speech, the rest was left to our natural sagacity. I therefore do not suppose that men, when they first began to speak and write, did put together many words in sentences; nay, I do not believe that when they first began to articulate, they put together many syllables in words. And I think the Chinese language is a living proof of this: For it consists entirely of monosyllables, and without any change, in these monosyllables, of the order or position of the letters, or any thing resembling what we call flection; and the only variety they give them, is by different tones, so different, that they make the same monosyllable sometimes signify nine or ten different things. Now the Chinese language, as well as the nation, is certainly of very great antiquity; and, I believe, it was the original language of Egypt long before the Shanscrit was invented; and from Egypt it travelled into India, and from India came with some other Egyptian arts

CHAP. II. PROGRESS OF LANGUAGE. 109

into China *. Nor should this slow progress of language appear wonderful to those who consider the imperfect state of languages at this day, many of which have not all the elemental sounds; or rather there are few that have them all. The Chinese language wants several of them; and even our English wants one of them, namely, the Greek *ypsilon*, or French *u*, instead of which we pronounce the Greek diphthong ευ.

Such being the progress, therefore, of the invention of letters, syllables, and words, there must, I think, have been a similar progress in the composition of words. The sense must have been at first concluded in a few words; and the composition would consist of a number of these short sentences, not connected toge-

---

* See Salmasius *Hellenistica*, p. 390. and 391. where he maintains, as I do, that the most antient languages consisted of words only of one, or very few syllables. Of this he gives several examples from the antient Greek.

ther by the sense, but independent of one another. If this were only conjecture, I should think it a most probable one, and I think even necessarily deducible from the nature of the thing. But it is proved by fact as well as by reasoning: For the most antient book extant is the writings of Moses, which are composed almost all in that stile, without long sentences, or any thing that can be called a period, keeping the sense suspended through many words. For proof of this, we need go no farther than the first verses of the first chapter of Genesis, where we have the creation of the world described in short sentences, without any thing of what we would call composition.

This stile, which was necessary before the art of composition was invented, is simple and pleasant. But when it was studied, as a beauty, by Sallust and Tacitus and their modern imitators, it is, I think, very bad writing; for it is impossible that it can be beautiful, wanting art and that variety which is essential to beauty.

But in Salluſt I think it is tolerable; and though I cannot praiſe it, it does not give me offence. But where there is point and turn affected, and a ſtudied obſcurity, which is the caſe of Tacitus*, and ſome of his modern imitators, I think it is the worſt ſtile that can be written. There are, I know, readers that delight in decyphering ſuch enigmatical ſentences†, and flatter themſelves that they not only read but invent. But for my part, I have no ſuch pleaſure; and any time that I may have beſtowed upon expounding thoſe oracles of wiſdom that are ſuppoſed to be contained in the ſhort ſentences of Tacitus, I have thought very ill employed, not

---

* See what I have written on the ſtile of Tacitus, in vol. 3d. of this work, chap. 12. p. 210.

† This appears to have been the taſte of ſome readers in the days of Quintilian, who ſays, in his *Inſtitutiones Oratoricae*, lib. 8. cap. 2. *Pervaſit quidem jam multos iſta perſuaſio, ut id jam demum eleganter atque exquiſite dictum putent, quod interpretandum ſit. Sed auditoribus etiam nonnullis grata ſunt haec, quae cum intellexerint, acumine ſuo delectantur, et gaudent non quaſi audiverint ſed quaſi invenerint.*

finding in them at all that wifdom which fome think they difcover in him; but only a very common fenfe, and perhaps not a true one, or not belonging to the fubject.

CHAP. III.

Composition in short sentences does not deserve the name of composition.—Of Composition in longer sentences.—The figures belonging to that composition of three kinds;—figures of the Syntax—of the Sense—and of the Sound.—The difference of the arrangement of words in the learned languages and in the modern.—Words at a distance from one another connected together, in the learned languages, by genders, numbers, and cases.—This produces a great effect in composition.—Milton has availed himself of the few cases we have in English, to compose some fine periods.—The artificial composition in the learned languages not introduced at once.—A simpler composition used at first.—Our language is so crouded with consonants and monosyllables, that no composition could make it so pleaſant as the Greek and Latin.—Objection to the artificial compoſition, that it makes the ſenſe obſcure.—This anſwered, and ſhewn that it has the contrary effect.—This artificial compoſition, ſo very various, has its bounds.—A bad art in this matter, as well as in other things.—Of the Figures of Syntax.—Some of theſe only proper for poetry.—Three of them may be uſed in oratory.—Elipſis, Parentheſis, and Repetition.—The Elipſis much uſed by Demoſthenes, and other Attic writers;—it gives a terſneſs and neatneſs to the ſtyle.—Parentheſis, a beautiful figure—much uſed by Demoſthenes;—in ſpeaking it has a wonderful good effect.—Repetition, moderately uſed, has likewiſe a good effect.—Of the figures of the ſenſe.—Theſe divided into three kinds, ſuch as are Pathetic, Ethic, and, laſtly, ſuch as only vary the form of the ſtile, ſo as to make it different from common ſpeech.—Of the Pathetic kind are Exclamation, Hyperbole, Epithets, Proſopopoea, and painting the ſubject.—Of the different uſe of theſe by

Cicero and Demosthenes.—Of the Ethic kind, as many figures as there are manners and characters to be imitated.—Difference betwixt Poetry and Oratory with respect to these figures.—Of the Figures of Sense of the third kind, without passion or characters.—These without number.—An example given of the variety of this figure.

AFTER having given an account of the first words that were used by men, when a language of art came to be formed, and of what nature the first composition of words in speech or writing was, I come now to treat of the several figures which diversify composition, after it was formed into sentences of some length: For a composition in short sentences of a few words, though making a complete sense, hardly deserves the name of composition.

The figures observed by grammarians are divided into three kinds, the figures of

Syntax or conſtruction; 2*dly*, figures of the ſenſe, that is, ſuch as affect the ſenſe of the words; and, *laſtly*, thoſe which may be called figures of the Sound, relating to the rhythm and melody of ſuch languages as the Greek and Latin.

Before I begin to ſpeak of theſe ſeveral figures, I think it is proper to ſay ſomething of the order and arrangement of words in Greek and Latin, compared with the arrangement of them in modern languages, ſuch as the Engliſh. This arrangement of the words is no figure of ſpeech, except where the tranſpoſition is violent and uncommon, and then it is called *Hyperbaton**, and may be reckoned among the figures of ſpeech: But, even where it is not ſo violent, it is proper to be taken notice of, as it makes the ſtile very different from common ſpeech.

From the great excellency of the grammar of the learned languages, which have

---

*. See what I have ſaid of the Hyperbaton, vol. 4. p. 221.

numbers, genders, and cafes, and thereby connect their words together, it is evident that thofe languages are not under the neceffity of placing the words befide one another which are joined together in conftruction, but may have them at a confiderable diftance from one another, and in different order, fometimes the one before the other, and fometimes after*; whereas our language, wanting thefe three ways of connecting words, is obliged to connect its words chiefly by juxta-pofition, which makes the compofition in our language very much ftinted, and tedioufly uniform, compared with the Greek and Latin †.

* See what I have further faid of the variety of antient compofition, p. 218. and following, of vol. 4th. and p. 245. and following of vol. 5th. where I have treated pretty fully of the difference betwixt antient and modern compofition.

† In the fine fpeech of Satan, in the beginning of the fecond book of Paradife Loft, we have an example of what may be done in compofition by the variety of cafes of nouns. In Englifh we have that variety only in our pronouns, and Milton has availed himfelf of it to make one of the fineft periods in

But this artificial compofition in the learned languages, was like other things of art, not brought to perfection at once, but by degrees. A much fimpler compofition would at firft be ufed, and which was preferved, even in later times, in laws, edicts, and decrees, and in familiar epiftles *, in which the ftile is much fimpler, in this refpect, than the oratorial, hiftorical, or even the didactic. But when writing and fpeaking came to be formed into an art, it would, in procefs of time, be difcovered, that the tranfpofition

Englifh, and which otherwife could not have been near fo fine. It begins thus,

 Me tho' juft right and the fixt laws of Heaven,
 Did firft create your leader,———

I will fay no more of it here, becaufe I have commented largely upon it in the 3d chap. of the 3d book of vol. 2d. and alfo in the 9th chap. of vol. 3d of this work, except to obferve, that if the pronoun of the firft perfon *I* had not had an accufative different from the nominative, it would have been impoffible for Milton to have given the period that roundnefs and compactnefs which it has.

 * See p. 218. and 219. of vol. 4.

Chap. III. Progress of Language. 119

of words from the natural order of syntax, produces an agreeable variety in the compofition; and when melody and rhythm came to be ftudied, it was in fome fort of abfolute neceffity. But though our liberty of compofition were as great as in Greek and Latin, we have fo many monofyllables in our language, and words with fo many confonants crouded together, and thefe fo different from one another, as not eafily to coalefce together in the fame found, that it would be impoffible, by any arrangement, to make a compofition fo pleafant as that of Greek and Latin *.

It may be ojected to this artificial compofition, that though it no doubt give a great variety to the ftile, it makes it obfcure. But this objection I think I have anfwered in the third differtation, which

---

* See what I have further faid upon this fubject, in the 2d vol. of this work, book 3. chap. 5. and 6. where I have fhewn at what pains the Greeks were to make their language fmooth and pleafant to the ear.

I have annexed to my second volume, where I think I have shewn, that in the best Greek oratorial compositions, such as those of Demosthenes, the words are so arranged, that they draw the attention of the hearer or reader, and have more weight and emphasis than if they were placed in what we would call the natural order. It is true, that it is difficult for one, who knows only English or some other modern languages, to understand the words arranged in a manner so different from that to which he has been accustomed: And though he may understand the words separately and by themselves, he will not be able to make out the meaning of them composed in a sentence, till they are put into the order to which he has been accustomed, that is, the order in which a school-boy construes them. But, according to the Greek proverb, ' Fine things ' are difficult.' Use, however, makes them easy; and, as we are commonly taught the learned languages when we are young, we are soon reconciled to a composition which at first appeared so unnatural to us. And it becomes at laſt not only more pleaſant to our ears, but it conveys the meaning more clearly and forcibly to us, eſpecially if the compoſition be in good periods, than any other arrangement of the words.

But we are not to imagine that this arrangement, however various it may be, (and it was certainly very various, eſpecially in their oratorial compoſitions), was without bounds and limits: For it is not every artificial compoſition that is claſſical; and there is bad art in this matter as well as good. To be convinced of this, we need only compare the compoſition of Ammianus Marellinus, or of the later Latin writers, with the compoſition of Cicero, Julius Caeſar, or any writer of the Auguſtan age. And if ſuch a compoſition as that of Ammianus is critically compared with theſe compoſitions of a better age and taſte, it will be found that what makes the difference chiefly is, the poſition of the words, which in the one are so placed, as to answer best to the sense, and at the same time to make the stile numerous and pleasing to the ear.

I come now to speak of what is properly called Figures of composition, beginning with the figures of construction. Of these I have treated so fully, in volume 3d. chapter 6. that I have very little to add here, except that there are many Figures mentioned there, which are not at all proper for prose composition, but are used by the poets, particularly Homer, which give a variety to the poetic stile, and yet at the same time do not make it obscure, as I think I have shewn from the examples I have given. The *Paronomasia*, and the *Parisosis*, are very much used by poets and by some orators, but I think ought to be very sparingly used by those who speak upon business, and not for mere show and ostentation, which was the case of the Epideictic orators. And I think there are only three of the figures which I have mentioned that are proper for all orations: And these are, the *Ellipsis*, the *Parenthe-*

Chap. III. Progress of Language. 123

ſis, and *Repetition*. As to *Ellipſis*, it is a figure much uſed by the Attic writers of all kinds, as well as their orators. And indeed it is a diſtinguiſhing mark of that dialect, which gives it a terſeneſs and neatneſs, free from all kind of froth and ſuperfluity; and by Demoſthenes particularly it is very much uſed, and, I think, contributes not a little to that δεινοτης, as it was called, which condenſed his ſtile ſo much, and brought it ſo forcibly home to the hearers. The parentheſis, too, he has very much uſed; and ſometimes even parentheſis within parentheſis *, of which I have given an example †. It is alſo much uſed by poets, and particularly by Milton, from whom I have given moſt beautiful examples of it: And indeed I know no figure that adorns any kind of writing more. In ſpeaking it has a wonderful effect, if it be well compoſed and well pronounced. And even in writing, though not intended for ſpeaking, it varies the

---

* See vol. 3d. of this work, p. 74.
† Ibid.

ſtile agreeably: For the teſt of good writing, as I have elſewhere obſerved, is reading it, and what does not pleaſe the ear when well read, I ſay, is not well written. But beſides pleaſing the ear, if the matter of it be of weight, I ſay, that matter is more forcibly conveyed to the reader, ſtanding by itſelf, than if it was mixed with the reſt of the ſentence. But in our modern writing this figure is much out of faſhion: There is hardly a parentheſis to be found in the French books now publiſhed; and I have heard it obſerved of our faſhionable writer Mr Gibbons, that in his hiſtory, at leaſt in the firſt volumes of it that were publiſhed, there is not a parentheſis to be found. And I think it is likely to be true, as it is very well known that he has formed his taſte of writing upon the French authors.

The laſt figure I mentioned is *Repetition*, which is a figure uſed in all kinds of writing and ſpeaking. Of this, too, in the chapter above quoted, I have given ſome beautiful examples: But it may be intemperately ufed, as well as any other figure; and of this likewife I have given an example from Cicero *.

I come now to fpeak of the figures of the fenfe or meaning. Thefe, fays Quintilian, are fo many that they cannot be numbered: But I think they may be reduced to certain claffes, and accordingly I have divided them into three; *firſt*, fuch as exprefs fome feeling or emotion of the mind; *ſecondly*, fuch as exprefs the character or manners of the fpeaker or writer; and, *thirdly*, fuch as without expreffing either of thefe, give a turn and form to the thought and expreffion, different from what is ufual in common fpeech. Under one or other of thefe heads may be ranked, as I imagine, every figure of this kind that can be devifed †.

Of all thefe three kinds I have, in the chapter below quoted, mentioned different

---

* See vol. 3d. of this work, p. 80.
† Ibid. chap. 6. p. 107.

figures, beginning with those belonging to the Pathetic, of which kind one is *Exclamation*, little used by the orators of Greece, and not at all by Demosthenes, but very much by Cicero. Then I speak of *Hyperbole*, not very much used by the best poets, and hardly at all by such orators as Demosthenes. Next I mention *Epithets*, more proper for the poetical stile than the oratorial, and therefore not much used by orators who write a chaste and correct stile. Then I speak of *Prosopopoea*, a figure entirely poetical, and not used by any Greek orator, as far as I can recollect: But Cicero has thought proper to adorn his stile with it *.

The last figure of the Pathetic I shall mention, is what is called in Greek διατυπσοις, that is, a particular and circumstantial description of a thing, such as may be called painting it, for the purpose of exciting any passion. It is a figure belonging more to poetry than oratory. It is how-

* Vol. 3d. p. 115.

Chap. III. PROGRESS OF LANGUAGE. 127

ever sometimes used by orators, and I have given an example where it is used by Demosthenes; but with a difference which I have observed betwixt the poetical and oratorial use of this figure *. But Cicero has not observed this distinction, as I have shewn, in a description of his, which may be called a piece of Dutch painting †.

As to the figures of the Ethic kind, these I have explained in the eight chapter of the same third volume, where I think I have made the proper distinction betwixt describing a character and imitating a character. It is a figure belonging both to poetry and oratory; but in different respects: For it is chiefly his own character which the orator represents; whereas the poet has nothing to do at all to appear himself in his piece. One species of this figure is very well known, viz. *Irony*; but there are as many speciefes of it, as

* Vol. 3d. p. 118.
† Ibid. p. 119.

there are different characters and manners to be imitated *.

The last figures of the sense, according to my division of them, are such, as without expressing either character or passion, give a turn or form to the thought and expression, different from what is usual in common speech: Of these I have mentioned some particular figures, such as interrogation, antithesis, simile, and allegory †. But of the figures of this kind it may be truly said what Quintilian says of all figures of the sense, that they cannot be numbered. Of this I think I have given a proof from Milton, in Satan's speech in the council of the devils ‡, which I have taken down and put up again in three different ways, shewing how the same sense may be varied by different compositions.

* P. 136. of vol. 3d. and following.
† Ibid. chap. 9. p. 143.
‡ Ibid. p. 138. and following.

CHAP. IV.

Of the third class of the figures of language which affect the sound, viz. the Melody and the Rhythm.—The measured Rhythm or versification of the antient languages, to be treated of in the book upon Poetry;—but of the Rhythm of their prose, something to be said in this book.—Of the melody of speech.—The difference betwixt that melody and the melody of music.—It has a greater resemblance to the Recitativo of the Italian opera, than any other music we know;—but differs from that also.—The Melody therefore of Language, a musical tone flowing through the whole speech, not rising too often nor too high.—No language perfect without it.—Origin of the Melody of Language. —Singing more natural to man than speech.—This the most difficult of all human inventions.—Men therefore sung before they spoke.—Language, as well as the race of men, came from the south and east.—People of these countries more musical than the people of the north and west.—When men began to speak, they joined music with their articulation.—Of the melody of the Chinese language.—This a most wonderful language.—Particular information which the author had concerning that language.—The Chinese first used musical tones, before they learned to articulate.—This they learned from Egypt.—Progress of the art there.—Answer to those who deny that ever a language existed with melody.—This proved from facts.—The melody of language lost in all degenerate languages.—Of the variety of melody in the Greek language.—Not the same variety in the Latin.—Melody, therefore, not so much studied in the Latin composition.

Chap. IV. Progress of Language. 131

I COME now to speak of the third class of figures of composition, according to the method in which I have ranked them; these have nothing to do with the syntax, or the sense of the words, but relate altogether to the sound; for they belong to the prosody of the learned languages, which makes what the Halicarnasian calls the Melody of Language, and to the rhythm, of which the antients composed their verse and numerous prose. Of this last I propose to say something in this part of my work, leaving what I have to say of the antient verse to the last volume of this work, in which I am to treat of the Stile of Poetry. As to the prosody or melody of the antient languages, I have said a good deal in the fourth chapter of the second book of the second volume of this work. But, as it is so little understood at present, even by those who call themselves scholars, that some deny even the existence of it, and do not believe that any people ever spoke, or that they could speak, as I suppose the Greeks and Romans did*, I think it is neceſſary to add here a good deal more upon the ſubject.

In the firſt place, as I have obſerved in the above mentioned fourth chapter, p. 271, there are many who value themſelves much upon their knowledge of Proſody, yet do not ſo much as know what the word means: For they confound it with rhythm, and think it denotes the quantity, or length and ſhortneſs of the ſyllables; whereas it has nothing to do with that, but relates to a thing quite different, viz.

---

* See what I have ſaid upon this ſubject, in vol. 5th. of this work, p. 443, where I have ſhewn not only that it is poſſible to ſpeak in this way, but that there is a nation actually exiſting in North America, who do at this day ſpeak ſo. If the reader will not believe this fact, let him attend to the way in which the Cuckow pronounces his name, and he will find that there is both melody and rhythm in that pronunciation: For the accent upon the firſt ſyllable is a *third* above the tone of the laſt ſyllable, but which is longer than the firſt, and in the ratio of *two* to *one*, as far as my ear can judge. Now I think we may ſuppoſe, that ſuch muſical nations as the Greeks and Romans, had as much, or more, muſic in their pronunciation than the Cuckow.

Chap. IV. Progress of Language. 133

the mufical tones which the Greeks and Latins gave to the fyllables of their words, and which made their language truly melodious, and is therefore very properly called by the Halicarnafian, the *Melody* of the Language. The Latins have a word compofed in the fame manner as the Greek word προσῳδια, and denoting precifely the fame thing, I mean the word *accentus*, which does not mean, as fome ignorant people may think, what we call *accent*, a thing fo entirely unknown to the Greeks and Romans, that they had not fo much as a name for it*.

There are others who do not diftinguifh betwixt the melody of fpeech and the melody of mufic; fo that they fuppofe the antients fung or chaunted when they fpoke. This miftake I have alfo taken notice of in p. 286, of the fecond volume, and have fhewn, from authority which cannot be difputed, that the difference betwixt the two was, that the melody of

* See vol. 4th. p. 32.

speech was συνεχης or εν ρυσει, that is, *proceeded by slides*, whereas the melody of music was *diastematic*, as they expressed it, that is, *the notes did not run into one another, but were distinguished by perceptible intervals*. The likest thing we have in modern times to the antient melody of speech, is the Recitativo of the Italian opera, which I hold to be a very valuable remain of the antient theatrical music. But it differs from that Recitativo in this material point, that the notes of the recitativo are distinguished from one another by perceptible intervals, and not running into one another like the melody of antient speech. It is therefore no more than music more simple than the music of the songs of the opera, and therefore better accommodated to narrative, for which purpose it is chiefly used; whereas the songs are expressive of sentiment and passion.

The melody, therefore, of Greek and Latin consisted of musical tones, which flowed through the whole composition, with the variety of high and low, without

Chap. IV. Progress of Language. 135

which there can be no mufic of any kind, but the high never rifing above *a fifth*, and being not too frequently repeated; for there is never more than one acute accent upon the fame word, though confifting of feveral fyllables. This, I think, muft have made a fweet and fimple melody, with variety enough, as the high tone does not always return at the fame interval. I will only add further upon this fubject, that without a melody of one kind or another, no language can be perfect; for the voice, as Ariftotle has obferved[*], is the moft imitative faculty belonging to us, and therefore it fhould be employed to its full extent; and fhould not only imitate fentiments and paffions, but alfo mufical tones.

And, if we ftudy the hiftory and philofophy of man, and can afcend to the origin of this wonderful art of language, we fhall find that the firft language fpoken by man muft have been mufical; for finging is natural to man as well as to fome birds;

[*] *Rhetor.* lib. 3. cap. 1.

whereas language is so far from being natural to man, that it is a work of the greatest art, and most difficult invention (if it was invented by men) of all the arts we practise. For setting aside the grammatical art, even articulation, which furnishes only the materials of language, is of itself not only of difficult invention, but so difficult in the practice, requiring so many various positions and actions of the organs of pronunciation, that nothing but continued practice from our infancy can make it easy for us: And therefore, as I have observed elsewhere*, language is the most wonderful of all the arts we have invented, as we have produced not only the art, but furnished the materials of it; whereas, in the other arts we practise, nature has given us the materials.

If, therefore, there ever was a natural state of man, and if he did not come into this world practising all the arts that he now practices, it is evident that he did not,

---

* Vol. 4th. p. 176. and following.

in his natural state, speak: But he sung; for having a voice capable of variety of tones, and being naturally pleased with those tones put together, though in the most rude and artless manner, he would make some kind of music with his voice, that is, he would sing: Or, if we will not believe that instinct would direct him to do that, we may suppose, as Lucretius does, that he learned it by imitating the birds *.

Further, history informs every man who studies it in the grand and comprehensive view of the history of the species, that language and the race of men came from the south and east. Now, the people there are much more musical than in the north and west, where they appear to have almost quite lost those musical talents,

* This notion of Lucretius was confirmed to me by what the wild girl, whom I saw in France, told me: For she said, the music in her country was an imitation of the singing of birds.

which they brought with them from the south and east: And the further north they have gone, the more they have lost of those talents; so that, as Lemmius, the Danish missionary among the Laplanders, informs us, these people, though undoubtedly they came from a country far to the east *, could hardly be taught the common

* This is evident from the language they speak, which is now known, with great certainty, to have come from a very remote country in the east, lying betwixt the Euxine and Caspian seas; for there is a book written by one Sainovicks, a member of the Royal Society of Denmark, printed in 1770, (it is a rare book, of which I had the use from the King's library, when I was last in London), where the author proves, I think demonstratively, by comparing the two languages together, that the Hungarian and Lapland languages are both dialects of the same language, and consequently, that the people must be originally the same. The affinity of the two languages he proves, not only by their having so many words in common, not less than an hundred and fifty, (p. 35.) but by idioms of syntax and composition, which could not be accidental, (p. 61.) Now, if they were originally the same people, it is the greatest migration of men that we read of in the history of man, greater than the migration of the Cimbers from the Tauric Chersonese to the Cimbric, or of the Goths from

Chap. IV. PROGRESS OF LANGUAGE. 139

church tunes. But there is a southern and eastern nation, with which we are pretty well acquainted, I mean the Chinese, who retain the musical genius of their country so much, that they have a much greater variety of musical accents upon their syllables than the Greeks had: For the same

Crim Tartary to Germany and Sweden: For the Hungarians, who call themselves *Majars*, came from a country betwixt the Euxine and Caspian seas, where there is a people of that name (see the second edition of vol. 1st. of this work, p. 594. in the note) and who, we must suppose, speak the same language, as they bear the same name. Now what a migration this was, from the Caspian sea, at least from beyond the Euxine, to Lapland, whether we suppose them to have come directly from their parent country to Lapland, or, what I think more probable, from Hungary to Lapland. This shews how much the study of language is connected with the history of man; since by it we discover the connection of nations with one another, and their migration from the most distant countries to the countries which they now inhabit. I will only add, concerning the language of these two nations, that it is a language of art, having one art belonging to language, which no other language in Europe at present has, that of forming cases of nouns by flection. This is a proof, that not only the race of men came from the east and south to the west and north, but that they brought with them a language of art.

monosyllable among them, by being differently accented, signifies nine or ten different things; so that their language, consisting of no more than three hundred and thirty words, serves all the purposes of a highly civilized life. Mr Bevin, the gentleman whom I have mentioned in my fifth volume *, was so obliging as to let me hear him speak some Chinese, and, as far as I could observe, their tones did not rise so high as the acute accent of the Greeks; but the notes were very much divided, and the intervals very small, so that the music of their language resembled, in that respect, the singing of birds. Whether they did not vary their monosyllables, by pronouncing them longer or shorter, I forgot to ask him; but I think it certain, that as rhythm is an essential part of music, they could not have had so much music in their language without rhythm; and I am persuaded that they distinguish in that way the sense of several of their monosyllables, as we know the Greeks distinguished

---

* P. 444.

some of their words, by the length or shortness of the syllables.

Of the Chinese language I have spoken in page 108. of this volume; and I will only add here, that it is the greatest phenomenon of the language kind that is to be found on this earth: For it is a language without any of the three arts of derivation, composition, and flection, without one or other, or all of which, I should have thought it impossible to have formed a language, which could serve the purposes of a life of civility and arts, such as that of the Chinese. It is, as I have observed in the passage above quoted, in that infantine state of articulation, when men had only learned to articulate single syllables, but not to put them together in words; for there must be a progress in all arts, from what is simplest and easiest, to what is compound and more difficult.

The first words, therefore, were as simple as possible, being only monosyllables;

and there, I think, it is natural to suppose that they would stop a while; and by giving tones and rhythms to those syllables, express their wants and desires, and so keep up an intercourse with one another. In this state, I imagine, the language remained for some time, even in Egypt, where I suppose it to have been first invented: And while it was in that state, it found its way to China, with other Egyptian arts, and particularly hieragryphical writing, which M. De Guignes has shewn came from Egypt to China. See vol. 34. of the Memoires of the French Academy. The Chinese, who, I believe are, as Dr. Warburton has said, a dull uninventive people, have preserved both the language and the writings of the Egyptians as they got them. But in Egypt I do not believe that either of these arts continued long in so infantine a state. That alphabetical characters were invented there I think there can be no doubt, and also the three great arts of language, derivation, composition, and flection. When they had got so far in the art of language, words of many syllables became absolutely necessary: The tones and rhythms of the monosyllables were nevertheless still preserved; and in this manner was formed such a language as the Shanscrit, which is now discovered to have been the antient language of Egypt, and of which the Greek is a dialect. Thus was completed the most wonderful of all human arts, by which about five millions of words were so connected together, as to be comprehended in the memory, and readily used *, and at the same time pronounced with a beautiful variety of melody and rhythm.

But to return to the musical accents of the Chinese language. The question is, Whether they first learned to articulate their monosyllable, and then learned these musical notes by which they distinguish them one from another? or, whether they first practised music, and then learned articulation? And it appears to me very much

* See vol. 5th. p. 434.

more probable, that having firſt ſung, whether by inſtinct, or having learned it from the birds; and after that, having learned from ſome nation with which they had an intercourſe, to articulate a few ſounds, they ſtill continued to ſing, and, as it was very natural, joined their muſical tones to their articulate ſounds, and ſo formed a muſical language, and at the ſame time ſupplyed the defects of their very ſcanty articulation.

But we muſt ſuppoſe, that the melody of the Greek language was far ſuperior to that of the Chineſe, and I think we are very much obliged to the Halicarnaſian, for explaining, ſo accurately as he has done, the nature of the Greek accents. He is the only author, as far as I know, that has done ſo; and but for the account he has given of them, I might have thought them as much without rule, and as little muſical, as the Chineſe accents. But the Halicarnaſian has told us that they riſe to a fifth, and every ſyllable of the word has either a grave ac-

Chap. IV. Progress of Language.

cent, an acute, or both, which is called a circumflex, and this is all the variety which the nature of the thing will admit. This variety, however, is not without rule; for I know an English scholar, who, if you give him the accentuation of any one word, will tell you how all its derivatives, and all its different flections are to be accented. I thought the passage in the Halicarnasian of such importance, that I have given a translation of it at full length, which I very seldom do; and he makes the matter so clear, though a good deal removed from common apprehension, that no man who understands the language, and has learned the first principles of music, can have any doubt in the matter.

If we could have any doubt that the Greek language was pronounced with the melody which the Halicarnasian has so well explained, the example of a savage nation of North America, who at this day pronounce their barbarous language in the same manner that the Greeks did their polite and highly cultivated language, puts the matter out of all doubt, and shews, that not only such a pronunciation is practicable, but that melody and rhythm are coeval with language, and had been brought to some degree of perfection, while the grammatical part of the language continued still very imperfect; which is the case of the Iroquois language. Of this language I have said a good deal in my fifth volume, p. 443 and 444.

If, therefore, no language ever was spoken by a whole nation with melody and rhythm, those who have heard the Chinese speak in that way must have been mistaken, or willingly imposed upon us. Dr. Moyes must have lied concerning the Iroquois, for he could not have been mistaken; and so must the Halicarnasian, in what he has told us with so much accuracy concerning the Greek accents. But these testimonies are all rejected by some, singly for this reason, that they have no idea of any people speaking in that way; and they hold it to be impossible that there should be any beauty in speaking, or in any other art, of which they have no idea. I will not pretend to enlarge the ideas of such men, or make them less fond of themselves; but, if they will not be convinced by facts that are told them, I think they should be convinced by the testimony of their own senses. Let them listen to that common bird the Cuckow, who, as I have shewn *, articulates his name of two syllables with both melody and rhythm. The Cocketoo pronounces his name of three syllables in the same way; but whether he rises higher, or not so high as the Cuckow, I cannot tell. Now, is there any absurdity or impossibility in supposing, that a musical nation, such as the Greeks certainly were, should do what we see the Cuckow does—join to their articulation both melody and rhythm. Nor should we be surprised that the Greeks practised an art that we cannot practise, and indeed can hardly have an idea of: For it would have been

* P. 132.

the same with their statuary, had not the monuments of that art come down to us, without which we should have hardly had an idea of the grace and beauty of such figures as the Apollo of Belvidere or the Venus of Medicis. But the melody of their speech has not come down to us, except in the accurate description of it which the Halicarnasian has given us. From him, indeed, we may learn the science of it; but there is a great difference betwixt the science of any art and the practice of it: For, from knowing merely the rules of an art, we cannot judge truly of the effects it will produce, except we know also how it answers in practice. For the same reason, as we have no practice of the antient music, nor know any thing of it, except from the accounts given of it by antient authors, we can have as little idea of the beauty of it, as of the melody of their speech. All we know of it is, that besides the Diatonic music, which is our only music, but which, among them, was no more than the music of the vulgar, they had two other kinds of music, the Chromatic

Chap. IV. Progress of Language. 149

and the Enharmonic; both which, proceeding by much smaller intervals, must have been more refined. And, as we know that they cultivated and practised music more than any other art, we may reasonably suppose that they carried it to greater perfection than any other art.

It may be observed that in a degenerate nation, among the first arts that are lost is the music of language. In modern Greece they have lost both the melody and rhythm of their language. And the language of the philosophers of India, commonly called the Shanscrit, though the grammar of it (and a most wonderful grammar it is) be preserved among the Bramins, who also speak it among themselves, yet the melody of it is lost in common use. But the Bramins preserve the knowledge of it likewise, and use it when they read their sacred book, the Vedum, in which the tones are marked, as in our Greek books [*]. The nations

---

[*] This fact, as well as many others concerning the

that migrated from the east and south to the north, have also, as I have observed, lost the melody of their language, which I think may partly be ascribed to their climate, which has not only shrivelled and contracted their bodies, but has more or less impaired all their senses.

Though these ancient accents are all together disused in the modern languages, yet they made a great part of the beauty of the composition in Greek, so that the Halicarnasian has made the ευμελεια of the composition of Demosthenes, one of its greatest praises *; and he tells us,

Shanscrit language and the Bramins, I learned last time I was in London from Mr Wilkins, a gentleman who was sixteen years in India, and all that time studied the Shanscrit language under Bramin masters, and I believe knows more of it than any European now living. He told me a fact concerning their sacred book, the *Vedam*, which I thought very curious. That this book, with the accents marked in it, they called their *Psalm* Book; which shews, as well as many other instances he gave me, the connection betwixt the Shanscrit and the Greek.

* See what I have said further upon this subject, vol. 2d. p. 380. and following.

that the tones of the words ought to be varied as well as the rhythms, and words accented in the fame way ought not to be placed together, in order that there may be a proper variety in the melody. The Romans, however, do not appear to have made a ftudy of that part of the art of compofition: And they certainly had not that variety of accent which the Greeks had; for they never accented the laft fyllable of a word: Nor do I believe, that in pronouncing their language, they were fo attentive to melody as the Greeks were; for they certainly were not fo mufical a nation as the Greeks. We are therefore not to wonder, that in a paffage from Cicero, which I have quoted *, in his *Orator ad M. Brutum*, cap. 44. he requires only three things relative to the found of oratorial compofition, viz. the order or arrangement of the words; the period; and, laftly, the numbers or rhythms. Nor indeed do I remember that he any where fpeaks of the

* Vol. 3d. p. 48.

melody as making any part of the beauty of compofition.

Before we leave this fubject of ancient accents, I think it may not be improper to obferve how they were loft, and what came in place of them. As it is not eafy to pronounce any number of fyllables, or words, with a perfect monotony, or without any variation of the voice of any kind, it was natural that the people who had loft the melody of their language, fhould fubftitute, in place of it, what we call *accents*, by which we pronounce one fyllable of a word louder than the reft, and which is the only kind of accent now ufed in the languages of Europe. If this were only conjecture, I think it muft be allowed to be a probable one: But it is proved by fact; for the modern Greeks at this day have fubftituted this kind of accent in place of the antient accents; for not only in their common difcourfe, but in reading their antient Greek books, they obferve the accents as marked in them; but in place of founding them as mufical notes,

Chap. IV. Progress of Language. 153

they only accent them as we do our syllables, by pronouncing one syllable louder than the rest *.

I have been thus long upon the subject of the melody of the Greek language, as it makes a considerable part of the beauty of oratorial composition; and because it is very little understood, nor has not been explained by any modern critic or scholar. This is a complaint that I observe is made by Taylor, in his notes upon the oration of Demosthenes *De Corona* †, where he very candidly confesses that he knows nothing of the matter. And he there quotes a passage from a scholiast of Euripides, which shews that the Greek ear was so nice, that they could distinguish, by the pronunciation, whether two syllables were contracted into one, by what they called a συναλοιφη, or whether they were distinct syllables.

* See vol. 4. lib. 1. chap. 1. p. 297.
† P. 679.

CHAP. V.

Of Rhythm.—*This a word taken from the Greek—not used by Cicero, but by Quintilian.—Not well expressed by* numerus *in Latin, or quantity in English.—A definition of Rhythm.—We have no practice of it, any more than of the melody of language.—Difference betwixt music and language.—Music cannot be without melody and rhythm, but a language may be without either.—Of the rhythm in prose. —Of this we have no perception; but it was an essential part of the antient oratorial composition.—Reason why the antients must have practised rhythm in their prose.—The orations of Demosthenes, pronounced by him with all the variety of rhythm, must have given the greatest pleasure to the learned ears of the Athenians.—The composition of Demosthenes altogether different from common speech. —There must have been a beauty in it, as pronounced by him, of which we can hardly form an idea.—This would have been the case of other arts, if monuments of them had not come down to us.—We should not by this be discouraged from the study of the antient arts.—By that study not only the beauty of Arts is to be learned, but the beauty of Manners and Characters.—A perfect character not otherwise to be formed.—Of Periods.—Both the sense and the sound of them better than of short sentences.—Without Periods our Rhetorical Stile must be nothing but vulgar speech.—A Period makes the sound more beautiful, as well as conveys the sense better.—This expressed in Aristotle's definition of a Period.—Periods must not be too long; nor must all be periodised.*

I COME now to speak of the Rhythm of these languages; and what I have to say upon this subject will be confined to the rhythm of the prose of Greek and Latin; for that only belongs to rhetoric.

As to the rhythm of their verse, I will explain it in the next volume, in which I am to treat of poetry.

Of rhythm in general I need say nothing here, as I have treated of it very fully in the 5th chapter of vol. 2d. of this work, where I think I have, upon philosophical principles, explained the nature of rhythm, and distinguished the different speciefes of it. It is a word which we have very properly borrowed from the Greek language: And I think the Romans, among many other terms of art which they took from the Greeks*, should also have taken this, instead of using the generic word *numerus*, which is the only word that Cicero uses to denote rhythm (though I observe that, when Quintilian wrote, the word *rhythmus* began to be naturalized among the Romans); and our word *quantity*, by which we express the rhythm of language, is also a word much too gene-

---

* See what I have said upon this subject in the beginning of this volume.

Chap. V. PROGRESS OF LANGUAGE. 157

ral, applying to every thing having parts or dimensions of any kind.

That the rhythm of language, or quantity as we call it, consists of long and short syllables, every man who has the least tincture of classical learning must know, though he may not be able exactly to define what a long and a short syllable is, and though he have no practice of it, any more than of their melody, neither in reading the prose of the learned languages, nor even in reading the verse, as I shall shew in the next volume upon the subject of poetry: For though we mark, as we sometimes do, a long syllable by accenting it, that accent does not make the syllable longer, but only louder. Who, therefore, denies the existence of the melody of those languages, because he has no practice of it, may, for the same reason, deny the existence of their rhythm.

What makes the rhythm of long and short syllables, is the ratio of the long to the short, which is as *two* to *one:* For without ratio or relation of one kind or another, there not only could be no science of rhythm, or of any thing else, but there could be no beauty or pleasure in the perception of it. It is therefore an agreeable mixture of syllables, having this ratio to one another, which makes what we call verse in the antient languages, or numerous prose.

From this definition it is apparent, that rhythm has nothing to do with the elevation or depression of the voice in musical cadence, and therefore is quite distinct from the melody of language. Every man who knows any thing of music, will readily make the distinction betwixt the two. But there is this difference betwixt music and language, that music cannot be without both melody and rhythm, but language may be without either, though not a perfect or complete language; but if a language has melody and rhythm, it agrees with music in this particular, that its rhythm is of more consequence than its melody. For rhythm, as the antients say,

Chap. IV. Progress of Language. 159

is every thing in mufic; and in language of the rhythm, as I have faid, verfe is compofed, and numerous profe.

That the antient verfe was made by the rhythm of long and fhort fyllables, though we do not pronounce it in that way, every fcholar muft acknowledge; but there are many fcholars, at leaft who think themfelves fo, that have no idea of the rhythm of profe. That we have no practice of this rhythm, nor any perception of it, any more than the other, is certain: But it is as certain that it was practifed, and very much ftudied by the antients; and it affected their ears fo much, that Cicero fays, ' He does not deferve
' the name of a *man* who has no percep-
' tion or feeling of it*.' And both he and the Halicarnafian, and even Ariftotle the philofopher, have given us rules for the compofition of this profe rhythm, without which Cicero fays, all compofition

---

* See the paffage quoted in vol. 2d. p. 410. See alfo p. 409. 411. where the effects of thefe oratorial

is loose and dissolute, and no better than the language of vulgar men *.

That numbers in prose were studied by the antients is not to be wondered ; but, on the contrary, it would have been matter of wonder, if, in a language composed of long and short syllables, and in which there must have been a concourse of rhythms of that kind in their prose as well as their verse, they had not endeavoured to make that concourse as agreeable to the ear as possible. And, indeed, if my ear were formed to that kind of rhythm, I believe I should like it better than the rhythm of their verse, as having more variety in it, and not regularly returning at certain intervals. I should therefore have believed, even without those great authorities of ancient au-

numbers, upon the people of Rome, are described, and an account given of the origin and progress of them.

* Vol. 4th. p. 258, and following—p. 262.—265. in which last page I have mentioned examples of this prose rhythm, given us by the Halicarnasian, by Demosthenes.

thors, that the antients did study those numbers in their prose as well as in their verse.

The orations of Demosthenes are so much varied in the composition, by an arrangement of words very different from that of common discourse, and so much adorned with variety of rhythm and melody, that when they were pronounced by him, with all the grace of action, in which he excelled so much, they must have given a delight to the learned ears, and even the eyes of the Athenians, (setting aside the weight of matter in them), of which we can hardly form an idea; and for my own part, if I had lived in those times, I am persuaded that I should have been more pleased with the speeches of Demosthenes than with the verses of Homer recited by the rhapsodists, or even with their finest theatrical entertainments.

It was this variety in his composition, by which not only the arrangement of the words was such as I have mentioned, but the melody and rhythm was so varied, that words accented in the same way were not joined together, nor words of the same rhythm or quantity *; which has made the Halicarnassian say, that it was acknowledged by every body, that there was no part of the orations of Demosthenes that was not some way adorned and varied from common speech †.

---

* See vol. 2d, p. 382. where I have translated a passage of the Halicarnassian, in which he informs us of this wonderful variety of the antient composition, and which must appear almost incredible to men such as we, who have no practice of melody or rhythm of language, nor ever heard any language pronounced in that way.

† The words are, Ουδεις ἁπλως τοπος ἱς ουχι πεποικιλται ταις τε ἐξαλαγαις, και τοις σχηματισμοις. (Περι της του Δημοσθενους διιοτητος, cap. 50. *in fine*). Where I understand by 'ἐξαλαγαι, not figures of speech, which are denoted by the word σχηματισμοι, but an uncommon order and arrangement of the words: For it is impossible to maintain that every passage in Demosthenes is adorned with tropes and figures; but, on the contrary, the stile of Demosthenes is for the greater

Chap. V. Progress of Language. 163

As it is impoffible to vary our ftile, as Demofthenes has done his, by an artificial arrangement of the words, or to adorn it with a noble melody, or a rhythm of dignity, as the Halicarnaffian expreffes it*; and, as we have no practice of that kind, nor ever heard a language pronounced in that way, I do not much wonder that even fcholars can hardly believe that in any age or nation men fpoke in that way; and indeed it is impoffible for us to form any

part very fimple, and, more than any other author, he has diftinguifhed himfelf, by making of common words an uncommon ftile. Now this was chiefly done by the ufe of that figure which rhetoricians call *Hyperbaton*, which, as the term implies, was the tranfpofition of words from their natural order to an artificial one:— See vol. 4th of this work, p. 221.; and alfo p. 218. and 219. where I have obferved the difference betwixt this artificial arrangement of words, and the common arrangement in converfation and familiar epiftles, and a difference ftill greater in the ftile of their laws and decrees. See alfo what I have faid upon this fubject, in my third volume, book 4. chap. 5. p. 102. 103.

* Μίλος ευγενης, ρυθμος αξιοματικος. See vol. 2. p. 382. of this work.

very clear or distinct idea of such speech. But we ought not for that reason to disbelieve what so many authors tell us of the Greeks speaking in that way, nor to reject that part of the Greek grammar, which treats of prosody and quantity, not only as quite useless to us, but which was never used even by the Greeks themselves. For, as I observed before *, there were other arts practised by the Greeks, of the beauty of which we never could have had any idea, if monuments of them had not come down to us. And I gave for instances their sculpture, to which may be added their architecture, and I may further add, the art of their language: For, if their writings had been all lost, as many of them are, I deny that any man of modern times could have formed so much as an idea of a language so perfect as the Greek. Now, as the pronunciation of that language has not, nor could not come down to us, I say it is impossible that we

* P. 148. of this volume.

can form any perfect idea of the melody and rhythm of their language, any more than of their music, of which I am persuaded our idea is very imperfect, for the same reason*.

But we should not be discouraged from the study of antiquity, because there was a beauty in some of their arts which we cannot imitate, nor form any perfect idea of. By those arts, of which monuments have come down to us, we are sure that they had ideas of beauty which we have not; and not of arts only, but what is more important, of manners and characters. These we ought carefully to study and imitate; for I hold, that no perfect character can be formed, any more than a fine statue, picture, or stile, except in imitation of the antient models. And this is a beauty of which we may certainly at least form an idea, and imitate as far as

---

* See what I have said further of their music, ibid.

our natural faculties will admit. But for this purpose we must live in the antient world; for we can only imitate men with whom we live and are intimately acquainted *.—But to return to our subject.

With the antient rhythm, I think, is very much connected the composition in periods, which was of absolute necessity in the rhetorical stile: For the rhythm would certainly please the ear more, when the sentence was rounded and compacted into a period, which, as I observed, is the completion of the art of composition, the beginning of which is first short sentences, then longer sentences, and last of all periods †. Of these I have spoken pretty fully in several passages of this work ‡, and

---

* See what I have said upon the subject of antient arts and manners, vol. 4th, p. 257. and 258.

† Of the progress of composition, see p. 109. 110.

‡ Vol. 3d. chap. 5. p. 57, and following, where I have given Aristotle's definition of a period, compared with Cicero's. See also vol. 2d. p. 360. where I have given a philosophical reason why a period conveys

have given sundry examples of them. And I will only add here, that a man, who pretends to speak as an orator without periods, does not know what oratory is: For I have made it part of the definition of rhetoric, that its stile must be different from common speech. Now, we cannot diversify our stile by melody and rhythm, as the antients did, nor by various arrangements of the words, and therefore, unless we have a mind to make the stile poetical, we must compose in periods, otherwise our language will be common speech. Nor will composition in long sentences supply the place of periods: For, unless such sentences are compacted and rounded, so as to bring the sense altogether to the hearer at the end of the period, they become obscure; and I have heard several speakers in such long sentences, whom I thought

sense and argument, better than if it were broken down into short sentences. An example of this, from Demosthenes, is given in p. 574. of the same volume. See further upon periods vol. 4th, p. 238. 408. and 409. where I have accounted why a period is more beautiful than a short sentence.

hardly intelligible, as you are apt to lose the connection, and to forget the beginning before you come to the end. Whereas a period well composed and well pronounced, connects the beginning with the end, so that it is very properly made a part of the definition of a period by Aristotle, that it has a beginning and end. And not only does the period properly conclude the sense, but if the period is well composed, the words, too, conclude with a proper cadence, so that the ear is filled, and finds nothing wanting in the sound any more than in the sense. But Aristotle concludes his definition with what ought carefully to be attended to in the composition of periods, 'That it be not too long, but of a moderate size *.' And I will add,

---

* Aristotle's words are, Λιγω δι περιοδον, λιξιν ιχου-σαν αρχην και τελιυτην, αυτην καθ' 'αυτην, και μεγεθος ευ-συνοπτον, *Rhetor.* lib. 3. cap. 9. where the reader will observe the words αυτην και 'αυτην, which appears to me to apply particularly to what I have observed concerning the sound of the period, and to distinguish this composition from what Aristotle calls the λεξις ειρομενη, which, with respect to the sound, has nei-

that there muſt be a variety in this matter, as well as in every thing elſe belonging to ſtile; for the whole compoſition muſt not be periodiſed; but there muſt be thrown in, here and there, ſhort ſentences, commonly in the form of interrogations, after the manner of Demoſthenes.

ther beginning nor end in itſelf, but is only terminated by the ſenſe, as is evident from the examples of that kind of ſtile which Ariſtotle gives in the paſſage of his Rhetoric above quoted. Of this ειρομενη λεξις he gives us this definition, 'Η ουδεν εχει τελος καθ' 'αυτην, αν μη το πραγμα λεγομενον τελειωθη: Which I think explains the words 'αυτην καθ 'αυτην, in the definition of the period, to relate not to the ſenſe, but to the ſound.

VOL. VI.   Y

CHAP. VI.

A taste for writing, as well as for other fine arts, to be formed only by the imitation of the antients.—Reason for this.—The Romans learned to write in that way, therefore we ought not to be ashamed to do so.—We cannot learn properly at second hand from the Romans.—They did not excel in any of the fine arts, though they learned them all from the Greeks;—could not even write their own history properly.—Reasons why the Romans did not excel in the fine arts.—First, want of genius for them;—In this the Greeks excelled all the world, as the Egyptians excelled in sciences and philosophy:—Next, their manners and occupations;—great economy and penurious living, absolutely necessary for them in the first ages of their state;—That in process of time produced the love of money, and the accumulation of it by the Patricians.

—*The consequence of which was a division in their state.—Description of their antient state by Horace.—They did not apply to the arts till after the Punic wars were ended, when they had got money and could live at their ease;—began then by translating.—Soon after that the wealth of Asia came among them, with luxury and the love of money.— Their youth bred to count money.—The consequence of this was, that no arts could flourish among them.—The pleasures of the Romans, as well as their occupations, were such, that arts could not flourish among them.—Of their Circus and Amphitheatre.—Comparison of the occupation and manners of the Athenians with those of the Romans.—War and arms the only occupation of the Athenians.—Their Theatre the finest entertainment that ever was.—No Amphitheatre among them.—Such being the case, impossible that the Romans could equal the Athenians in arts.—The Athenians, praeter laudem, nullius avari.—Horace could not have been so great a poet, if* he had not *studied in Athens.—He there learned Philosophy, and to write Lyric Poetry and Dialogue better than any other Roman.—Degeneracy of the Roman taste, after the days of Augustus, by their forsaking the imitation of the Greek models.—The Romans, therefore, Horace only excepted, models for no kind of writing—least of all for the oratorial.—Their taste in it entirely spoiled by the schools of declamation, which were unknown in the better times of Greece.—The Greek writings, therefore, are the models for stile.—There, both the ornaments of speech, and the proper use of them, are to be learned.—The imitation of the Greek authors should begin with translation.—This more pleasant from Greek to English than from Latin to English.—Of the Ridiculous Character of Stile.—The nature of the Ridiculous, and why Laughter is peculiar to man.—Not common among men who have a high sense of the beautiful in sentiments and manners.—This exemplified by the Indians of North America.—An account of the behaviour of those Indians,* both in their public assemblies and in their private conversations.—The true objects of Ridicule are the vain of our own species.—Men addicted to laughter should consider how they look when they laugh, and what a noise they make.—This Character of Stile should be very little used in oratory—is not consistent with gravity and dignity.—Both Cicero and Quintilian say a great deal too much of it.—But the orator may be pleasant and facetious, though not ridiculous.—That does not make men laugh, which is a pitiful ambition.—Wit, if rightly understood, may be used in oratory; but there must not be too much of it.—Humour altogether improper.—Young orators apt to exceed in the ornaments of speech.—The cure for this is the practice of business; but of real business, not fictitious.—The great art of an orator is to conceal art.—The attention of the hearers must not be drawn to words from things.

I WILL conclude this book with some general observations upon *Stile*, to which every man, who would distinguish himself as a speaker, should attend.

And, in the first place, as writing is an art, and I think one of the fine arts, I hold it to be certain that no man can excel in it, any more than in painting, sculpture, or architecture, except by studying and imitating the antient models of those arts; for it is not given to us, inhabitants of the north and west of Europe, to invent any thing of value in the fine arts. Nor should we be mortified with this reflection: For we cannot pretend to be a finer people than the Romans, who got all their arts, as well as sciences, from the Greeks *; for which, as I have observed elsewhere †, they had not so much as names,

---

* See what I shall say further upon this subject in this chapter.

† P. 8. of this vol. and also p. 156.

Chap. VI. Progress of Language. 175

except what they got from the Greek language. And, as to the writing art, I think we should not be ashamed to form a stile, as Cicero did, by translating from Demosthenes, Plato, and Xenophon*: For as a man, who would be a sculptor or painter, must not only see and admire the antient statues, but must copy them most diligently and carefully; so I hold that a man, who would be a good writer, must exercise himself in a translation from the antient authors, and particularly from Demosthenes, whom I hold to be the greatest artificer of prose that ever wrote, and the most perfect model upon which he can form his taste of the oratorial stile.

But there are many who think we may learn to write very well, at second hand from the Romans, without studying the Greek and the authors who write in that language; and this is a notion very preva-

---

* Taylor's notes upon the Orations of Æschines and Demosthenes, *De Corona*, in the beginning, p. 593. and following of vol. 2d.

lent in a country such as that in which I write, where the Greek language is very little understood, even by such as think themselves scholars. But I am of opinion that the Romans, though they were taught by the best masters, and had the finest models in the world to imitate, excelled in none of the fine arts. That they never produced a sculptor or painter of any value, is a fact that cannot be disputed: And though they applied more to the writing art than to any other of the fine arts, yet I do not think they excelled in it, not even in a stile much easier than the oratorial, I mean the stile of history, in which they are very far inferior to the Greeks, as I have elsewhere observed *; so that though they performed the greatest actions, and established the greatest empire that ever existed, they were not able to write properly their own history, which we learn better from the Greek historians than their own. And I think I have shewn, that even where they have translated from the

* Vol. 5th. p. 223.

Greek, they did not perfectly underſtand the original*.

But it will be aſked, what is the reaſon that the Romans who had ſuch excellent maſters to teach them, and ſuch fine models to imitate, did not excel more in the arts? And I anſwer, firſt, that they wanted the *ingenium*, which, Horace ſays, the muſe had beſtowed upon the Greeks, in the verſes which I have choſen for the motto of ſome of my volumes of this work: For I hold that there is a great difference of genius, not only among individuals of the ſame nation, but of nations themſelves compared with one another. The Greek nation was more favoured by the Muſes and Graces, than any nation that I believe ever exiſted; and therefore they have produced the fineſt works of art in the world: Nor can any thing fine of that kind be produced, except in imitation of them. The Egyptians, on the other hand, excel-

---

* Vol. 5th. p. 64. and following.

led in science; and I hold it is from that country that we derive ultimately all the science and all the philosophy that is now in Europe. The Romans, through the medium of the Greeks, got some of their philosophy; but it was not carried far among them, not so far, I think, as the arts, and not near so far as the Greeks carried it; of which we need no other proof than this, that they had no schools of philosophy among them, such as the Greeks had.

But there was another reason, which perhaps contributed still more to the little success of the Romans in arts and sciences, and that was their manners and their occupations. In the first ages of their state their only business was war and agriculture. To this last they were obliged to apply themselves most assiduously, having no more than two *jugera* for each man, that is, about an acre and a half, for the maintenance of themselves and families; and which they were obliged to cultivate with their own hands. This penurious way of living made great economy abfolutely neceffary. Now, from great economy naturally arifes the love of money, and the accumulation of it, which began among the Romans as foon as, by the fuccefs of their arms, they had acquired more land and more wealth. Of thefe the Patricians, or chief men of the ftate, as was natural, acquired moft: And accordingly we fee that they firft began to accumulate, by lending money to the poorer fort at a high intereft. And this produced the firft diforder in the Roman government: For a warlike and free people could not bear to be thus oppreffed; and therefore they became unruly and tumultuous, and at laft made a feceffion to the Sacred Mountain, as it was called. Nor could they be brought back again otherwife than by allowing them to have magiftrates of their own to protect them, I mean the Tribunes; which divided them fo much from the Patricians, as to make two ftates of one.

Horace has very well defcribed the antient manners of the Romans in thefe lines,

> Romae dulce diu fuit et solenne, reclusa
> Mane domo vigilare; clienti promere jura;
> Cautos nominibus certis expendere nummos;
> Majores audire, minori dicere per quae
> Crescere res posset, minui damnosa libido.
>
> *Epist. 1. lib. 2. v. 103.*

While the Romans were thus employed, labouring, as it might be said, for their subsistence, they had not time to cultivate the arts, if they had had genius and inclination for them. They did not therefore begin to imitate the Greek arts, till they had acquired wealth by their conquests, and were living, as we would say, at their ease. This was not till after the Punic wars were ended, as Horace tells us,

> Serus enim Graecis admovit acumina chartis:
> Et, post Punica bella, quietus quaerere coepit
> Quid Sophocles et Thespis et Aeschylus utile ferrent.
>
> *Epist. 2 lib. 2. v. 161.*

But though they began late, they began in the proper way: For they began by translating.

> Tentavit quoque rem si digne vertere posset.
>
> *Ibid. v. 164.*

And one of the best works, in my opinion,

that has come down to us from the Romans, are the comedies of Terence, which are, I believe, almoſt altogether tranſlations from Menander; for they have nothing Roman in them, the ſcene being in Athens, and the manners and names of the perſonages Greek.

But the interval was very ſhort betwixt the end of the Punic wars and the wealth of Aſia coming in among them, and with wealth, its neceſſary attendant luxury: Then money, which was before wanted for their ſubſiſtence, became ſtill more neceſſary for ſupplying the demands of a luxurious life. And, in this ſtate, I am perſuaded, their love of money was very much greater than when they were living upon their two *jugera*; for the love of money increaſes in proportion, and more than in proportion, to the accumulation of it. And accordingly, in the days of Horace, when they might be ſaid to be in poſſeſſion of the wealth of the world, their love of money was come to ſuch a height, that it appears to have been almoſt their only passion: And they taught their children little else but to count money.

> Romani pueri longis rationibus assem
> Discunt in partes centum diducere: dicat
> Filius Albini, *si de quincunce remota est*
> *Uncia, quid superat?* poteras dixisse, *Triens. Eu!*
> *Rem poteris servare tuam: redit uncia: quid fit?*
> *Semis.*———
>
> *De Arte Poet.* v. 325.

And not only were the children of the vulgar educated in this way, but those of the better sort, *pueri magnis centurionibus orti* *. When such were the character and manners of the people, Horace very properly asks the question,

> ———An, haec animos aerugo et cura peculi
> Cum semel imbuerit, speramus carmina fingi
> Posse linenda cedro, et laevi servanda cupresso?
>
> *De Arte Poet.* v. 330.

And for the same reason he might have asked, whether it was possible they could excel in any other art, or in any science.

Such was the occupation of the Romans

---
* Lib. 1. sat. 6. v. 70.

Chap. VI. Progress of Language. 183

as late down as the days of Auguſtus, when it is ſuppoſed that arts and ſciences flouriſhed moſt among them.

Let us next conſider what their pleaſures and amuſements were, by which, as much as by any thing elſe, we may judge of the genius and taſte of a people. Theſe, among the Romans, were the horſe races in the Circus, and their combats of gladiators in their Amphitheatres. The entertainment of the theatre they learned from the Etruſcans. But it does not appear to me that ever the Romans took ſo much delight in theatrical repreſentations, as in the two entertainments I have mentioned.

Now let us compare the manners of the Romans with thoſe of the Athenians. Their occupation was arms and government; for they do not appear to have ever applied much to agriculture. What they practiſed of that was chiefly by their ſlaves. And as to their pleaſures and entertainments, theſe their theatre furniſhed them, which I believe to have been the moſt elegant entertainment that ever was among men: For it confiſted of three of the fineſt of the fine arts, poetry, muſic, and the imitation of paſſions and ſentiments by motion to muſic, which they called Dancing. They got, too, philoſophy from Egypt; which came to them through the Pythagorean ſchool in Italy, and alſo directly from Egypt by Plato, who was there ſeveral years. And they took to philoſophy ſo much, that it became a paſſion among their young men, who, inſtead of counting money, as the youth of Rome did, addicted themſelves to philoſophy ſo much, that among the frugal and induſtrious it became a praiſe for a young man not to frequent the ſchools of philoſophers: And accordingly Simo in Terence commends his ſon for not being addicted to horſes or dogs, nor to *philoſophers* *. As to bodily exerciſes, they had in their public or national games, ſuch as the Olympic or Iſthmian, chariot races

---

* Andr. act. 1. ſcen. 1.

and exercises of every kind, the victors in which were highly honoured, and entered the cities to which they belonged in a triumphal chariot drawn by four horses, in the manner a Roman general did, who had conquered a nation, or won a great battle, and were maintained all the rest of their lives at the public cost*. And they had in those games also exhibitions of genius and learning; but as to the barbarous spectacle of men killing one another, such as the Gladiatorian shows in Rome, it was utterly unknown in Greece.

Thus I think it appears, from the account here given of the occupations, manners, and taste of the Romans and Athenians, that it was impossible, by the nature of things, that the Romans should have excelled, or even equalled their masters the Athenians in any art or science. And there

---

* See the preface to book 9th of Vitruvius.

is one part of the Greek character which I have not yet mentioned, which of itself was sufficient to set them above the Romans in arts and sciences; and that is, that they were, as Horace tells us,

———praeter laudem, nullius avari.

which was just the reverse of the Romans: So that, with the change of one word, we may apply the line to them, and say,

——— praeter *nummos*, nullius avari.

for from the account that Horace, in sundry passages, gives us of their manners in his age, money was every thing among them *: So that they deserved no longer the praise which Livy bestows upon them,

---

* O cives, cives! quaerenda pecunia primum est;
Virtus post nummos: haec Janus summus ab imo
Perdocet; haec recinunt juvenes dictata senesque,
Laevo suspensi loculos tabulamque lacerto.
Lib. 1. epist. 1. v. 53.

Scilicet uxorem cum dote, fidemque, et amicos,
Et genus et formam regina pecunia donat.
Lib. 1. epist. 6. v. 36.

of being the people among whom poverty continued longeſt honourable*; for in the days of Horace it was the greateſt reproach †.

When ſuch was the character of the Romans, even in the moſt learned age, which was certainly under Auguſtus Caeſar, it is not to be wondered that they produced nothing extraordinary even in the way of poetry, to which they appear to have applied more than to any of the fine arts, except Horace, who, in my opinion, is the greateſt poet they ever had. But he could not have been ſo eminent, if he had not been educated by his father in a manner very different from that in which peo-

Et genus et virtus, niſi cum re, vilior alga eſt.
Lib. 2. ſat. 5. v. 8.

* In proœmio.

† Magnum pauperies opprobrium, jubet,
Quidvis et facere et pati,
Virtutiſque viam deſerit arduae.
Lib. 3. od. 24. v. 42.

ple of his rank were educated, as he tells us himself,

> Causa fuit pater his; qui, macro pauper agello,
> Nolluit in Flavî ludum me mittere, magni
> Quo pueri magnis e centurionibus orti,
> Laevo suspensi loculos tabulamque lacerto,
> Ibant octonis referentes idibus aera.
>
> Sat. 6. lib. 1. v. 76.

He began his Greek learning at Rome, where he was taught by a schoolmaster, whom he calls *plagosus Orbilius*,

> Iratus Graiis quantum nocuisset Achilles.
>
> Sat. 2. lib. 2. v. 43.

But if he had not prosecuted those studies in Athens, he never would have been the fine writer he was. There he not only formed his taste in poetry, but he learned philosophy; an obligation which he acknowledges to Athens,

> Adjicere bonae paulo plus artis Athaenae;
> Scilicet ut curvo possim dignoscere rectum,
> Atque inter sylvas Academi quaerere verum.
>
> Ibid. v. 44.

From Athens he brought the Lyric Poetry to Rome, and perfected himself in what I think still finer writing, I mean *Dialogue*, which he learned from Plato and Menander*, and from

> Eupolis atque Cratinus, Aristophanesque, poetae,
> Atque alii quorum comedia prisca virorum est.

And accordingly he has produced some of the finest pieces of that kind that are extant, particularly his dialogue with Damasippus, where there is a fable or story, and a very pleasant one, which makes it truly a poem; and I do not hesitate to pronounce it the finest little poem in Latin.

After the days of Augustus they seem to have given up, in a great measure, their Greek masters, and to have set up for standards of fine writing some of their own authors, such as Virgil for a poet, and Sallust for an historian; and then they produced such poems as the Pharsalia of

---

* Damasippus mentions his carrying Plato to the country with him, in company with Menander which he calls *stipare Platona Menandro*. Lib. 2. sat. 3. v. 11.

Lucan, and such histories as the Annals of Tacitus*.

In this manner I think I have shewn, that the Romans, Horace only excepted, ought not to be our standard for fine writing of any kind, and particularly not of the oratorial kind. Their taste in that sort of composition was entirely spoiled by their schools of declamation, where they harangued upon fictitious subjects, and in a stile quite different from the stile of business, and fit only to draw the admiration of the vulgar. This was a practice entirely unknown in the best times of Greece, when Athens could boast of nine great orators, and did not begin, as Quintilian tells us, till about the time of Demetrius Phalerius. In Rome it was so much practised, that it infected the stile not only of their oratory, but of every other kind of writing, *ut ne vel carmen sani coloris enituit,* as Petronius Arbiter says; and accor-

---

* See more upon this subject, vol. 5th. p. 222. and following.

dingly, in the speeches of Virgil, we have a great deal of the quaint short sentences, the *vibrantes sententiolae* of Portius Latro *.

Thus I think I have shewn, that though the Romans were the first people in the world in arms and government, it was impossible that they could equal the Athenians in any of the fine arts; and particularly in oratory they must have been much inferior to them. It is therefore by the study of the Greek authors that the scholar must form his taste of stile and composition: For in those authors he will not only learn all the ornaments of speech, but he will learn to use them properly and discretely;

Descriptas servare vices operumque colores;

and not to mix them all together in every kind of composition; so that his prose will

---

* Upon the subject of the schools of Declamation, and the influence they had upon the taste of the age, see vol. 3. p. 258. and following.

not be poetry; and in his prose he will distinguish betwixt the historical, the didactic, and the rhetorical stile, and not jumble all these stiles together, as is very common in our writings at present.

But we must not only study those ancient authors, but we must imitate them, beginning, as the Romans did, with translating: And we shall have more pleasure as well as more profit, in translating from the Greek than from the Latin, the idiom of our language coming nearer to the Greek than to the Latin; for we have that significant and most emphatical part of speech, the Article, which the Latins want; and, besides that, we have a past participle active, formed indeed by an auxiliary verb, but the Latins want it altogether *. This makes our language fall more easily into the

---

* It is surprising that our English translators of the Bible have not availed themselves of this advantage, which our language has over the Latin. See what I have said on this subject, in vol. 4th, p. 123.

Greek idiom: And for that reason I have always had more pleasure in translating from the Greek than from the Latin. And I am persuaded the practice which Queen Elizabeth was taught by her preceptor, Roger Ascham, of double translation, or retranslating, from the Greek or Latin to the English, and back again (at some distance of time no doubt) from the English to the Greek or Latin, will be very useful for making the young scholar perfectly acquainted with the idioms of these several languages, and their conformity or disconformity with one another. But I believe this is practised by no body at present*.

Of the different characters of stile I have

---

* See what I have said upon this subject in a note upon p. 389. of vol. 3d, where the reader may see how learned an age that of Queen Elizabeth's was, when kings and queens learned Greek with so much labour and care, and in which there was a lady not only that wrote the Greek very well, but spoke it; I mean Lady Jean Gray.

said a good deal in the third volume, which I will not here repeat. I will only add something to what I have said on that character of stile I call *the Ridiculous**. It is a kind of stile which, according to my observation, is becoming every day more and more common, both in private conversation and public speaking: And people laugh now at so many different things, that it is not easy to say at what they laugh. Quintilian has bestowed a long chapter upon the Ridiculous: But I think he has not explained it so well in many words as Aristotle has done in two, where he says that the γελοιον, or *Ridiculous*, is αισχος ανωδυνον, that is, *the deformed without hurt or mischief* †. And with this definition of Aristotle Cicero agrees, when he says, that *Locus autem et regio quasi ridiculi, turpitudine et deformitate quâdam continetur* ‡. It is

---

* Vol. 3d. book 4th, cap. 16. p. 228.

† Vol. 3d, p. 303.

‡ Lib. 2. *De Oratore* cap. 58,

therefore the oppofite of the Beautiful; and as there is the fame knowledge of contraries, fo that we cannot know any one thing without knowing at the fame time what is contrary to it, this accounts for Laughter being peculiar to our fpecies, as no animal upon this earth, except man, has any fenfe of the Beautiful, and confequently of the Deformed. And the higher our fenfe of beauty is, the more lively, and the more correct at the fame time, will our perception of the Ridiculous be; whereas thofe, who have not a correct tafte of the Beautiful, will be difpofed to laugh at they do not know what; and hence it is, that laughter is fo common among vulgar men. But men of exalted minds, and who have a high fenfe of the Beautiful and Noble in characters and manners, are very little difpofed to laugh; for, though they perceive the Ridiculous, they are not delighted with it. This we obferve among the Indians of North America, whom we call Savages; for not only in their public affemblies, where they deliberate upon state affairs *, there is the greatest gravity and dignity of behaviour observed, but in their private conversation there are none of those violent bursts of laughter which we see among us; nor do you observe in a company of them so many people laughing and speaking at the same time, that one can hardly understand what is said, or what is the subject of the laughter. This I have been assured of by several persons, who have lived for years among them, understood and spoke their language, and conversed familiarly with them †. Those people, we must, I am

---

* Dr. Franklin in a pamphlet, which he has published, containing, among other things, *Remarks upon the Savages of North America*, says, that in these assemblies they behave with the greatest order and decency, without having any need of a speaker, such as in our House of Commons, who is often hoarse with calling *to order*. Every speaker in those Indian assemblies is heard with the greatest attention, and after he has sat down, before another rises they wait a while to know whether he has any thing to add.

† I know three gentlemen who were in the service of the Hudson's Bay Company, and lived in that

Chap. VI. Progress of Language. 197

afraid, allow, have a higher sense than we of what is beautiful, graceful, and becoming in sentiments and behaviour. The generality of men among us are so much disposed to laugh, that they do not distinguish properly betwixt the subjects of laughter and those of admiration. Thus we commonly laugh at a witty or clever saying; whereas we should admire it, and approve of it with a smile expressing pleasure *. Such men do not appear to know, that the passion which excites laughter is contempt; and the proper object of contempt is vanity, without which the meanest animal

country, one of them twenty nine years, another twenty-four, and the third seventeen. The first gentleman I mentioned was three years by himself, without any other European, among a nation of Indians far to the west of Hudson's Bay, who ride on horseback, and are from thence called Equestrian Indians, by whom he was most hospitably entertained, provided with every thing he wanted for food and raiment, and all without fee or reward.

* See the chapter above quoted of vol. 3d, p. 306 and 307, where I have distinguished betwixt a laugh and a smile.

that God has made is not contemptible; And therefore we do not laugh at the foolish absurd things which an ideot says or does; but if he is vain, and thinks he is speaking and acting very properly, we despise and laugh at him. The objects, therefore, of ridicule are confined to our species, as well as the sense of it. And in this way I understand what both Aristotle and Cicero say of it.

I would have those who indulge themselves so much in laughter, look at themselves in the glass when they laugh, and attend to the noise they make; for there are many people who have faces not otherwise disagreeable, but which they disfigure very much when they laugh. And some of them make a noise upon that occasion which is very disagreeable, and indeed is hardly human. It is true that the *dulce loqui*, and the *ridere decorum*, qualities which Horace says he possessed when he was young, are the gifts of nature; but such men, though they be obliged to speak, whatever their natural tone of voice may be, are not obliged to laugh. And they should consider that men of genius and an exalted mind are not at all delighted with the ridiculous, though, as I have observed, they must perceive it; but their delight is in the beautiful, which, as I have shewn elsewhere*, is the only pleasure of our intellectual nature.

As to the use of this character of Stile in oratory, if it be true, as I think it is, that nothing adds so much weight to the councils and arguments of an orator as gravity and dignity, it should be very sparingly, if at all used. Quintilian, indeed, has recommended it much; but he confesses that it was his admiration of Cicero, who dealt so much in it, that made him so fond of it †. He has given us several of Cicero's jokes in his orations against Verres ‡: And he was so full of them in pri-

---

* Ant. Metaph. vol. 2. book 2. chap. 5. 6. and 7.

† Lib. 6. cap. 3. p. 242. edit. Rollin.

‡ Ibid. p. 251.

vate conversation, that his freed man Tyro published three books of his jests, or, as some say, he published them himself*. Whether that be true or not, if he had not been exceedingly fond of that kind of wit, it is impossible that he would have dwelt so long upon it, in his second book *De Oratore*, longer than even Quintilian. But though I think the orator should not be ridiculous, that is, speak to make men laugh, (which, as I have observed in the chapter above quoted of the third volume of this work, is the classical signification of the word), he may, upon proper occasions, be pleasant and entertaining, and may have the *molle atque facetum*, which Horace commends in the Pastorals of Virgil †. But it is a pitiful ambition to speak to make men laugh. If, however, that be his aim,

---

* Ibid. p. 242. It is Macrobius who relates, that some said the books were written by Cicero himself.

† See Quintilian's observations upon this expression of Horace, p. 245. where he very well explains the word *facetum*, saying that *Decoris hanc magis et excultae cujusdam elegantiae appellationem, puto.*

and if he have any degree of parts or cleverness, he is sure to succeed, as the taste of the Ridiculous is so generally prevalent at present in Britain, in every popular assembly. But a great speaker will think it below him to attempt it; and it is a great praise, I think, of the eloquence of our minister, that he never so much as aims at raising a laugh: And the antient Greek orators were so chaste in this respect, that there is not in all the orations of Demosthenes one jest to be found. And even in the comedies of Menander, which Terence has translated, there is hardly any thing, as I have observed elsewhere*, that can provoke a laugh.

But what shall we say of *Wit?* Is it a proper ornament of the Rhetorical Stile? If it be confounded with the *Ridiculous,* as it is by many, I think it is not at all proper for an oration. But if it be distin-

* Vol. 5th, p. 23.

guished from the *Ridiculous*, as I have done *, and made to consist in great sense expressed in few words, and with an uncommon turn of expression, I think it may not be improperly used upon some occasions; but not too often, lest it should appear like an affectation of *Wit*; which is offensive to men of sense and good taste, and takes away both from the weight of the arguments and the credibility of the narrative. As to *Humour*, if it be as I have defined it †, *the imitation of characters ridiculous*, it is altogether improper in an oration, as it makes a mimic of the orator.

The young orator, if he have genius and fancy, and be likewise a scholar, will be apt to exceed much in the ornaments of stile. I know no better cure for this than that he should be a man of business, and particularly should apply to the business of the bar; for there he will soon

---

* Vol. 3d, p. 318.

† Ibid. p. 345.

learn that buſineſs is not to be carried on by figures of ſpeech. Demoſthenes and all the great orators of old were men of buſineſs: For, if they did not plead cauſes, which moſt of them did, they were employed in the buſineſs of the ſtate. But if, in place of real buſineſs, they had employed themſelves in pleading fictitious cauſes, as they did in the ſchools of declamation in Rome, they would not have been ſuch orators as they were; for I know nothing more proper for ſpoiling the taſte of an orator.

I will conclude this ſubject with obſerving, that the greateſt art in ſpeaking and writing is to conceal art, and particularly the art of words; which, if it be obſerved and ſtick out, *(extra corpus orationis eminet,* as Petronius expreſſes it), will take a great deal from the weight of the matter. The greateſt beauty, therefore, that I know in the ſtile of either writing or ſpeaking is, that the words ſhould not draw the attention of the reader or hearer from the ſenſe and matter.

BOOK III.

Of Action *or* Pronunciation.

CHAP. I.

Of Pronunciation, *or* Action, *as the antients called it.*—*Three things comprehended under Action.*—*One of them the most important of all, viz. the management of the voice.*—*The sayings of Demosthenes, and Antonius the Roman orator, upon the subject of Action.*—*To excel in Oratory both nature and art must concur.*—*Of the requisites from nature.*—*These divide into qualities of the mind and of the body;*—*and first, of the qualities of the body.*—*Rhetoric distinguished from all the other fine arts by requiring these qualities.*—*The first bodily quality of a speaker, size and figure.*—*Quotation from Milton on this subject.*—*A voice sweet and expressive of feeling; or if not, strong and commanding.—A good speaker ought also to be well winded.—Of the qualities of the mind which the orator requires;—And first, a sense of the* Pulchrum *and* Honestum.—*This peculiar to human nature.—A quotation from Cicero on this subject.—The extent of this sense—it goes to every word and every action.—Quotation from Milton and Tibullus on this subject.—The taste of the French very elegant in this matter.—If not bestowed by nature, no teaching can give it.—The Grave and Dignified also belong to the orator.—This likewise from nature.—Also genius and natural parts.—A perfect orator ought to be superior to his audience.—This was the case of Pericles.—Recapitulation of the natural qualities of mind required to make an orator.—What Art bestows, next to be considered.*

IN this book I am to treat of a most important part of the Rhetorical art, so important, that it gives to it the name of *Eloquence;* what I mean is the Elocution or Pronunciation of Speech. It is a noted saying of Demosthenes, than whom no man knew better in what the beauty and excellency of the art consisted, that the first, the second, and third quality of an orator was Action; and if he had been asked what the fourth was, I believe he would have made the same answer. Now, under action the antients comprehended not only what we call action, that is, the gesture of the body, but the look, the action of the features of the face in speaking, and principally the management of the voice, the most important of all the things I have mentioned*. And it is as difficult as it is necessary; which made Marcus Antonius, the Roman orator, a cotemporary of Lucius Crassus, say, *disertos a se visos esse multos, eloquentem autem neminem;* by which I understand he meant, that though he had seen many orators who excelled both in the matter and the diction of their speeches, yet he never saw any whose elocution he could praise.

* Upon the subject of *Action*, see vol. 4th, p. 280, where I have given Cicero's definition of it.

To excel in this principal part of the art, there are many things required: And firſt there are certain talents which every great ſpeaker muſt have from nature; for we can excel in no art, if we are not fitted by nature for the practice of that art. But as nature alone will not make a man perfect in any art or ſcience, ſo in oratory we muſt join to nature, art and education, and aſſiduous practice under the beſt maſters we can find, and according to the beſt rules. I will begin with the qualities which we muſt derive from nature, and without which no art or teaching will make us great ſpeakers. Theſe I divide into qualities of mind and of body: For it is peculiar to eloquence, and diſtinguiſhes it from all the other fine arts, that certain qualities of the body, as well as of the mind, are neceſſary to make us excel in it:—With the qualities of the body I will begin.

And, in the firſt place, a great ſpeaker ſhould have ſize and figure; for a little deformed man can hardly be ſeen in a great aſſembly, if he could be heard. A great speaker, therefore, should seem, when he rises to speak, like Beelzebub in Milton, *a pillar of state*, and should stand

> With Atlantean shoulders, fit to bear
> The weight of mightiest monarchies———.

He should also have a look, which

> Draws audience and attention still as night.

Such a figure and such a look would prepossess an audience wonderfully in favour of the speaker. There should be also something naturally graceful and becoming, and expressing a good and great character in the movement of his features while he speaks, and in the gesture of his body. But above all his voice should be sweet and clear, strong and commanding attention. There are some people who have a tone of voice so sweet, pleasant, and so expressive of their sentiments, that every thing they say touches your heart. This is what Cicero calls *suavitas quae exit ex ore;* which he distinguishes from the *suavitas verborum* *. And it was by this sweet tone of voice that the Athenians

---

* *De Oratore*, lib. 3. cap. 11.

were diftinguifhed not only from the Afiatics, but from the other Greeks*. But this is a gift which nature has beftowed upon very few; and I believe it is not to be acquired by any art or teaching, at leaft in any great degree. There are fome who cannot properly be faid to have any tone of voice at all; but fpeak fomewhat like the beating of a drum, by thumps and ftrokes; and if they fpeak very faft, which often happens, it is like the ruff of a drum. But though a well-tuned voice is given to very few fpeakers, a ftrong commanding voice is neceffary for any man who would excel in the art. He fhould alfo be, like a good horfe, well winded; fo as to be able to pronounce a long period in one breath, *una continuatione verborum*, as Cicero has expreffed it.

Thefe are the qualities of body which a great fpeaker muft have from nature. But

---

* *De Oratore*, ibid.

in this art, as in every thing elſe belonging to man, mind is principal. And the firſt quality of mind which is required, is a ſenſe of what is Graceful and Becoming, or in one word, of what is *beautiful*, without which no man can excel in any of the fine arts, and leaſt of all in oratory. And I ſay further, that he cannot be a man of worth or goodneſs; and indeed I think that he hardly deſerves the name of a Man: For I hold, that a ſenſe of the *pulchrum* and *honeſtum* in ſentiments and in actions, diſtinguiſhes us more from the brute creation than any thing elſe*; and accordingly it appears in us before our reaſon begins to exert itſelf in any great degree. This doctrine,

---

* This is the opinion of Cicero, who, in the general definition which he gives us of the *decorum*, ſays, *in omni honeſtate verſatur*, and that it belongs to every thing that is *pulchrum et honeſtum;* and he adds, that it is that, *quod conſentaneum ſit hominis excellentiae, in eo, in quo natura ejus a reliquis animantibus differat :* (*De Officiis*, lib. 1. cap. 27. *in fine.)*: Which is juſt ſaying what I ſay, that it is the *honeſtum* and the *decorum* which principally diſtinguiſhes us from the brutes.

I know, will appear very ſtrange to thoſe who have learned the philoſophy of Mr Paley, in his book upon Morals, which is the only book of ſcience that has been publiſhed in England of a great while, but which, I think, does no honour to the nation; for it takes away not only the foundation of Virtue and of Morals, but it puts an end at once to all the fine arts; for if we have no ſenſe of what is Beautiful, Graceful, and Becoming in ſentiments and actions, I think it is impoſſible we can have it in outward forms, the chief beauty of which confiſts in the expreſſion of what is Beautiful and Fine in the diſpoſitions and ſentiments of the mind *.

---

* From Mr Paley's book I could only learn one thing; that he himſelf had no ſenſe of the Beautiful and Graceful, any more than Mr David Hume, whoſe philoſophy of Morals he has endeavoured to revive, making the principle of it *utility*, or the computation of profit and loſs; for a man who has that ſenſe, which all men of genius muſt have, can no more doubt of the exiſtence of it, than of his own exiſtence. Nor is it an uncommon thing to ſee men in this age intirely void of it; for in a much better age,

As this sense is congenial to our nature, and indeed predominant in it, it extends to every thing we do; *Status, incessus, sessio,* (says Cicero), *accubatio, vultus, oculi, manuum motus, teneant illud decorum**. And a man, who himself possesses this sense of the Graceful and Becoming in any high degree, will perceive it in another in every the the least thing he does or says.

> Speaking or mute, all comeliness and grace
> Attends thee, and each word each action forms;

says the Angel to Adam in Milton: And the poet says of his mistress,

and even among the Greeks, a people more favoured by the Muses and Graces than any other that ever existed, Aristotle tells us that there were many who had not the least idea of the το καλον, though we do not find that there was any philosopher, or any writer of any kind among them, who denied or doubted the existence of it. See what I have said on this subject in Ant. Metaph. vol. 2d, book 2d, and the three last chapters of that book.

* *De Officiis*, lib. 1. cap. 35.

*Illam quicquid agit, quoquo vestigia movet,
Componit furtim subsequiturque decor* *.

where the reader of taste will observe, how properly the word *furtim* is applied to express that the Graceful must not be studied or affected, or, as it were, sticking out, but must animate every word and action; or, as Milton expresses it, *form them* †.

This sense, therefore, of the Graceful and Becoming, must appear in every word, every look, and every motion of the ora-

---

* Tibulli lib. 4. carm. 2. v. 8.

† The French, who study grace more, I think, than any other nation in Europe, at least in outward deportment, say of a woman that is very graceful, " Qu'elle est toute petrie de graces;" that is, *The graces are kneaded into her*: And such is their taste of beauty, that they think this a higher eulogium upon a lady than any thing they can say of her face or person: And speaking of a man, they think the greatest praise they can bestow on his person is, that " Il a " l'air noble;" and the worst thing they can say of his appearance is, " Qu'il a l'air ignoble." See p. 296. of vol. 4th.

tor. And though, no doubt, it, as well as every other sense belonging to us, may be improved by culture and practice, if we have it not from nature, no art or teaching can give it us.

Connected with the Graceful and the Becoming, is the Grave and the Dignified. This, too, must be from nature; for an affected gravity and dignity, when the natural character is that of a buffoon or a vulgar man, is ridiculous.

To make an orator, nature must also furnish genius and good natural parts. These undoubtedly may be very much improved by art and culture; but nature must have laid the foundation.

Lastly, to make a perfect orator, there is something more, which nature must furnish; and that is a great and elevated mind. And in this respect I maintain, that a perfect orator ought to be above the audience to whom he speaks, and should be in some degree a being superior to them;

Chap. I. Progress of Language. 215

though it may be proper, in order to obtain what is the end of all oratory, persuasion, that he should seem to submit his judgment to theirs, and to court their approbation. Such an orator, I believe, Pericles was, the greatest speaker, by what we hear of him, that perhaps ever existed, whose superiority, in the powers of speech, is well expressed by what is said of him, " That, he thundered and lightened when " he spoke."

These are the qualities with which, I think, an orator must be born; and if so, I think we may say, *oratores nascimur*, as we say *poetae nascimur*; and I believe more of the gifts of nature are required to make an orator than to make a poet: For setting aside those talents of the mind which I have mentioned as necessary for the orator as well as the poet, there are qualities of the body which, as I have shewn, the orator requires, but with which the poet has nothing to do. In the next chapter I shall speak of what it is necessary that education, art, and teaching should furnish to the orator; and in this respect I am persuaded it will appear that the art of oratory is, as Cicero says, *incredibili magnitudine et difficultate**.

---

* See what I have said further upon the difficulty of the art in vol. 4th, p. 285. and 286.

CHAP. II.

Education, *absolutely necessary for making a speaker.—Should begin early, even with the nurse and the mother.—Examples of the advantage of a mother speaking well.—All those that are about children should have nothing faulty in their pronunciation.—After the child is come to be a boy, his pronunciation must be formed with great care.—Our schools defective in that article.—The consequence of that is, that men speak ill, who would otherwise have spoken well. —To speak well in private conversation, a necessary prelude to public speaking.— This, in boys, should be carefully attended to.—Natural defects by that attention may be corrected.—An affected tone and manner of speaking to be carefully avoided.*

THAT a proper Education is neceffary for a man that is to be a fpeaker, every body will admit. I will add, that it ought to begin very early; Quintilian fays with the nurfe*, who, he fays, ought to have nothing faulty in her fpeech. If the mother happen to be the nurfe, fo much the better for the child in every refpect: But though fhe do not nurfe him, he is more with her after he is weaned than with any other; and for that reafon it is of great importance that fhe fhould fpeak well. It was to their education under their mother Cornelia, that the two Gracchi chiefly owed their reputation as orators. Some letters of hers were extent in Cicero's time, and from them, he fays, it appears, *Filios non tam in graemio educatos quam in fermone matris* †: And I had occafion to know a very young boy, whofe fpeaking

---

* Lib. 1. cap. 1. paragraph 2.

† Cicero De Claris Oratoribus, cap. 58.

Chap. II. Progress of Language. 219

would have surprised me extremely, being very different from the language both of the family and country, if I had not known his mother, who spoke remarkably well. Both Cicero and Quintilian require also, that the paedagogues, that is, those who attended children when they were very young, should speak well*. And I will add, that all the servants, and in general every body with whom they converse, should have nothing faulty in their pronunciation; for as it is by imitation that we learn to speak, children of necessity imitate those whom they hear. And it is true what Quintilian observes, that we are most tenacious of what we learn very young, and more tenacious of what is bad than of what is good; for what is good is easily changed for the worst, but it is not easy to make the change contrarywise †.

When the child grows up, and becomes what we call a boy, the Romans employ-

* Cicero, ibid.—Quintil. ibid,
† Quintil. ibid.

ed men of genius, even poets, to form his pronunciation,

<blockquote>Os pueri tenerum balbumque Poeta figurat,</blockquote>

says Horace*. This business, among us, is committed to schoolmasters, who ought to labour nothing more than to teach the boys to pronounce distinctly, neither too fast nor too slow, and with proper variations of tone. And I maintain, that a boy incapable of learning any art or science, may be taught to read or speak any thing he understands, as well as it is possible, that is, as well as his natural faculties of speech will admit. And the reason is, that speaking is learned, as I have said, by imitation. Now in that way we learn better in our childhood and early youth, than at any other time, of our life. But I am afraid our schoolmasters are at more pains to teach our children the grammar of the learned languages, than to pronounce well their own: And I doubt many of themselves are not masters of the art of pronun-

---

* Lib. 2. Epist. 1. v. 126.

ciation. But whatever be the cause, so it is, that I have known several boys who had their language made worse at school, though taught at Westminster or Eaton, so far from being improved in their speaking; and there are men, whom I have heard speak in public, that, I am persuaded, would have been orators, if they had been properly taught to speak at school.

Before a boy begins public speaking, he should learn to talk well in private conversation, without which no man ever was or ever will be a good public speaker. His conversation, therefore, should be carefully attended to; and he should be taught not only to smile, but to laugh agreeably, which will make him a pleasant companion, though he should never be a public speaker. The *dulce loqui* and the *ridere decorum*, which I mentioned above*, are very amiable qualities. And though nature must furnish the materials there, and of every thing else belonging to us, yet art and

* P. 198.

teaching can do a great deal; for though we cannot alter the features of our face, nor the action of those features in speaking or laughing, yet we may correct, in some degree, their natural imperfections*. And, if we have the sense of the Graceful and Becoming, we may make even an ugly face not disagreeable.

* I knew a lady who was very handsome, and a celebrated toast, but whose smile was really a grimace. Now this, I am persuaded, might have been corrected in some measure, if it had been early attended to, and her face would have been thereby much improved: For a smile is, I think, the most pleasant action in the human face, and the most expressive of agreeable sentiments. It is very different from laughing, which very often deforms the countenance, and very seldom expresses any sentiment that is agreeable; yet the Latins have no word to distinguish it from the laugh. And in this respect not only the Greek, but even the English is a richer language than the Latin: For in Latin they could not express what Sappho says of Venus,

Μειδιασασ' αθανατῳ προσωπῳ.

Nor could they express what the English poet has said in his translation of another ode of Sappho;

If we, naturally or from habit, speak fast and inarticulately, we may, by care and attention, correct that fault: And if we are addicted to immoderate bursts of laughter, we may certainly learn to laugh with more decorum, and not to speak and laugh at the same time; or, what is worse, to laugh, speak, and eat all at once, as I have seen some people do. Boys should also be carefully taught to repeat verses well, and to try to procure that *suavitas oris* of Pomponius Atticus, which, as I have observed elsewhere, made him so agreeable to the great men of Rome*.

Before I quit this subject of private con-

" And hears and sees thee, all the while,
" Softly speak and sweetly smile."

for a laugh may have decorum in it, like Horace's laugh, but it cannot have sweetness. Of the difference betwixt laughing and smiling, and how properly Homer has marked that difference, see vol. 3d, p. 306, and 307.

* See vol. 4th, p. 301. See also what I have said in general upon the Stile of Conversation, and what is necessary to make it agreeable. Ibid. p. 293, &c.

verſation, I muſt obſerve, that I have known ſome young people, who, ſtudying to ſpeak much better than others, have acquired a tone and manner of ſpeaking uncommon and unnatural. They ſpeak with a voice which the Italians call *voce finta;* and they appear as if they were acting a part, and ridiculing ſome body who talked in that affected way. Theſe gentlemen ought to know that nothing is good or pleaſant that is not natural; and even a rough ill-tuned natural voice, is better than ſuch a voice as they affect. Our young orator, therefore, ought to ſtudy to ſpeak, as Cicero directs, *ſono vocis recto et ſimplici, ut nihil oſtentationis aut imitationis afferre videatur* *.

---

* *De Oratore,* lib. 3. cap. 12.

CHAP. III.

Of the Education *necessary to make a speaker.—Of action in speaking, and what is comprehended under it.—Of the tone of Public Speaking.—The difference betwixt* Speaking, Talking, Prating, *and* Prattling.*—A voice and ear for Speaking as well as for Music.—The difference betwixt* Speaking *and* Talking *is in the tone of the voice.—What that difference is.—The young scholar to be exercised in speaking, talking, and prating the same thing.—Of the tones of passion and sentiment.—Without these there is a Monotony in speaking.—Even where there is no variety of passion or sentiment, difference of* matter *requires different tones—especially in composition in periods with parentheses.—-Of Periods.—The sense conveyed more forcibly by being sus-*

pended, till it comes out at the end of the Period.—This Suspense must be marked by the voice.—Practice of composing and speaking Periods to be acquired by reading antient orations.—The student of oratory should know the difference betwixt languages, and their excellencies and defects.—Our language superior to the French, by having accents—Those accents too strong in common use, so as to obscure the following syllables.—They should therefore be softened by the speaker.—Of Emphasis.—Use of it too common in public speaking—it hurts both the sense and sound of a Period;—if very loud and frequent, it makes barking *of speaking.—Oratory should not study too much the pleasure of the ear by the use of the figure Parisosis.—The nature of this figure.—Intemperately used by Cicero.—Of the look, mein, and action of the features of the face in speaking.—Art may do something in that matter, but nature more.—Of the gesture of the body;—this from nature—but may be governed by art.—The orator must not be a pantomime, nor*

Chap. III. PROGRESS OF LANGUAGE. 227

even a player.—Of the use of gesture among the French and Italians.—Among us not so much of it.—But there must be some.— It should not be insignificant nor too violent.—Of the appearance of Ulysses in Homer, when he began his speeches;—this not an idea formed by Homer of a great speaker, but a portrait of Ulysses.—Such an appearance not to be recommended to an orator.—The arts of Action and Pronunciation ought not to be neglected even in speaking upon subjects of science to men who understand the science.

IN this chapter I am to treat of the Education which is necessary to form a speaker, and particularly to make him excel in the most difficult parts of the art, I mean the Action; under which I include, as I have said, not only the motion and gesture of the body, but the look and appearance of the speaker, and above all the management of his voice*, which, as it is

---

* This is the definition given of Action by *Cicero de Oratore*, lib. 1. cap. 5. I have given the words in vol. 4th, p. 280.

the organ conveying to the hearer the sense and sentiments of the speaker, must needs be principal in the art, as without it there could be no such thing as an art of speech of any kind.

The first thing, in my opinion, that a young speaker should learn, is to distinguish betwixt the tone of private conversation and Public Speaking, or betwixt *Talking* and *Speaking*; or, as the Latins expressed it, *Loqui* and *Dicere*, to which I think the English words *Talking* and *Speaking* correspond. And, accordingly, when we say that a man is a speaker, we mean that he is a public speaker. And, I think, our young student should learn also to make the distinction betwixt *Talking* and *Prating*, and also betwixt *Prating* and *Prattling*, which I hold to be the diminutive of Prating; so rich is our language in words expressing the different tones and manners of utterance, richer than any other language that I know.

That there is both a voice and an ear

for speaking as well as for music, I think it is impossible to deny: And though a man may not have a voice that fits him for public speaking, yet, if he has the sense of hearing, and any degree of taste or feeling, he will readily distinguish betwixt the tone of public speaking and private conversation. To such a man, if any one in company assumes the tone of public speaking, it will give offence; and also, if a public speaker shall descend to *talk*, and much more if he shall *prate* or *prattle:* But, however apparent these distinctions may be, there is nothing more common than to hear our speakers *talk*, and, I am afraid, sometimes *prate*: And so little is the art studied and cultivated in Britain, that there are but few who have the tone of public speaking, or are able to distinguish betwixt *talking* loud, or vehemently, and *speaking*. Now, to make this distinction, is one of the first lessons that our young speaker should learn: For he should be taught to swell his voice, and to make it more deep and solemn, without making it louder; and his master should exercise him in reading or speaking the same thing, first in the tone of public speaking, then of talk or conversation, and last of all, to make him prate or prattle. And if he is well exercised in this way, his ear will soon be formed to perceive the difference, and he will neither declaim in private company, nor will he talk or prate in public.

The next thing that our young speaker should learn is the different tones of passion or sentiment: For, as variety is required in every thing of which there is any art, a monotony is offensive even in private conversation, and much more in public speaking: For even where there is no passion or sentiment expressed, yet, in conveying the sense in a sentence of any length, and of some variety in the matter, a change of tone is necessary to convey the sense clearly. And if the composition be of the rhetorical kind, that is, in periods, with sometimes a parenthesis, if the tone of the voice be not changed according to the variety of the sentiment and the matter, it will not be intelligible. In place of vary-

Chap. III. Progress of Language. 231

ing the tone, many speakers sink their voice, and often when they mean to be very pathetic. But instead of expressing passion, they express nothing at all; for they are not heard, at least not distinctly.

As I have mentioned periods, I will say something of them. To compose a Period well is not an easy matter; but, according to my observation, it should seem, to pronounce them well is still more difficult: For I have heard discourses composed in periods, particularly sermons, so ill pronounced, that I thought it would have been better if the periods had been broken down into short sentences. The great beauty of a period is, that it keeps the sense suspended, perhaps for some considerable time, till at last it brings it out at the end with more force than it could otherwise be conveyed; for by the suspense it makes a greater impression than it would otherwise do; and very often the impression is made greater by surprise, something not expected at the beginning of the Period, or even in the progress of it, being brought out in the end. Now this suspence must be expressed by the voice; and if the matter of the different members of the Period be various, so as to require different tones, and if the members be distinguished from one another by proper pauses, but still preserving the continuation of the sense, it is the greatest beauty of pronunciation, as it both pleases the ear, and conveys the sense and argument in the most forcible manner; for it brings it all together to the mind, in which way only an argument can be rightly understood; for all argument is by syllogism. Now we cannot apprehend the truth of a syllogism, unless we have the premises and the conclusion in our view at the same time. And the δεινοτης of Demosthenes, as they called it, was, I am persuaded, chiefly owing to his collecting his arguments in Periods, and bringing them out so forcibly upon his hearers [*].

To teach the scholar both to compose

---

[*] See what I have further said upon Periods, vol. 4th, p. 408. and the passages there referred to.

and pronounce Periods, it is neceſſary that he ſhould be trained to read and to repeat antient orations, (for he can never be an orator if he is not a ſcholar), particularly thoſe of Demoſthenes, the beſt compoſed of any I know: And it muſt be his daily exerciſe; which in time will make both the compoſition and pronunciation of Periods eaſy to him, ſo that even when he ſpeaks extempore he will ſpeak in Periods. It was in this way, as I have elſewhere obſerved *, that the Duke of Wharton was trained by his father to be ſo great a ſpeaker.

Our young orator ſhould be taught to know the advantages and diſadvantages of the language in which he is to ſpeak. This is beſt known by comparing it, firſt, with the learned languages, and then with ſome modern languages, ſuch as the French. By comparing it with the learned languages he will find it defective in many things which adorn oratorial com-

* Vol. 4th, p. 244.

position, such as melody and rhythm, and that variety of arrangement of words which the more perfect grammar of those languages admits, and which gives a wonderful beauty and variety to composition in Greek and Latin. But the English has one thing in its pronunciation which the learned languages had not, and that is what we call Accent, by which the voice is raised and made louder upon one syllable of a word than upon another.* This I do not state as a defect of those languages; on the contrary, I should have thought it a blemish in them, if with the melody and rhythm of their language they had mixed the beatings and thumpings of our accents, in which if there be any music, it is the music of a drum. But I think it is a defect in the French language, being without melody or rhythm, as well as ours, not to have them: For they give a variety to our pronunciation which the French have not, and enable us to make (what I think the finest composition in modern times) such verse as that of Milton, of which he has

---

* See vol. 4th, p. 32.

made the best orations that are to be found in any modern work. But this advantage of our language above the French, is attended with this disadvantage, that it makes the pronunciation of it rough, and not unlike, as I have said, the beating of a drum; and it makes the pronunciation of our words not clear and distinct, and indeed hardly intelligible to foreigners when they begin to learn our language; for the vehemence of our accents is such, that it obscures the following syllables of the word, of which we need no other example than the word *syllable* itself. This vehemence of accent is certainly not necessary in our language; for the Italians have accents such as ours, and accordingly make blank verse as well as we; but they pronounce distinctly the following syllables of the word, as well as the accented syllable*. I would therefore advise the young

---

* I have reason to think that this vehemence of accentuation, which distinguishes the English language so much from the Italian, and, I believe, from every other language in Europe, was not practised formerly in England so much as it is at present; for I have been

speaker not to aggravate this blemish of the language, by founding our accents too violently, but rather to soften them in the pronunciation, and thereby give as much smoothness to his utterance as the language will admit of.

Besides this violence of our accents, there is a thing very much practised by our public speakers, and sometimes even

told by some gentlemen who have been in America, and particularly by one who was there many years, that the people of New England do not accent syllables with near so much violence as the people of Old England do at present; and for that reason they speak more clearly and intelligibly. The fact appears to be, that the people of New England have preserved the language they brought with them, which was the language spoken in England in the days of Milton, when men both spoke and wrote better in England than they do now: For I am afraid that nothing is improved in England since that time, but, on the contrary, has grown worse, and among other things language; and I have elsewhere observed, that since I was educated, among English gentlemen at a foreign university, half a century ago, the language is worse, both in the phraseology and the pronunciation, particularly as it is spoken by the younger people. See vol. 4th, p. 116. 118. and 119.; and also p. 167. and following.

Chap. III. PROGRESS OF LANGUAGE. 237

in private converfation, called Emphafis, by which one word in a fentence is founded much louder and ftronger than the other words. Whether this was in ufe among the antients, I will not pretend to determine: All I know is, that it is not mentioned in any antient book upon the fubject of grammar or rhetoric: And the Greeks had particles, fuch as μεν, δε, γε, δη*, τοι, μεντοι, and the like, by which

---

* This particle δη is of great emphafis, and is ufed to denote that, what follows deferves the particular attention of the reader or the hearer. The Latins fupply the want of it very clumfily, I think, by the word *fcilicet*: As in a paffage of Virgil, in the fecond Georgic, where he fays, fpeaking of the life of farmers, and the way they paffed their holidays,

 Hanc vitam veteres olim coluere Sabini,
 Hanc Remus et frater; hinc fortis Etruria crevit,
 Scilicet et rerum facta eft pulcherrima Roma.

which laft line might be thus tranflated into Greek,

 Και ΔΗ εγενετο καλλιστη πολις Ρωμη.

The particles γε and τοι ferve alfo to excite the attention of the reader. The others I have mentioned ferve for the purpofe of connection. See further upon the fubject of thefe particles, vol. 4th, p. 63. and following.

they excited the attention of the hearers to certain parts of the sentence more than to others, so that they did not need to excite that attention by raising their voice above the level of the speech, and so making their language bound, as it were, and hop. But be that as it will, it is certain that our accents and our emphasis, joined together, do destroy all smoothness and roundness in the speeches of many of our orators, and make them resemble barking rather than speaking: And particularly they destroy altogether the pronunciation of a period; for they call off the attention of the hearer from that continuation of the sense, which it is necessary he should carry on to the end of the period. And besides, it destroys the roundness and flow of the sound of the period. This I have observed, particularly in hearing some men read the periods of Milton's Paradise Lost, which they made hardly intelligible by their many and violent emphases, though they imagined that they made in that way the sense much clearer and stronger, which,

I believe, is the reason that they are so much used: But where there are many emphases, even though they be not extraordinarily loud, there are truly none at all. I do not, however, advise our young speaker to pronounce no words more emphatically than others. An emphasis, upon some words in our language, is necessary, to call the attention of the hearer to the thing signified by them, and thereby to supply the want of such particles in Greek as I have mentioned. But they should not be too frequent, nor too loud or vehement, so as to destroy the roundness and smoothness of speaking.

The oratorial composition, as it should not be rough and unpleasant in its sound, so it ought not to study too much the pleasure of the ear by the too frequent use of the figure which the Greeks call παρισωσις, by which *like* is referred to *like*, *contrary* to *contrary*, and words of the same form and structure made to answer one to another. Of this figure of speech I have spoken at some length in the third volume of this work*, where I have shewn that Cicero has used it very intemperately, even in speeches of business; for in epideictic orations, which are composed only to please and entertain, they may not only be tolerated, but considered as an ornament suited to the subject. But even Isocrates (I have observed) in his panegyrical orations, has not been so immoderate in the use of them as Cicero. And thus much may suffice for what may be called the vocal part of Action.

As to the other part of Action, relating to the look, the air, the mein, and the action of the face in speaking, nature must be the governing principle, and must do almost the whole. Yet art will do something; for if we have a sense of what is becoming and dignified, without which art can do nothing, the face and mein may be composed to express gravity and dignity suitable to the subject of the oration. And if there be any thing aukward or un-

---

* P. 85. and following.

Chap. III. PROGRESS OF LANGUAGE.

gracious in the action of our features when we speak, that may in some measure be corrected, at least so far as to express nothing vulgar or mean. But if the speaker have no natural gravity nor dignity, he had better not try to assume it; for an affectation of that kind is more offensive, and makes the speaker more contemptible than his native vulgarity. At the same time, if he be a man of abilities, and a good actor as well as speaker, he may venture to imitate gravity and dignity, and, like Belial in Milton, seem at least

"For dignity compos'd and high exploit;"

and *if his tongue drop manna*, and if he can, like Gorgias the Sophist,

———————— make the worse appear
The better reason,——————

he will attain to great reputation as an orator, and will acquire wealth, and place, and power, which are the things now aimed at by speaking.

As to Gesture, the last thing to be considered belonging to Action, nature certainly no doubt prompts us to express our sentiments by some action of the body. But this, as well as other things that are natural to us, may be governed and regulated by art. There was a great art among the antients, by which all sentiments and passions were expressed by the action of the body alone, without the voice. This was the art of the *Pantomimes*, once the great delight of the people of Rome. But in rhetoric the action of the body never can be separated from the words: But these may be accompanied with proper gestures, corresponding to the things signified by them. And this was beginning to be formed into an art among the Greeks, as Aristotle has informed us in the first chapter of his third book upon rhetoric; and he gives it the name of ʽυποκριτικη, or the *Players Art*: And if the orator was not too much of a player, I am persuaded it must have had a great effect upon the people to whom he spoke, and accordingly Aristotle tells us that it had.

That there was a great deal of this action in later times, both among the Greeks and Romans, we are sure. Quintilian speaks a great deal of the gestures of the orator, and particularly of the action of his hands, without which, he says, all other action is weak and imperfect. How many motions the hands have, he adds, cannot be expressed: For, says he, other parts of the body assist the speaker, but they may be said to speak themselves; for with them we ask, we promise, call, let go, threaten, supplicate, abominate, interrogate, deny, express joy, sadness, doubt, confession, and repentance, with a good deal more to the same purpose; and he concludes with saying, that in such a difference of languages in different nations, this seems to be the common language of men*. In modern times there is a good deal of gesture among the French and Italians, and not only in public speaking, but in private conversation, they express a

* Lib. 11. *Institutionum* cap. 3. p. 461. of the edition Roline.

great deal by gesture*. In Britain there is much less of it; but it is so natural a kind of expression, that there must be some of it even in private conversation; and I think there ought to be more of it in public speaking, in order to give life and animation to what is said. If a man was to harrangue, with his arms hanging down by his sides, like an Egyptian statue, or suppose a little action with one hand, but the other in his breeches, which I have seen, he certainly would not move the passions of his hearers, nor engage their attention, at least by his attitude and gesture. Or, if he were to clasp his hands, and move only his thumbs, which is the only action I have observed of a celebrated preacher, he could not, I think, much move his audience †. But though

---

* See concerning the action of the antient orators, and of the pleaders in Italy at this day, vol. 4th, p. 280.

† As our arms and hands are very useful, and indeed of absolute necessity in the practice of the arts of life, so the action of them may be very graceful and

such an action be so gentle as to be quite insignificant, there is a rude and noisy action which I like worse, such as that of beating upon any form or bench that

becoming; or, on the contrary, very awkward and ungraceful. Ovid advises a lady,

Si vox est, canta; si mollia brachia, salta.

And it is well known that the antients danced as much, or more, with their arms, as with their feet: And motion to music, expressing sentiments and passions, was called by them *Dancing*. Now the grace of motion is, as I have observed elsewhere, (vol. 4th, p. 295 and following), much too little studied in Britain. The fashion was sometime ago, (what it is now I know not), that the ladies danced even country dances, with their arms hanging down by their sides, as if they had been pinned to them. The men, in walking, instead of making the motion of their arms correspond with the motion of the legs and of the body, as it naturally should do, dispose of their arms and hands in various ways. Some I have seen hang their arms from their arm-pits by the thumbs: Others put their hands into their breeches; others into their waistcoat pockets, with the thumbs exerted, which they sometimes move like the preacher above-mentioned; and I have seen some hide them in the pockets of their coats, which they make project before them as they walk. And all this, it is evident, they do from an affectation of what is graceful and becoming.

happens to be near the speaker, (and I have known some of these orators who beat a ruff upon the bench); for if this be joined with a violent emphasis, which is commonly the case, it is barking and thumping, not speaking. The action, therefore, should be moderate, natural, and graceful: And it should have nothing of mimickry in it, as Quintilian, in the passage above quoted, has very well observed; for an orator should not be a pantomime, nor even an actor. He should not, therefore, endeavour to imitate by his gesture any thing that he may have occasion to describe. This Quintilian has very well illustrated by a passage from Cicero[*].

With respect to this kind of action, there is a remarkable passage in Homer, describing the appearance of Ulysses rising to speak among the Trojans, when he was sent by the Greeks along with Menelaus to demand the restitution of Helen. It is in the speech of Antenor to Helen,

[*] Ibid. p. 462.

Chap. III. PROGRESS OF LANGUAGE. 247

in the third Iliad *. He says, when he first rose, he looked down, fixing his eyes upon the ground, and stood without moving his sceptre at all, either forward or backward. ' This (says Antenor) made ' him look like a man senseless or out ' of his wits; but when he began to utter ' his great commanding voice, and the ' words fell from him, thick as a shower ' of snow in winter, then we found that no ' other man could contend with Ulysses ' in eloquence, and quite forgot his figure ' and attitude when he first rose to speak.'

This description of Ulysses is, I am persuaded, a portrait taken from an authentic account which the poet has had of the manner of Ulysses, and not an ideal figure, representing what the poet thought beautiful and graceful in speaking; for it is only Ulysses that he has described addressing himself to his audience in that manner, not any other speaker either in the Iliad or Odyssey: And I think it is very suitable to the character of Ulysses, who was the most

* Ver. 203.

artful of men, practised in all kinds of deceit and imposition,

Ειδως παντοιους τε δολους και μηδεα πυκνα.

And no doubt his stupid appearance, when he first rose, would make his eloquence more surprising and striking when he began to speak. This, however, I would not advise any modern orator to imitate; nor do I know that it was imitated by any Greek or Latin orator in later times. At the same time I think the contrary extreme of appearing too bold, assuming, and arrogant, is more to be avoided.

I will conclude this subject of Pronunciation and Action, with observing, that though Action have so great an effect upon a popular audience, that it is the chief part of oratory, yet it is not to be neglected in speaking upon any subject of art or science, such as law, even to a few judges who understand the science; for though Aristotle say that the arts of oratory, relating to the stile and the pronunciation, are chiefly intended for the people, yet we should speak even to men of science, so as not to offend their ears*. But I will add, that we ought even to please their ears, though that to be sure ought not to be our chief study; for an argument in flowing language, well pronounced, and coming from a graceful person, will affect the coolest judge more than the same argument in rough and unpolished language, ill pronounced, and coming from a person that has neither dignity nor grace. The arts therefore of pronunciation ought not to be neglected by any speaker of any kind, whether upon subjects Deliberative, Judicial, or Panegyrical.

* *Rhetoricor.* lib. 3. cap. 1.

BOOK IV.

Of those who have excelled in the Rhetorical Art.

CHAP. I.

Subject of this Book.—Examples of those who have excelled in this art, taken chiefly from the Greeks.—The first example from Homer.—The eulogiums upon Homer by the Halicarnassian, Hermogenes, and Quintilian.—Of the speeches in the Iliad—more in number than in any other poem.—Examples of them;—and first, Agamemnon's speech to the army, in the second book:—That a most artful speech:—The speeches of Ulysses and Nestor upon the same occasion—different, but well suited to their characters:—In the ninth book, containing the embassy by the Greeks to Achilles, there is the finest speaking to be found in the Iliad;—the speeches of Ulysses, Phoenix, Ajax, very different from one another—but wonderfully suited to their characters and the occasion:—The composition in the speech of Achilles, remarkably distinguished from any other composition in Homer.—The character of Diomede very well marked by his speaking on two important occasions:—The different effects of his speaking, upon the Greeks, compared with the effect which the speaking of Nestor and Ulysses had upon them:—Diomede's character also marked by his not speaking.

HAVING, in the preceding part of this work, delivered the precepts of the Rhetorical art, I come now to speak of those who have excelled in it. And, as I hold that the ancients have excelled us in all the fine arts*, and as it is from

---

* See what I have further said upon this subject, vol. 4th, book 2. cap. 2.

them that I have given the precepts of the art, so it is by examples taken likewise from them, that I intend to illustrate those precepts: And these examples will be chiefly taken from the Greeks; for I think I have given very good reasons why the Greeks excelled the Romans in all the fine arts *.

I will begin with Homer, as the standard of perfection not only in poetry, but in rhetoric, and indeed in every kind of composition. For he was the father of letters and the fountain of all learning among the Greeks: And they compared him to the ocean, from which, as Homer himself tells us, all fountains, all rivers, and all seas are derived †. And Hermogenes has said, that he has excelled all poets, rhetoricians, and writers of every kind, in every species of writing ‡. And

* Chap. 6th of book 2d of this volume.
† Dionysius περι συνθεσεως, cap. 24.
‡ Hermogenes, περι ιδεων. tom. 2. περι πολιτικου λογου.

Quintilian has made an eulogium upon him, which I will give in his own words, as I think it is one of the best things that Quintilian has written: ' Igitur, ut Ara-
' tus ab Jove incipiendum putat, ita nos
' rite coepturi ab Homero videmur. Hic
' enim (quemadmodum ex oceano, dicit
' ipse, amnium vim fontiumque cursus ini-
' tium capere), omnibus eloquentiae parti-
' bus exemplum et ortum dedit: Hunc
' nemo in magnis sublimitate, in parvis
' proprietate superaverit. Idem laetus ac
' pressus, jucundus et gravis, tum copia
' tum brevitate mirabilis; nec poeticâ mo-
' do sed oratoriâ virtute eminentissimus.'
And a little after, ' Quid? in verbis, sen-
' tentiis, figuris, dispositione totius operis,
' nonne humani ingenii modum excedit?
' Ut magni sit viri virtutes ejus, non emu-
' latione (quod fieri non potest) sed intel-
' lectu sequi; verum hic omnes sine du-
' bio, et in omni genere eloquentiae procul
' a se reliquit *.'

* Lib. 10. cap. 1.

To shew that these authors are not mistaken, in praising Homer so much for his excellence in rhetoric, I will give some few instances from the many speeches that we have in the Iliad, more I believe than in any other narrative poem: For though in the Odyssey Ulysses speaks through five books, and Æneas in Virgil through two, these speeches are not of the rhetorical kind, but of the narrative, and therefore are plainly historical.

The first speech in Homer I shall mention is the speech of Agamemnon to the army in the second Iliad, which is the most artful speech I ever read, and a perfect masterpiece of the kind; For he there uses arguments to persuade the Greeks to leave Troy and return home, which ought to have persuaded them to stay. Now this shews him to have been a king who knew perfectly well how to manage a popular assembly. He knew how unpopular a thing he had done by quarrelling with Achilles, and that if he had directly advised them to take the field without him, they would not have been difposed to liften to him; and befides, he would have made himfelf anfwerable for the ill fuccefs of the war. At the fame time to have ufed ftrong and conclufive arguments to perfuade them to go, would have been imprudent: For they might have made fuch an impreffion upon them, that the other leaders could not, as was concerted, have perfuaded them to ftay. This concert I think was a mafter-piece of policy, and fhews that Homer underftood the art of government as well as he did the art of war*.

* That he underftood very well the art of *Tactics*, is evident from a paffage in Iliad 13th, v. 711. and following, where he relates that the Locrians, who followed Ajax of Oïleus, not being heavy armed men, but only bowmen and archers, were drawn up in the fecond line behind the heavy armed men, over whofe heads they annoyed the Trojans fo much by their miffiles, that they broke their phalanx. This is an advantage, and I think a very great advantage, that the bow and arrow has over our fire arms: And by availing himfelf of this advantage, William the Conqueror gained the battle of Haftings and the kingdom of England; for he himfelf, at the head of his

In the same book we have a specimen of the eloquence of Ulysses and of Nestor, the two greatest orators among the Greeks. Ulysses, in his speech to the people, dissuading them from going, advises them, and argues with them, persuading them to trust to the omen he mentions, and the interpretation given of it by Calchas. Nestor, on the other hand, assumes a tone very different, for he scolds them, and threatens them; and advises Agamemnon to use his authority, and to order and arrange them properly in the battle, by

---

horse, charged the Saxon foot, who were drawn up in a very deep phalanx, upon which he could make no impression; but he broke them by his Norman archers, who were drawn up in the second line behind the cavalry, and over their heads poured down such a shower of arrows upon the Saxon phalanx, that they could not keep their ground; and Harold their king was killed by an arrow. See a very accurate account of this battle in Lord Lyttleton's history of England. This coincidence betwixt the tactics of Homer and those of William the Conqueror is the more remarkable, that I do not know that such an order of battle has ever been used from the time of the Trojan war, till it was used by the Conqueror.

dividing them into nations and tribes. Such a speech was suitable to the age of Nestor, and the authority which it gave him; but it would have been improper from the mouth of Ulysses.

But the finest speaking in the Iliad, and which best distinguishes the characters of the speakers, is in the ninth book, where we have an account given us of the embassy to Achilles, and of the speeches of the three ambassadors, and of Achilles to them. Ulysses's speech there is of the same kind as that above-mentioned in the second book, a speech of reasoning, containing many arguments to persuade Achilles to join the army, such as the imminent hazard both fleet and army were in of being totally destroyed—the glory he would acquire by saving them, when no other means of doing that could be devised—the presents offered him by Agamemnon, which he enumerates very particularly—the regard he ought to have for the other Greeks, who honoured him like a god, though he had none at all for Agamemnon—and, laſtly, he tells him, that if he now took the field, he would have the glory of killing Hector, who would now encounter him, being ſo elated with his ſucceſs, that he thought no Greek was a match for him. Achilles's anſwer is as much in character as poſſible. He ſets out with declaring, that he always ſpoke his mind freely, and that he hated every man who thought one thing and ſpoke another. This character which he gives himſelf, is directly oppoſite to that of Ulyſſes, who exceeded all men in artifice and cunning, and, as we ſee from the Odyſſey, where he is the hero, very frequently told ſtories that he knew to be falſe. Achilles then proceeds to relate his own ſervices to the common cauſe, and to expreſs, in the ſtrongeſt terms, his reſentment againſt Agamemnon, who had treated him ſo ill in return for ſuch ſervices. And here we may obſerve Homer uſes very properly a ſtile not only quite different from that of his narrative, but from that of any other of his ſpeeches; for he has in one place a string of interrogations, to the number of four, all following one another *. And in another place he has a string of short unconnected sentences, to the number of seven, very uncommon in Homer †. The speech of Phoenix follows that of Achilles, and is of a kind very different from that of Ulysses. He begins it crying; and the whole of it is supplicating more than reasoning. He tells him that if he was positive to go, he should not go without him: then he relates how his father Peleus had given him the charge to instruct him, and how accordingly he had done so, having taught him both to act and speak. Next he relates his own story, and how kindly he had been received by Achilles's father Peleus, and how he treated Achilles, when an infant, as if he had been his nurse. Then he uses religious motives with him, and concludes with the story of

---

* Iliad 9. v. 337 and following.
† Ibid. 375. and following.

Meleager, who had quarrelled with his friends, as Achilles had done, but was appeafed, and by his valour faved his country. The effect of this fpeech was fuch upon Achilles, that he defired that Phoenix would ſtay with him when the other ambaſſadors went away; and inſtead of going to-morrow, as he faid to Ulyſſes he would do, he was to deliberate, when the morning came, whether he ſhould go or not.

After this Ajax fpeaks; and it is as much in the character of a rough blunt foldier as can well be imagined. He addreſſes himfelf, not to Achilles, as the other fpeakers had done, but to Ulyſſes; and advifes that they ſhould go away and give an account of their ill fuccefs to the Greeks. Then he fpeaks of Achilles in the third perfon, and reproaches him with being more obſtinate and inexorable than a man whofe brother had been killed by another. And he concludes with addreſſing himfelf to Achilles, and requeſting him to have a regard to his roof and to

Chap. I. Progress of Language. 261

his greatest friends among the Greeks who were under it. This manner of speaking of Ajax, so different from that of the other speakers, makes a most agreeable variety: And it had an effect upon Achilles, very different from that of the speech of Ulysses, and such as might be expected from his character, which resembled much more the character of Ajax than of Ulysses *.

---

* There is an excellent observation on the different characters of these speakers in a *Scholium* of Victorius, a Florentine, a great Greek Scholar of the 16th century, to be seen in Barnes's edition of Homer, p. 366. upon v. 618. of Iliad 9 All his *Scholia* upon this 9th book of Homer, are well worth the reading, not only for the matter, but for the stile, which is excellent Greek: For Greek in that very learned age, the most learned that has been since the restoration of letters, was commonly written, and even spoken by men of letters, who conversed in that language with the refugee Greeks, that came from Constantinople and could not speak Latin, that tongue being entirely lost in Greece. Of the Italians who wrote Greek with the greatest purity, there was Strozza, a Florentine nobleman, who writes a very good supplement to Aristotle's books of Polity, in such excellent Greek, that I cannot distinguish his stile from that of Aristotle,

I will only mention one other character, which, I think, is wonderfully marked by

(See vol. 3d of Ant. Metaphysics, p. 45 of the preface): And Aristotle's books of *Economics*, we have preserved to us, only in the Greek translation from a Latin translation, (the original having been lost) by one Tuscanus (vol. 5th of this work, p. 370.) Of the same century is also Wolfius, a professor in Switzerland, who writes a *prœmium* or introduction to Demosthenes's Orations, which Taylor, in his edition of Demosthenes, has published. The next I shall mention is Lambinus, a professor in the University of Paris, who has published an edition of Demosthenes, which he has dedicated to Henry III. of France, with a Greek epistle, which, for elegance of the stile, and the perfect purity of the language, is inferior to very few things that have come down to us from antient times. Nor was this study and knowledge of the Greek confined to Italy and France: For in England there was in that age, not only private men and professors in universities, but persons of the highest rank, who were famous for their Greek learning: For, besides Chancellor More, there was Queen Elizabeth; and Lady Jane Grey, not only understood and wrote the Greek, but spoke it.—See p. 193. of this volume, and p. 258. of vol. 4th.

That the writing of Greek, as well as the speaking of it, is now entirely disused, is, I am afraid no good sign of the learning of the age, any more than of the

Chap. I. PROGRESS OF LANGUAGE. 263

his speaking. It is the character of Diomede. When the ambassadors from Troy came to the Greeks, and offered them, in the name of Paris, to restore all the wealth he had carried away with Helen, and more besides, but not Helen herself; the Greeks, upon this offer, sat silent a long while, deliberating what they should do. At last Diomede arose, and made a very short speech, saying that they ought not to receive neither the wealth, nor even Helen herself, if she had been offered. The effect of this speech upon the Greeks is described in the following lines:

Ὡς ἔφαθ'· οἱ δ' ἄρα πάντες ἐπίαχον υἷες Ἀχαιῶν,
Μῦθον ἀγασσάμενοι Διομήδεος ἱπποδάμοιο.
Iliad. Lib. 7. v. 303.

taste; for it is certainly a language much finer in every respect than the Latin. And even the little that is now written in Latin in Europe, is so written, that it had better been written in any other language, except in Italy, where we have several writers of this century, who write most elegant Latin: So that I begin to consider Italy as not only the country of fine arts, but of learning.

where we may obferve how different the effect of this fpeech of Diomede was upon the Greeks from the effect of the fpeeches even of Neftor and Ulyffes; for when they fpoke it is only faid of the Greeks,

———'Οι δ' αρα τον μαλα μεν κλυον ξδ' επιθοντο.

There is another fpeech of Diomede, much of the fame kind, related in the beginning of the ninth book, where Agamemnon, in a fecret council of the chiefs, advifes them to leave Troy and take to their fhips, not feignedly as he did in the affembly in the fecond book, but fincerely, as their affairs were then in a very defperate fituation: After this fpeech the Greeks fat filent a long time, till at laft Diomede rofe, and putting Agamemnon in mind how he had reproached him with being weak and cowardly, tells him, that the fons of Greece were not fo unwarlike as to take his advice, and to return without taking Troy. But, fays he, if you have a mind to go, the way is open, and your fhips are ready to carry you back to Mycene. The other Greeks will stay and take the town: Or if they will go likewise, let them go, Sthenelus and I will stay and take the town *. And this speech of his was received with the same acclamations, as the speech above-mentioned. As Julius Caesar was an excellent scholar, as well as a great general, I think it is probable that he had this passage of Homer in view, when, in the speech which he made to his soldiers, to encourage them to march against Arioviſtus and his Germans, and not to be frightened with the terrible reports they had heard of them from the Gauls, he concludes, like Diomede, with saying, that if the rest of the army would not follow him, he and the tenth legion would go against the Germans.

And not only does Diomede shew his character in this manner by speaking, but also by not speaking: For, in the fourth

---

* Iliad 9. v. 32. and following.

Iliad *, when Agamemnon, making the round of his army, came to where Diomede was posted, and finding him not advancing to engage, reproached him with being a degenerate son of so brave a father, one of whose exploits he relates. To this, Homer says, Diomede made no answer, from respect and reverence to the king: and not only did he not speak himself, but he rebuked Sthenelus, who answered Agamemnon, by telling him that he lied, for that they were better men than their fathers.

* V. 370, &c.

CHAP. II.

Of the Orators of later times in Greece and Rome.—Of the difficulty of excelling in that art, greater than in any other art;—therefore so few eminent orators either in Greece or Rome.—Yet it was an art very much practised, not only in peace but in war.—Pericles the greatest orator that ever was in Greece.—Nothing of him come down to us.—Demosthenes the next greatest in Greece, and Cicero in Rome.—These two compared together.—Quintilian's judgment of Cicero.—The high eulogium bestowed upon him by that critic.—Not much regard to be paid to the stile of the writers in Quintilian's age, nor to their taste and judgment.—Cicero had not that magnanimity and elevation of mind which is necessary to form a great orator;—Therefore he spoke with fear and trembling before a people whom he despised as the dregs of Romulus.—The vanity of Cicero another reason why he could not excel in his art.—Examples of this vanity.—Besides the vanity of the individual, he had a national vanity, which made him speak of the Greeks with contempt.—Of the poetry of Cicero.—Connected with his vanity, was his taste for the ridiculous.—This taste he has considered as necessary for an orator, and has given precepts for it at great length.—Quintilian has collected many of the jests in his orations.—Difference betwixt Cicero and Demosthenes or even the best comic writers.—Of the qualities of body possessed by Cicero.—By nature weak and infirm.—That increased by his too great vehemence in speaking.—A very bad account given of his action and pronunciation by himself.—To correct this manner he travelled to Athens and to Asia.—Returned very much improved.—He learned therefore not only to write from Greek masters, but also to speak and pronounce.—One defect in the pronuncia-

tion of Cicero, that he does not appear to have studied the melody, but only the rhythm of his language.—In this respect his pronunciation very different from that of Demosthenes.—The way, that Cicero learned the art of speaking, such, that he could not have been an orator like Demosthenes.—It was by practising declamation that he learned.—Of the nature of that kind of speaking.—Of the difference betwixt the Greek and Latin rhetoricians.—Of the figures of composition relating to the sound.—These ought not to be much studied in speeches of business.—But one thing relating to the sound much studied by the antient orators, viz. the rhythm.—Of the rhythm of their prose.—The nature of it.—Some denied the existence of it.—Of the melody of the Greek language, and the variety of that melody.—Cicero says nothing of the melody of the Latin language.—His oratory therefore defective in that respect.—Of the music of Demosthenes's composition—not such an ornament as could draw the *attention of the hearer from the matter. Cicero appears to have had no idea of the melody of oratorial compoſition.—He has adorned his ſtile by other figures of the ſound, which are of the poetical kind.—An account given of theſe figures :—Alſo with figures of the ſenſe that are poetical, ſuch as* Exclamation *and* Proſopopoea.—*The Halicarnaſſian's opinion of Demoſthenes. —The Author's opinion of Cicero, the reverſe of that of Quintilian.—Cicero's critical works very much better than his Orations.—Praiſe of his dialogue* De O-ratore.—*His ſtile extremely copious.— Very well imitated by ſome late Italian writers in Latin.*

I DESCEND from Homer, and thoſe antient times, to ſpeak of the famous Orators of Greece and Rome of later times. As eloquence is an art requiring ſuch eminent qualities not only of mind but of body, by which it is diſtinguiſhed, as I have obſerved, from all the fine arts *, and ſo is truly,

---

* See chap. 1. of book 1. of this volume.

what Cicero has said it is, an art *incredibili magnitudine et difficultate*, it is no wonder that so few have excelled in it, many fewer than in any other art or science: For we read of many great generals in Greece and Rome, many fine poets, sculptors, and painters, philosophers, too, and men eminent in different sciences; but we hear of very few great orators: Athens, when it was in all its glory, and when it might be said to be the domicile of arts and sciences, produced only ten great orators. And as to the Romans, there is only one of any great reputation, whose orations have come down to us, I mean Cicero: And yet all public business, both among the Greeks and Romans, was carried on by speaking; and in Athens no man could be sure either of his life or fortune, unless he could speak: For men there were not allowed advocates to plead their cause; but were obliged to defend themselves both in civil and criminal causes: For though they used orations composed by others, they were obliged to speak them themselves. Even in military affairs, oratory was practified, especially among the Romans: Julius Caesar frequently harangued his soldiers, particularly before his battle with Ariovistus, in order to allay that fright into which the Gauls had thrown his soldiers, by telling them such frightful stories of the size and strength and valour of the Germans. And upon occasion of the loss which he suffered in the civil war, at Dyracchium, he likewise made a speech to his soldiers. And also he harangued his men, when they were drawn up to fight the great and decisive battle of Pharsalia: And, he says, it was *ex more militari;* that is, it is customary to do so upon such occasions.

The greatest orator, I believe, that ever was in Greece or Rome, was Pericles*: But of him nothing remains. Of all the other orators of Greece, Demosthenes was undoubtedly the most renowned: And of him many orations have come down to us, both in public and private causes. Cicero, as I have said, was the most

---

* See p. 215. of this volume.

eminent orator that Rome has produced: and of him a great many orations of different kinds have been preserved to us. And I am now to compare together these two orators, and give my opinion which of them I think the best.

If we were to be determined by the judgment of Quintilian in this matter, the preference must be given to Cicero, of whom he speaks, in several passages of his *Institations*, in the highest stile of admiraion. In one passage, he says, his eloquence was divine*; in another passage he denominates him *praecipuus in eloquentia vir*†.— The last passage I shall quote is from book

---

* Lib. 10. cap. 2. sec. 2. where he is talking of that common clausule of Cicero's periods, *esse videatur;* and which he used *usque ad nauseam*, as was observed by his cotemporaries. Quintilian's words are, 'Noveram quosdam, qui se pulchre expressisse genus illud coelestis hujus in dicendo viri sibi viderentur, si in clausula posuissent, *esse videatur*.'

† Lib. 6. cap. 3. sec. 1.

10. cap. 1. sec. 3. where he makes his eulogium in these words: 'Mihi videtur
'Marcus Tullius, cum se totum ad imita-
'tionem Graecorum contulisset, effinxisse
'vim Demosthenis, copiam Platonis, ju-
'cunditatem Isocratis; nec vero, quod in
'quoque optimum fuit, studio consecutus
'est tantum, sed plurimas, vel potius om-
'nes, ex seipso, virtutes extulit immortalis
'ingenii beatissima ubertate. Non enim
'pluvias (ut ait Pindarus) aquas colligit,
'sed vivo gurgite exundat, dono quo-
'dam providentiae genitus, in quo to-
'tas vires suas eloquentia experiretur.'
And accordingly he appears to have studied Demosthenes but very little; at least almost all the examples and illustrations of his precepts are taken from Cicero. But I do not admire the stile of Quintilian, or of any writer of that age; neither have I any high opinion of their taste or judgement of authors: And therefore I am very clearly of an opinion different from that of Quintilian, and have not the least hesitation to prefer Demosthenes to Cicero.

Chap. II. Progress of Language. 275

And, in the first place, there were some things in the character of Cicero, which made it impossible for him to come up to the idea I have formed of a perfect orator. This idea I have given in the first chapter of the third book of this volume *, where I have described him to be a man of a great and elevated mind, much above the audience to whom he speaks. Now that Cicero was not such a man, but on the contrary a man of a weak and timid mind, is evident from what he tells us of himself; for he says, he never began to speak in public without fear and trembling. In his speech *pro Aulo Cluentio* he has these words, ' Hic ego, cum ad respondendum ' surrexi, quâ cura, Dii immortales! quâ ' solicitudine animi? Quo timore?' And he adds, ' semper equidem magno cum ' metu incipio dicere †.' And, in another place, he expresses his pusilanimity in this matter in terms still stronger, and calls the

---

* P. 214.

† Orat. pro *Aulo Cluentio*, sec. 18.

gods to witness for the truth of what he says. 'Ita Deos mihi velim propitios, ut,
'cum illius diei mihi venit in mentem,
'quo die, citato reo, mihi dicendum sit,
'non solum commoveor animo, sed etiam
'toto corpore perhorresco *.'—And this before a people whom he calls the dregs of Romulus *(ex faece Romuli)* †; and indeed they were no better in his time.

There is another part of Cicero's character, which, I think, makes it impossible that he ever should have arrived to any great perfection in any art, and that is—his vanity; for a very great artist never can be vain of any performance in his art, because he cannot be a great artist, if he come up to the idea he has formed of the perfection of his art, which must be always something beyond what he can come up to in practice, otherwise the work

* Orat. in *Quint. Caecilium*; *Divinatio*. sec. 13.

† Lib. 2. epist. 1. *ad Atticum*: Where, speaking of Cato, he says, 'Dicit tanquam in Platonis πολιτεια, non tanquam in *Romuli faece*, sententiam.' p. 100. Ed. Oliveti.

cannot be of very great excellency. It is for this reason that the statuaries of old considered their works as unfinished; and therefore they inscribed upon their statues, that such a man εποιει, not εποιησε or πεποιηκε; that is, that he *was a-doing it, but did not do it, nor has not done it.* Now that Cicero was vain is well known; and he has furnished, himself, an example of it, (such as I think is not to be parallelled), in a letter of his to one Lucceius*, who was writing a history of the Italic war, and of the civil war betwixt Marius and Sylla. The abilities of this writer he commends highly; and as, he says, he desired very much to be praised by him, and to have his name in that way transmitted to posterity, he entreats him to make a separate history of the Cataline Conspiracy, of his consulship, and of all that happened to him after his consulship till his return from banishment, and not to mix his history with the general history of the times: ' For,' says he, ' when you are wholly employed on one

---

* Ad *Familiares*, lib. 5. epist. 12.

'subject and one person, your narrative
'will be more copious and more ornament-
'ed.' Then he proceeds to entreat ' That
'he would praise him even more than he
'thought he deserved, and more than truth
'allowed, without regard to the laws of
'history *.'

* This is so remarkable an instance of Cicero's vanity, that I will give the reader his own words : ' Ne-
'que tamen ignoro, quam impudenter faciam, qui tibi
'tantum oneris imponam, (potest enim mihi denegare
'occupatio tua), deinde etiam, ut ornes me, postulem.
'Quid, si illa tibi non tantopere videntur ornanda?
'Sed tamen qui semel verecundiae fines transierit, eum
'bene et naviter oportet esse impudentem. Itaque te
'plane etiam atque etiam rogo, ut et ornes ea vehe-
'mentius etiam quam fortasse sentis, et in eo leges his-
'toriae negligas : gratiamque illam, de qua suavissime
'quodam in procemio scripsisti, a qua te deflecti non
'magis potuisse demonstras, quam Herculem, Xeno-
'phontium illum, a voluptate: ea si me tibi vehemen-
'tius commendabit, ne aspernere; amorique nostro
'plusculum etiam, quam concedet veritas, largiare.'—
The reader may see a translation of the passage in Dr.
Middleton's Life of Cicero, (sec. 6.) and also the apology which the Doctor endeavours to make for him, but
which does not at all satisfy me. In one thing, however,
I perfectly agree with the Doctor, that the stile and composition of the letter is most elegant; and I am per-

He applied himself also to philosophy when he was not employed in pleading, in declaiming, or in state affairs; that is, when he had nothing else to do. And he boasts that he had proceeded an orator, not from the shops of rhetoricians, but from the walks of the academy. And he has written a great deal upon philosophy, when he could do nothing else, which was the case during the civil war betwixt Marius and Sylla, and under the Dictatorship of Caesar; and he has given us the reason for his writing so much on that subject, that he thought it, *magnificum, Romanisque hominibus gloriosum, ut Graecis de philosophia literis non egeant: quod assequar pro-*

suaded it was very much laboured by him, for it is very different from the other letters to his friends contained in this collection, and also from his letters to Atticus, the greatest part of which appear to me to be extempore productions, with very little regard to the stile or composition, so that they are rather what we would call *cards* than *letters*. But this letter, I think, deserves the praise which he bestows upon it himself, in a letter to Atticus, (lib. 4. cap. 6.) where he calls it *valde bella*.

fecto, si instituta perfecero*. Whether he has accomplished this, those, who have studied the Greek philosophy in the Greek books, will be best able to judge. For my own part I am of opinion, that the best use the Romans made of the Greek philosophy, was to form, upon the principles of it, a system of the law of private property, which the Emperor Justinian has preserved to us, in the *Corpus Juris* that we have got from him, and particularly in the *Institutes* and *Pandects*; and it is singular enough, that the Romans were the only antient nation who made a science of the law of private property. It may also be observed, that all the systems of law in Europe, that have been formed in later times, are upon the plan of the Roman law.

From what I have last mentioned, it appears, that besides his vanity as an individual, he had a great deal of national va-

---

* De Divinatione, lib. 2. sec. 2.

nity, which he carried so far as to maintain, that the Latin language was a richer language than the Greek. This he has expressed in one passage by an exclamation, in which he has apostrophised Greece in this manner: *O verborum inops interdum, quibus abandare semper putas, Graecia* *! And this national vanity made him so ungrateful to the Greeks, from whom he and all the other Romans had learned every thing they knew, that he calls them *Graeculi*, and speaks of them as idle and talkative people, *Otiosi et loquaces*; he adds, indeed, *fortasse docti atque eruditi* †.

Besides his philosophic and rhetorical studies, he attempted also poetry: And we have several fragments of that kind preserved to us, which Olivet has published

---

* Quaest. Tusculan. lib. 2. cap. 15. See also upon the same subject *De Natura Deorum*, lib. 1. cap. 4. et *De Oratore*, lib. 2. cap. 4.

† Lib. 1. *De Oratore*, cap. 22. See also Orat. pro *P. Sextio*, sec. 51.

in his last volume of Cicero's works. One of his poetical performances was in three books, on the subject of his own consulship; of the second book of which, we have some fragments preserved, where we have that line which, I think, is so justly ridiculed by Juvenal,

  O fortunatam, natam me consule, Romam!

From this specimen we may perceive that his stile in verse had those affected ornaments which I shall show his prose had, and that vanity was his predominant passion in every thing that he wrote, whether in verse or in prose.

With vanity is necessarily connected a delight in the ridiculous; for every vain man is very much disposed to laugh at the folly of another. And the chief reason why laughing gives us so much pleasure, is our vanity in thinking that we are free from the blemish or deformity that we laugh at, and therefore are so far superior to the objects of our laughter [*]. Of this

[*] See vol. 3d. of this work, p. 305.

character of ſtile I have ſaid a good deal in my third volume *; where I have diſtinguiſhed betwixt the claſſical ſignification of the word *ridiculous*, and the ſenſe in which we commonly uſe it †. And to what I have there ſaid, I have made ſome additions in the ſixth chapter of the ſecond book of this volume ‡.

For the reaſons I have given, we ought not to be ſurpriſed that there is ſo much of the ridiculous to be found in Cicero's Orations. But I am a little ſurpriſed that he has ſaid expreſsly, and has laid it down as a precept of the art, that it is the buſineſs of an orator to excite laughter: *Eſt plane oratoris, movere riſum* §. And accordingly he has given us a formal treatiſe upon it, in his ſecond book *De Oratore*, dividing it into that which ariſes from

---

* Book 4. cap. 16.

† Ibid. p. 299.

‡ P. 194.

§ *De Oratore*, lib. 2. cap. 58.

things, and that which arises from words; and, in explaining the several particulars which fall under those two heads, he has employed no less than twelve chapters in that book *. Quintilian, in his chapter *de risu* †, has not been so full upon it, and has given the orator some very proper cautions in the use of it, which Cicero has not given. He tells us that Cicero, *non solum extra judicia, sed in ipsis etiam orationibus, habitus est nimis risus affectator* ‡. His book of Jests in private conversation, written by himself or his freed-man, I have mentioned in this volume §. And as to his Orations, Quintilian, in the end of his chapter upon laughter above mentioned, tells us that there were many jests (some of which he mentions) in his oration against Verres; and in his oration for Muraena there were so

---

* Chap. 59.—71. inclusive.
† Lib. 6. cap. 3.
‡ Lib. 6. cap. 3. sec. 1.
§ P. 200.

Chap. II. PROGRESS OF LANGUAGE. 285

many of them, upon the subject of the Stoical philosophy, that I think Cato's saying upon the occasion was not at all improper, *Quam ridiculum consulem habemus* *. How much Cicero differs from Demosthenes in this respect, I have elsewhere observed †. In him there is nothing that has the least tendency to excite laughter; and even in the comic writers of the best kind, such as Menander and Terence, there is, as I have said ‡, scarcely any thing to be found of that kind. So that here we have a speaker, upon business of the greatest importance, more jocose than a comic writer. And, upon the whole, if there were no other proof that Cicero was not, nor could not be, perfect in an art that requires a great genius and elevated mind, I think his love of the ridiculous is sufficient; for I maintain, that there never was a man of great genius, who was a great

¶ Vol. 3. p. 299.

† Ibid. p. 308.

‡ P. 291. of this volume.

jester in private conversation, and much less in public speaking; for even the Indians of North America, whom we call savages, do not, as I before observed, delight in the ridiculous, even in private conversation*: And the reason is plain; for though a man, who has the highest sense of what is beautiful, graceful, and becoming, may, and indeed must perceive the ridiculous of things, he does not delight in it, but on the contrary turns his attention from it to that which his genius naturally leads him to contemplate;—I mean the dignified and beautiful †.

Such were Cicero's qualities of mind: As to those of his body, he tells us himself ‡ that he was of a very slender and infirm habit; and that if he had continued the manner of speaking in which he began, his health could not have held out: And in this passage he gives a very bad account

---

* P. 195. ibid.

† Ibid.

‡ *Brutus*, sive De Claris Oratoribus, cap. 91.

of his action and pronunciation: For he says, 'Omnia fine remiffione, fine varieta-
'te, vi fumma vocis, et totius corporis con-
'tentione, dicebam.' He was therefore advifed by his friends and phyficians to give over pleading; 'But,' fays he, ' thinking
' that I might avoid the hazard of hurting
' my health by moderating my voice,
' changing, and at the fame time improv-
' ing my manner of fpeaking, I determined
' to go abroad.' And firft he went to Athens, where he practifed under the directions of Demetrius Syrus, an old mafter of the art: Then he went to Afia, and applied himfelf to the moft famous rhetoricians there; and not content with that, he went to Rhodes, and there exercifed himfelf under one Molo, whom he had known in Rome. And he concludes the account of his travels by faying, that, after he had ftayed two years abroad, he returned to Rome, ' non modo exercitatior, fed prope
' mutatus; nam et contentio nimia vocis
' reciderat, et quafi deferbuerat oratio; la-
' teribufque vires, et corporis mediocris

'habitus accesserat *.' And thus it appears, that his stile was not only formed by the imitation of the Greek orators, but his pronunciation was corrected by practising under Greek masters, who gave a temperance to it, and a variety, which it had not before. So that he learned from the Greeks, or *Graeculi*, as he called them, the chief part, or what is principal in the rhetorical art;—I mean the action.

But there is one part of the pronunciation, which he does not appear to me to have studied, and that is melody. Every language, that is perfect of its kind, must be musical †. Now there can be no music without melody as well as rhythm. The Latin language was musical as well as the Greek, and had those accents or tones of music, which make the melody of speech. Now it cannot be a matter of indifference how those tones are disposed and arranged in speaking; and it must give a great

---

* *Brutus*, sive De Clar. Orat. cap. 91.

† P. 135. of this volume.

beauty to the pronunciation, if thefe as well as the rhythms are agreeably varied: And accordingly the Halicarnafian tells us that this ought to be done. Now Cicero ftudied very much the rhythm of his language, but he does not appear to have confidered at all the melody of it *. So that from all the many books he has written upon the rhetorical art, we cannot difcover that he had fo much as an idea of *the noble melody* †, which the Halicarnafian admired in Demofthenes.

But fuppofe his pronunciation had been as perfect as that of Demofthenes; fuppofe alfo that the materials of his art, I mean the Latin language, had been as fine a language as the Greek; and further, let me fuppofe that he had had all the qualities both of mind and body, which are required to make a perfect orator, yet he

* Vol. 2d. p. 382.

† P. 151. of this vol.

was educated and trained to speak in such a way, that it was impossible he could have been such an orator as Demosthenes; but must have had those faults, which are conspicuous in his stile, and of which I shall afterwards take notice. The education I mean is the exercise of declaiming, which he tells us himself he practised every day *. And Suetonius tells us that he continued the practice of declaiming in Greek down to his praetorship †; and in Latin, after he became an old man, he declaimed with Hirtius and Pansa, then consuls, whom he calls his scholars.

How much the practice of declamation contributed to spoil the taste of eloquence in Rome, and indeed of all writing of every kind, verse as well as prose, I have shewn at some length in the third volume of this work ‡, which the reader, though he may have read it before, will perhaps

---

* *Brutus*, cap. 90.
† Suetonius *De Claris Oratoribus*, cap. 1.
‡ Book 4. chap. 13.

think it worth the while to read again, as it contains many things upon the subject of eloquence which never were before published in English. I will only add to what I have said there concerning the practice of declamation, that when a man speaks upon a fictitious subject, so that he has not, for his audience, people whom he would persuade to act, or judges whom he would convince of the justice of the cause he pleads, but speaks only to be admired by those who hear him, it is impossible that such a speaker should not be more studious of the ornament of words, than of the weight of matter. To the arguments he uses, he will endeavour to give a smart witty turn: And he will be accustomed to answer only objections of his own invention, and which are made to be answered, not those made by a real adversary*. In Cicero's time they did not declaim in public, but only before a master, or in company with a few friends: But in

---

* See what one Montanus has said upon this subject, in a passage which I have quoted, vol. 3d. p. 263.

the days of Auguſtus there were public ſchools of declamation; and then, ſays Petronius, there was an end of eloquence. The practice was not at all known in Rome till a little before the days of Cicero, who, when he was a boy, heard the firſt Latin declaimer, one Lucius Plotius Gallus; for at firſt there were only Latin maſters of this declaiming art, which was not at all approved by the wiſer men at Rome; and it was prohibited by a decree of the ſenate, mentioned by Suetonius, in his book *De Claris Oratoribus*, and afterwards by an edict of the cenſors, Cn. Domitius Ahenobarbus, and Lucius Licinius Craſſus the orator, who mentions this decree in Cicero's third book *De Oratore*; and calls the ſchools of thoſe declaimers *ludi impudentiae*, the ſchools of impudence*. Now, though I am perſuaded that thoſe Latin rhetoricians were not, as Craſſus ſays, ſo learned as the Greek, and that the practice of declaiming in that language, enabled the young orator to en-

---

* Cap. 24.

rich his Latin ſtile more than he could have otherwiſe done; yet I think it is impoſſible but that, by daily practice upon feigned ſubjects, a man ſhould acquire a ſtile of ſpeaking very different from the ſtile of real buſineſs: And it is from thence that Cicero, though he practiſed chiefly even with Greek rhetoricians, has derived theſe faults which are to be obſerved in the ſtile of his orations.

Of theſe faults I have ſpoken at ſome length in my third volume, particularly in the ſixth and ſeventh chapters, and ſhall ſay ſomething more before I conclude this chapter. Here I will only add ſome general reflections upon thoſe figures of compoſition which affect the ſound.

That the ear is pleaſed with a ſimilarity which it perceives in ſounds, if they be diſtinguiſhed by proper intervals, and not continued without any ſuch diſtinction, is a fact that cannot be denied. It is in this way that the Greek and Latin verſe pleaſes us, by the ſame rhythm returning at the same intervals: And our own verse pleases us by the same number of syllables, accented in the same way, returning at certain intervals. And in prose, the figures I have mentioned in the 6th chapter of the 3d volume above quoted, such as *repetition, paronomasia,* and *parisosis,* please us in the same manner. But all figures, which only affect the sound, ought to be very sparingly used in speeches of real business, and business often of the greatest importance, such as deliberations upon public affairs, or trials, upon the issue of which the life or fortune of a citizen may depend. In such orations it is the figures of the sense, according to the division I have made of figures*, that ought to be chiefly used. And in general, the best compositions of every kind are those which draw the attention of the reader, not to the words, but to the matter: For whatever attention is bestowed upon the words, may be said to be lost as to the matter,

---

* P. 115. of this volume.

which, in every compofition of any value, ought to be principal.

There was one thing, however, in antient oratory, which, though refpecting the found only, was very much attended to by the orators, and, I think, with very good reafon: And that was, the *numbers*, or *rhythm*, as it is more properly called *. Of the rhythm of the antient profe I have treated at fome length in the 5th chapter of the 2d book of this volume, to which I refer my readers. It is a rhythm compofed of the fame feet as the rhythm of verfe is, but very different in this refpect, that it was not exactly meafured as the verfe was, and did not return at certain intervals; nor did the feet, of which it was compofed, follow one another in any certain order, as in verfe: But, as Cicero has told us, all the different feet are mixed together in this profe rhythm, but not without a choice or felection of certain feet rather than others upon certain

* P. 156. of this volume.

occasions, which Cicero has explained at considerable length*. And, instead of that uniformity which we observe in the antient verse, and without which it would not be verse, there was a very great variety; for, as the Halicarnasian has told us, the placing words of the same rhythm near to one another, was avoided †. It was therefore a beauty which did not stick out, or *eminebat extra corpus orationis*, as Petronius expresses it. And though it must have been felt by all, who had ears to hear, yet Cicero could not give a reason why it pleased so much ‡; and he tells us ‖, that there were some who denied that it existed. But Cicero, though he cannot give a reason why these numbers please so much, has not the least doubt of their existence; and he goes so far as to say, that a man who does not

---

* *Orator*, cap. 63. and following.

† Vol. 2d. of this work, p. 382.

‡ *Orator*. cap. 55.

‖ Ibid. cap. 54.

perceive them does not deserve to be called a man *.

But though Cicero has treated very fully of the rhythm of rhetorical compofition, he has not faid a word of the melody of it, though that muft have been perceived in the pronunciation as much as the rhythm, and have given equal if not fuperior pleafure to the hearer. For this I can give no other reafon, than that the Latins, not being fo mufical a people as the Greeks, did not attend fo much to the melody of their language: For that the Latins had acute and grave accents, as well as the Greeks, cannot be doubted, though they had not the fame variety in accenting their fyllables that the Greeks had; for they never laid an acute accent upon the laft fyllable of a word, which the Greeks frequently did. What, therefore, the Halicarnaffian reckons a great beauty in the compofition of Demofthenes, and mentions among the firft

* P. 159 of this volume.

things that diſtinguiſh his ſtile*, I mean the beauty of his melody, Cicero does not ſo much as mention. And yet I think it is abſolutely neceſſary, that if there be a melody in a language, the order and arrangement of the tones muſt give a beauty and variety to the pronunciation, as well as the order and arrangement of the ſhort and long ſyllables: And accordingly the Halicarnaſſian requires that there ſhould be the ſame variety in the melody as in the rhythm; ſo that words accented in the ſame way ſhould not be put together, any more than words of the ſame rhythm †. And he further ſeems to have thought that there was an expreſſion of ſentiment by the melody as well as by the rhythm: And therefore he ſpeaks of *a noble melody*, and *a rhythm of dignity* ‡. Here, therefore, we have two beauties of the pronunciation joined together, but which are ſo incorpo-

---

* See vol. 2d. of this work, p. 382.

† Ibid.

‡ Ibid.

rated with language as not at all to stick out, or to have any appearance of swell or affectation of pomp. The first orator who excelled in this way was, as the Halicarnassian tells us, Lysias, who, he says, was the best composer of plain speech without metre, having invented a particular harmony for such a composition, by which the sound of the words was both adorned and sweetened, without any appearance of study or art *. As no author expresses himself better upon such subjects, I have given his words in the note below †, where the reader will observe, that, though Lysias sweetened the pronunciation very much by his harmonious composition, his stile appeared to be altogether like to common speech, though exceedingly different

---

* *De Lysia Judicium*, sect. 3.

† Ὁμοίως δὲ τοῖς ἰδιώταις διαλέγεσθαι δοκῶν, πλεῖστον ὅσον ἰδιώτου διαφέρει· καὶ ἔπει ποιητὴς κράτιστος λόγων, λελυμένης ἐκ μέτρου λέξεως, ἰδίαν τινα λόγων εὑρηκὼς ἁρμονίαν, ᾗ τὰ ὀνόματα κοσμεῖ τε καὶ ἡδύνει, μηδὲν ἔχοντα ογκώδες μηδὲ φορτικόν.

from it, which I think is the best account that can be given of any stile in prose. And there is another passage in this work of the Halicarnassian (sect. 8.) where he commends Lysias for excelling in the greatest art of a speaker or writer, namely, the concealing of art; so that what has cost the composer the greatest pains and labour, appears to be altogether without study or art. And I am convinced, as I have said *, that if I had lived in that age, and had had an ear as delicate as the Athenian, I should have been as much, or even more pleased with the sound, not to speak of the sense or matter, of the orations of Demosthenes pronounced by himself, than with the verses of Homer repeated by the rhapsodists.

It was in this way, as the Halicarnassian tells us, in a passage which I have translated †, that Demosthenes made music of

* P. 161. of this volume.
‡ Vol. 2. p. 381.

Chap. II. Progress of Language. 301

his speeches, differing from the common music not so much in kind as in degree. By this music, he says, the ear was delighted with the melody, and moved by the rhythm; and at the same time that it was proper and suited to the subject, it had that variety without which no work of art can please. And it was an ornament to the speech, of such a kind, that it could not draw the attention of the reader from the matter to the words, any more than a song would do, if the music of it be simple and not too complicated and artificial, which is often the case of the music of the songs of the Italian opera: But on the contrary, by pleasing the ear so much, it will make the matter have the greater impression upon the hearers. And in this way he has made a style, of which no part is not some way adorned and varied from common speech*, not by tropes or figures of speech, of which Demosthenes is more sparing than any other orator I know; but by melody and rhythm, and that variety

* P. 162. of this volume.

of arrangement of his words, by which, as I have shewn elsewhere *, not only he pleases the ear, but conveys the meaning more forcibly.

Of the melody of speech, Cicero, as I have said, does not appear to me to have had so much as an idea. The rhythm he studied much: And there is no doubt a great deal of ornament of that kind in his orations. Whether in it he has succeeded better than Demosthenes, I have not an ear that can judge. All I can say is, that by the composition of Demosthenes the sense is better conveyed to me than by that of Cicero. But it is by the figures of which I have treated in the 6th chapter of volume 3d, such as *repetition*, *paronomasia*, and *parisosis*, that he has chosen to distinguish his stile from common speech, without adding any thing to the sense or emphasis, but on the contrary; and instead of pleasing the ear with variety, he tires and disgusts it by a disagreeable same-

---

* In the 3d. dissertation annexed to vol. 2d.

ness in the composition. Of this kind of unmeaning repetition, I have given an example from the oration *pro Archia Poeta**, where we have the word *quantum* five times repeated, without adding any thing to the sense, and merely for the pleasure of the ear; but in which he has not, in my opinion, succeeded. There is a passage in the same oration *pro Archia Poeta*, in praise of the *humaniores literae*, which I have also quoted †, where there is a sentence, (for I cannot call it a period, having nothing of the roundness and compactness of a period), divided into six or seven short members, of the same form and structure, corresponding exactly to one another. This, no doubt, gives a certain concinnity and prettiness to the sentence; but I hold it to be a puerility in stile, such as is not to be found in Demosthenes, or in any good Greek writer. And in his famous oration *pro Milone*, com-

* Vol. 3d. p. 80.

† Ibid. p 90.

posed by him when he was in the fulness of years and glory, (not when he was young, and defended Sextus Roscius Amerinus, where, upon the subject of the punishment of parricide, we have a number of very pretty little conceits thrown together, which he himself did not approve of when his judgment was more mature*), there is not only a string of antitheses†, but the words are made to answer all exactly to one another, both in the form of the case and tense, and in the sound; so that it is really a kind of poetry, and rhyming poetry: For not only the words terminate with the same syllable, like our rhymes, such as *scripta* and *r..*; but with two syllables, like the Italian rhymes. Thus you have *dicimus, accepimus, legimus*, corresponding to other three words terminated by the same two syllables, *arripuimus, hausimus, expressimus*; and there are other two rhymes of the

---

* Vol. 3d. p. 87.

† Ibid. p. 88.

Chap. II. PROGRESS OF LANGUAGE. 305

fame kind, *inſtituti* and *imbuti*. And from what he has ſaid in his *Orator. ad M. Brutum*, and elſewhere*, it is evident that he ſtudied ſuch gingling of words, and thought them a beauty of ſtile.

Not only did Cicero, in this manner, make the ſound of the rhetorical ſtile poetical, but he has figured the ſenſe and matter with ſuch poetical figures as *exclamation*, προσωποποιΐα, and διατυπωσις, or *particular and pictureſque deſcriptions of things*. Of theſe figures I have ſpoken pretty fully in the ſixth chapter of my third volume, and have quoted ſeveral examples of them from Cicero, and obſerved, that in ſome of them, particularly *exclamation*, he is more figurative than even Homer; and I have given a long quotation from him of the uſe of the laſt mentioned figure †, where we have a picture moſt accurately drawn;

* See the paſſages quoted in vol. 3d, p. 88. and following.

† Vol. 3d. p. 119.

VOL. VI.   Q q

but it is not what the French call the *belle nature*, which is there painted, but quite the contrary.

Upon the whole, I agree perfectly with the Halicarnaſſian in his opinion of Demoſthenes, whom he prefers to all the other orators of Greece: And particularly he admires his compoſition, (the greateſt art of ſtile), in which he was allowed to excel by all his cotemporaries, even by his greateſt enemy Æſchines *. But, as to Cicero, I differ ſo much from Quintilian, that what he ſays of him, *ille demum ſe profeciſſe ſciat, cui Cicero valde placet,* I would reverſe in this way, and ſay, *ille demum ſe profeciſſe ſciat, cui Cicero non placet.* I ſpeak of him as an orator, for in his critical and philoſophical works I admire his ſtile very much: And I do not retract what I have ſaid † in praiſe of his dialogue *De Oratore*, which I ſtill think an admirable

---

* Vol. 4th. of this work, book 2d. chap. 7.

† Dionyſius *De admiranda vi dicendi in Demoſthens,* cap. 35.

composition, both for matter and stile. I have lately read the discourse which he puts into the mouth of the elder Cato, upon the subject of old age, and which I would recommend to the study of every man as far advanced in life as I am. It is one of the finest things in the Latin language, and I do not wonder that Theodorus Gaza made it the only example of any work translated from Latin into Greek, by the learned Greeks who were then in Italy*. And I am persuaded, those faults that I have observed in his orations, arose from his practising declamation, in which more attention must necessarily be given to the words than to the things which have no real existence, but are mere fictions†. And there is a copiousness of words, and of good words too, in all his works, such as is not to be found in any other Latin author; and therefore I would advise every man, who desires to form a good Latin stile, to

---

* See vol. 4th. p. 335. and 336

† See what one Montanus has said further upon this subject, vol. 3d. p. 256. and 257.

study his works diligently. This I find has been done by some late Italian writers in Latin, particularly one Politus, a professor in the *Piae Scholae* of Florence, who has given us a translation of several books of Eustathius's Commentary upon Homer, with some dedications, prefaces, and dissertations, written in excellent Latin. It is a work that he has carried no further than the fifth book of the Iliad; but, imperfect as it is, I recommend it very much to the young student of Greek, who may not be so learned in the language as to understand Eustathius without a translation and notes. But not only is the study of Cicero useful for enabling a man to form a good Latin stile, but it will give him a taste for a rich and copious stile in any other language.

CHAP. III.

Julius Caesar a greater orator than Cicero.—His eloquence is praised by Cicero under the characters of Brutus and Pomponius Atticus.——Natural advantages which Caesar had, and which contributed much to make him excel as an orator:—first his birth—then his military genius—the beauty of his person—a fine voice, and a graceful dignified action.—To all these advantages Caesar joined great application to the art.—Studied at Mitylene under a great master, Cratippus, and practiced daily rhetorical exercises.—His speaking the most elegant of all the Latin orators.—This not owing so much to his domestic education as to his deep learning. —He wrote a book upon the Latin language, addressed to Cicero.—Pure Latinity the ground work of oratory.—This formerly learned by imitation of those who spoke well.—But the language, now cor-

rupted by the conflux of strangers, to be restored only by art and science.—These Caesar applied, and in that way he became so great an orator, joining the ornaments of eloquence with the purity of language.—Conclusion of the eulogium of Caesar's eloquence from the mouth of Atticus.—Caesar was the Pericles of Rome. —He comes up to the idea of a perfect orator.—And he was likewise the greatest and most amiable man of whom we read in history.

ALTHOUGH Cicero be the greatest Orator of Rome, whose speeches have come down to us, yet I think I should not do justice to the Roman eloquence, if I did not mention an orator of theirs, who, in my judgment, must have excelled Cicero very much, though no orations of his have been preserved, nor any thing of that kind, except some speeches, which he tells us he made to his soldiers, but which we cannot compare with the orations of Cicero. The orator I mean is Julius Caefar, of whofe excellence, as an hiftorian, I have fpoken in the preceding volume; and I think he excelled all his countrymen as much or more in oratory, than he did in writing hiftory. I fhall give an account of his eloquence from Cicero, who, I think, cannot be fuppofed to be partial to him; for he was of an oppofite party in the ftate, and, if he was not acceffory to his murder, he at leaft approved of it. It is in his *Brutus*, or book *De Claris Oratoribus*, that he fpeaks of Caefar as an orator; and introduces both Brutus and Pomponius Atticus praifing him highly.

Caefar had more advantages from nature to qualify him for excelling in that art than any other Roman we read of. In the firft place, he was of high birth, being of an heroic race; for he was defcended of one of thofe Trojan families, which, the Halicarnaffian tells us, were ftill preferved in Rome at the time he wrote, to the number of fifty *; and of the chief of them,

* *Antiquitat.* lib. 1. cap. 85.

for he was defcended of their king Æneas*. And as I hold that there is a great difference of races and families in our own fpecies, as well as in every other fpecies of animals, this was a great advantage which Caefar had over Cicero; and he was fuperior to him in another refpect, that he had an heroic fpirit worthy of his birth, was a foldier as well as an orator, and the greateft general of his age. He had, too, great advantages of perfon; Velleius Paterculus fays, that he was *formâ omnium civium excellentiſſimus* †. He had likewife a fplendid voice,

---

* Suetonius, in his life of Caefar, cap. 6. tells us that he fpoke a funeral oration upon his aunt Julia and his wife Cornelia: ' Et in Amitae quidem laudatione, ' de ejus ac patris fui utraque origine, fic refert. " Amitae meae, Juliae, maternum genus ab regibus or- " tum, paternum cum diis immortalibus conjunctum eft: " Nam ab Anco Marcio funt Marcii reges, quo nomine " fuit mater; a Venere Julii, cujus gentis familia eft " noftra. Eft ergo in genere, et fanctitas regum, qui " plurimum inter homines pollent, et ceremonia Deo- " rum, quorum ipfi in poteftate funt reges."

† Lib. 2. cap. 41. I will give the whole paffage from Velleius, who writes good Latin, and, as he lived fo near to the time of Julius Caefar, that is, under Au-

Chap. III. PROGRESS OF LANGUAGE. 313

as Cicero tells us, and great grace and dignity in his action*. With thefe advantages from nature, joined with his great genius and extraordinary abilities, it was impoffible that he fhould not have excelled in the oratorial art, if he gave fufficient application to it: And that he did fo, Cicero attefts by what he makes Brutus fay, that he faw him at Mytilene learning the art from one Cratippus, who, he fays, was a great friend of Cicero. And he adds, that he learned with great application, omitting every other ftudy, and was every day employed

---

guftus and Tiberius, he muft be fuppofed to be very well informed concerning the particulars he relates of Caefar. ' Hic nobiliffima Juliorum genitus familia, ' et, quod inter omnes antiquiffimos conftabat, ab An-' chife ac Venere deducens genus, forma omnium ci-' vium excellentiffimus, vigore animi acerrimus, muni-' ficentiae effufiffimus, animo fuper humanam et natu-' ram et fidem evectus, magnitudine cogitationum, ce-' leritate bellandi, patientia periculorum, magno illi ' Alexandro, fed fobrio neque iracundo, fimillimus.'

* *De Claris Oratoribus*, cap. 71.

in rhetorical exercises *; and in this way he acquired a great copiousness of choice words †. And Cicero makes Atticus say, that of all the Latin orators, he was the most elegant speaker ‡; which, says Atticus, was not so much owing to his domestic education, though that was not wanting neither, but to much deep learning which he had acquired by great study and diligence, and which made him excell so much in the art of language ‖; and here he takes occasion to mention a book which Caesar had written upon the Latin language, and addressed to Cicero. And he makes the same Atticus say a little after, that the ground-work and foundation of the oratorial art is a pure and correct Latinity §, which those, who formerly possessed it, did not owe to art or science, but to a good habit of speaking, which they had formed by

---

* *De Claris Oratoribus*, cap. 71.
† Ibid.
‡ Ibid. 72.
‖ Ibid.
§ Ibid. cap. 74.

Chap. III. Progress of Language. 315

imitation of thofe who fpoke well; for good fpeaking as well as virtue was the praife of that age. 'But, fays he, now by
' the conflux of ftrangers, who fpeak ill, the
' language both of Rome and Greece is,
' much altered for the worfe. To correct
' this abufe, and reftore the language to its
' purity, art and fcience muft, like a touch-
' ftone, be applied, and in that way bad
' ufe muft be corrected*. Now this
' rule Caefar has applied, and in that way
' has purified and refined his language; and
' when, to this elegance of words, (which,
' though you be no orator, but only a free
' born Roman citizen, is neceffary), he joins
' the ornaments of eloquence, he may be
' faid to fet a well painted picture in a good
' light.' And he concludes his eulogium with the higheft praife which I think he has yet beftowed upon him, and which I will give in the words he puts into the mouth of Atticus: 'Splendidam quan-
' dam, minimeque veteratoriam rationem

* *De Claris Oratoribus*, cap. 74.

'dicendi tenet, voce, motu; forma etiam
'magnifica et generofa quodammodo.' So
that he excelled in voice and action, the
chief quality of an orator: His form was
noble, magnificent, and generous; and his
manner of fpeaking liberal, without the appearance of cunning or art. This account
of his fpeaking, I think, may be depended
upon, as coming from men who muft have
often heard him fpeak; and there were alfo
feveral of his orations that were publifhed
and read by them*. In fhort, I think Julius
Caefar muft have been fuch an orator in
Rome as Pericles was in Athens; and he
muft, I think, have come up to my idea
of a perfect orator †, that is, a man who has
an underftanding and elevation of mind
fuperior to his audience, and which, therefore, muft ftrike them with awe. He
would not therefore fhake and tremble as
Cicero did, when he fpake before the dregs
of Romulus, as he calls them; though he
would no doubt treat them with that appear-

* *De Oratoribus*, cap. 76.
† P. 214. of this volume.

ance at least of respect which was necessary to persuade them; nor would he use these puerile figures to please their ears, of antitheses, and like sounding periods and members of periods, which Cicero uses so frequently.

I will not repeat here, what I have said elsewhere* of his great qualities; and I will conclude the chapter with saying, that he excelled so much both in acting and speaking, that I hold him to be the greatest man of whom we read in history, and at the same time the most amiable; for he was so much beloved by his friends, that it was a common oath of theirs, *Sic ego, vivente Caesare, moriar.*

* Vol. 5. cap. 2. of book 1.

BOOK V.

Of the Oratory *of Demosthenes, containing Observations on his Matter and* Stile.

CHAP. I.

Demosthenes the greatest orator in antient times, and greater than any that can be in modern.—Reasons why it is impossible that any thing can be composed to be spoken, so perfect as the composition of Demosthenes. —The greatest part of Demosthenes lost, as he is only read, not heard.—Praise of him by his rival Eschines.—Of the natural defects of the bodily qualifications of Demosthenes;—his habit infirm.— his voice weak;—and his articulation imperfect.—Of the wonderful industry and application by which he supplied those natural defects;—such as shutting himself up for months together in a habitation under ground—and speaking with pebbles in his mouth:—By these means he overcame nature, and transformed himself into another man.—He could not have done so, if he had not had a genius which led him to the study of Rhetoric in preference to all other studies.—The occasion upon which he shewed this natural propensity.—Of the education he had as an orator.—He may be said to have been self-taught.—He began the practice of the art, not in the school of declamation, but with real business:—Did not attend Isocrates but Isaeus; and studied Thucydides.—The best lesson of all, he got from a player.—To practice what he had learned from him, he shut himself up in a subterraneous habitation,—studied there the melody and rhythm of speech,—and to compose in periods.

I COME now to speak of Demosthenes, the greatest orator in antient times of those who have left any monuments behind them, that are come down to us, and greater than any orator can be in modern times; for though we may write very well, and compose what for the matter is excellent, yet the modern languages do not furnish materials of which we can make a composition to be spoken, such as that of Demosthenes: For there is a sweetness and variety in the sound of the Greek language, at the same time an arrangement of the words so various, as must have given great pleasure to the ear, and likewise conveyed the sense more emphatically and forcibly than could otherwise have been conveyed, as I think I have elsewhere shewn [*]. And when we join to all this the melody and rhythm of the Greek language, of the beauty of which, as we never heard it pronounced, we can hardly form an idea, I think it is not going too

---

[*] Dissertation 3d. annexed to vol. 2d. of this work.

far to say, that it is impossible, by the nature of things, to compose any thing in our language, or in any modern language, which will please so much when spoken, as the language of Demosthenes, who, as it is well known, excelled so much in action and pronunciation, that Valerius Maximus says very properly, that in Demosthenes, as we have him, *magna pars Demosthenis abest; quod legitur potius quam auditur* *. And when his rival Æschines read to the people of Rhodes (the place to which he retired after his banishment) Demosthenes's oration for Ctesiphon, and read it no doubt better than any man now living can read it, they admiring it very much, ' How much more,' says he, ' would you ' have admired it, if you had heard him ' pronounce it.'

Those, therefore, who have formed their taste of stile upon such authors as Demosthenes, will not, when they write or speak

* Lib. 8. cap. 10.

English, bestow much pains upon the ornaments of language, knowing that they never can make a composition of that kind which will please even themselves, compared with that of Demosthenes. Their only study, therefore, with regard to language, will be to express themselves in proper words, and as significant of their meaning as any they can find. They will take care not to make their stile poetical by the frequent use of epithets, which are the proper ornaments of poetry: and they will use none that are merely ornamental, and not tending to inforce the sense or the argument. Neither will they abound in antitheses or metaphors. But, above all, they will avoid the affectation of any thing like numbers in English prose; of which every scholar must know that our language is incapable. In this respect a great author in English is faulty, I mean Lord Shaftsbury, as I have elsewhere observed *; where I have shewn, that by concluding his sentences with two, and sometimes three

---

* Vol. 3d. p. 284, and following.

nouns, and their attendant epithets, he has given a kind of dancing cadence to his ſtile, to which you may beat time. But I have done this author the juſtice to obſerve, that this fault is only to be found in his Miſcellanies, and ſome other pieces he has written; but in his dialogue, entitled the *Morialiſts*, he has not wantoned with words in that manner, but the ſtile of it is chaſte and ſober*. It is therefore true what I have obſerved elſewhere †, and here repeat, that if we have a mind to adorn our proſe ſtile in Engliſh, it ſhould be chiefly by compoſition in periods, which, if well compoſed, will not only make the ſtile more a-

---

* Vol. 4th. p. 365. and 393. The reader perhaps may think it worth his while to read the whole chapter, which is upon the ſubject of this dialogue of Lord Shaftſbury, where I think I have beſtowed juſt praiſe upon the noble author, who, by this work, has, in my opinion, done a great deal of honour, not only to the Engliſh nation, but to modern times, which have produced nothing of the dialogue kind, (a compoſition of the greateſt beauty when well executed), that can be compared with it.

† P. 166. and the paſſages there referred to.

greeable to the ear when read or spoken, but will convey the sense more forcibly. But even in periods we may abound too much, and by that make our composition too uniform, and without that variety which is required to make every work of art beautiful. No man ever composed better periods than Demosthenes; but all his stile is not periodised, and there are thrown in, amongst his periods, many short sentences, commonly in the form of interrogations. And in that respect his stile is very different from that of another Athenian orator, Isocrates, whose composition is almost all in periods: And I would further observe, upon this subject, that periods are more proper for the oratorial, than for any other stile; and they are undoubtedly very proper for collecting together the several propositions of which an argument may consist, and bringing them out with great force in the end of the period. But in the historical and didactic stile they should be more sparingly used. Livy, in his Narrative, has, as I have elsewhere observed*,

---

* Vol. 5th. p. 230.

too many periods, and so composed as often to make his stile perplexed and obscure. Of the didactic stile I think Aristotle is the most perfect model. Now, in his works there is hardly any thing you can call a period, excepting the beginning of some of them, which he has adorned in that way; particularly, he has ushered in his book upon Poetry with a period very well composed, and which, I think, shews that he could have composed in periods, if the subject had required it *.

To conclude this subject of the ornament of language—I think it is true what

---

* He begins his book of Poetry thus: Περι ποιητικης αυτης τε και των ειδων αυτης, ητινα δυναμιν 'εκαστον εχει, και πως δει συνισlασlαι τους μυθους ει μελλοι καλως εξειν η ποιησις· ετι δε εκ ποσων και ποιων εστι μοριων· 'ομοιως δε και περι των 'αλλων, 'οσα της αυτης εστι μεθοδον, λεγωμεν, αρξαμενοι, κατα φυσιν, πρωτον 'απο πρωτων. And he begins his *Philosophy of Nature*, or Φυσικη ακροασις, as he calls it, with a still longer period, having a parenthesis in it of some length. There is also a period in the beginning of his treatise *De Anima*, much shorter, but very well composed. The rest of his stile is all plain didactic, without any ornament of the words or of the composition.

I have said above*, that in Rhetoric, as well as in other arts, the greatest art is to conceal art; for if the stile appear to be much laboured, it will not please a critic of good taste, even though the art be good; but if it be not so, which I observe is often the case, the author will appear to have laboured to write ill, which I think the greatest fault that any author can have.

That there are certain qualities of body required for the practice of oratory, not necessary in any other of the fine arts, I have elsewhere observed †: Now, in these, and some of them of the greatest importance too, Demosthenes was by nature very deficient; and as he supplied those natural defects by wonderful industry and application, he may be said to have in that respect more merit than any other great orator ever had.

He was very infirm of body, so infirm, that he did not frequent the Palaestra

---

* P. 203. † Vol. 4th, p. 285.

Chap. I. PROGRESS OF LANGUAGE. 327

when he was young, as all the other citizens of Athens of the same rank did; and for that reason he was thought to be of a character soft and effeminate, from whence he had the nickname of Βατταλος, the name of a musician who was remarkably delicate and effeminate*. The natural consequence of this infirmity of his habit was, that his voice was weak, which was a very great defect in an orator who was to speak to so many thousands of people: For an antient orator, who spoke to the people of Athens or Rome assembled, or a general who harangued a whole army, must have had a voice, such as I doubt is not now to be heard*. He was also so short-winded, that he could not speak a period of any length: And his articulation was natu-

* Libanius the sophist, in an epistle addressed to the proconsul Montius.

† Dapper, in his description of the Archipelago Islands, quoted by M. de Buffon, vol. 3d, p. 442. says, that in some of these islands the inhabitants have their voices so strong, that they can converse with one another at the distance of a quarter of a league, and some-

rally so defective, that he could not pronounce R, the first letter of the name of his art.

These so great defects he cured by application and industry, such as would ap-

times of a whole league. In the heroic age of Greece, when they had not the use in their armies of trumpets or drums to give signals, the epithet which Homer gives to some of his heroes, of βοὴν ἀγαθὸς, was a great praise, as it was only by the voice that any command could be given.—And here we may observe, in passing, how strictly Homer observes the manners of the age (or the *costume*, as the Italians call it) of which he writes: For though the σαλπιγξ, or trumpet, was known in his time, and is accordingly mentioned by him in one of his similies, yet he does not speak of it as used in the Trojan war. See Eustathius's Commentary, *p.* 1139. *lin.* 52. where he speaks of other things that were in use in Homer's time, and which he likewise mentions in his similies; but does not say that they were used in the heroic times. Virgil is not so accurate in this respect; for he makes men fight upon horseback in that age; which they could not do, for a very good reason, that the horses were not able to carry men of their size in war, or upon a journey, though sometimes they mounted them occasionally and for a short way, as Diomede and Ulysses did the horses of Rhesus. —Iliad 10.

pear incredible, if it were not very well vouched. He was in use to shut himself up, for two or three months together, in a dark habitation under ground, (which Plutarch says was to be seen in his time), with one half of his head shaven, that he might not go abroad or be seen by any body. There he amended the defect in his articulation, and learned to pronounce the letter R as well as any body else. He practised there also, as Plutarch informs us, the composition of sentences and periods: And it was in this retreat that I suppose he practiced a very strange method, by which it is said he improved his pronunciation: It was by speaking with pebbles in his mouth, which no doubt would cost him a great effort; but the consequence of it would be, that he would speak more distinctly and articulately when the pebbles were out of his mouth, than he could otherwise have done.

The shortness of his wind he cured by going up ascents quickly, and at the same time pronouncing many verses in one breath; by which exercise he enabled himself to pronounce without stop or hesitation, *una continuatione verborum*, as Cicero says, those beautiful long periods which we find in his Orations. And to accustom himself to bear the noise and tumult of the people assembled, he used to declaim upon the sea shore, amid the noise of the waves breaking upon the rocks. In this way he fought against nature, as Valerius Maximus says, and overcame her by obstinate perseverance; and he adds, *Itaque alterum Demosthenem mater, alterum industria enixa est* *.

He could not, I think, have thus triumphed over nature, nor transformed himself so much as he did, if he had not had a violent propensity for the art, and a genius that led him to the practice of it, neglecting all other studies. And accordingly we are told by Plutarch, that when he was very young, seeing a great confluence of

---

* Valer. Maxim, lib. 8. cap. 7.

people gathered together, to hear a famous orator of thofe days called Calliftratus, he defired leave of his pedagogue to be one of his hearers. And accordingly having, with the affiftance of the pedagogue, got into the court of juftice, he was fo charmed with the oratory of Calliftratus, that he gave over every other ftudy, and applied himfelf wholly to rhetoric *. And it was then, as it is faid, that he forfook Plato and the Academy, and addicted himfelf wholly to Oratory †.

As to the education, that he had to qualify him to make fo great a figure in Oratory, he may, I think, be faid to have been felf-taught, in the feveral ways above defcribed. He was inftructed, however, as Plutarch informs us, by a great Athenian orator of thofe times, Ifaeus, whom he admired and followed; for he had no occafion to travel as far as Cicero did, for inftruction in the art, which was better practifed in Athens

---

* Plutarch's Life of Demofthenes, in the beginning.

† Aulus Gellius, lib. 3. cap. 13.

at that time than any where else in the world. He appears, too, to have informed himself of the stile and manner of Pericles, whom he is said to have imitated; so that he formed himself upon the model of one of the greatest orators that, I believe, ever existed *. He began the practice of the art, not as Cicero did, by declaiming on fictitious causes, but with real business: For as soon as he was of age, he prosecuted his tutors for mal-administration of his estate, and recovered something from them, but much short of what they had embezzled †. He did not attend the school of Isocrates, because, as Plutarch says, he could not afford to pay him. But I do not think that he suffered thereby any loss; for though Isocrates might have made of him such a panegyrical orator as himself, he could not, by imitating him, have excelled so much in the judicial and the deliberative. He studied Thucydides very much, and transcribed him, as it is said, several times with his own hand. He

* P. 316.
† Plutarch, in the Life of Demosthenes.

Chap. I. Progress of Language.   333

learned from him, no doubt, that argumentative ftile which is fo eminent in Demofthenes, and to comprehend fo much matter in his periods; but his periods are much better compofed than thofe of Thucydides, and not fo much crouded, and often obfcured, with figures.

But the moſt important leſſon of all he got from a friend of his, who was a player, *Satyrus* by name. When he firſt began to fpeak to the people he was very ill received; for he could not pronounce his own periods, full of matter and argument, fo as to be diftinctly underſtood: And one day he was fo ill treated by the people, that he went out of the affembly with his head covered. It was then that his friend the player met him, to whom he complained, that though he had applied more to the ftudy of fpeaking than any other man, and had fpent the prime of his life in it, yet he was not fo well heard by the people, as low ignorant men, who practiced other trades, fuch as that of a failor, and lived idly and diffolutely. " What

'you say is true,' says Satyrus, ' And I
' will give you the reason for it, if you
' will repeat me any verses that you may
' remember of Sophocles or Euripides.'
Accordingly Demosthenes did repeat some
of their verses: And after he had done it,
Satyrus pronounced the same verses; but
so much more gracefully, and with a tone
and manner so different, that Demosthenes
hardly knew them to be the same: And
in this way he learned that the study of
the matter and composition of an oration
signified little, if it was not well pronounced. It was then, as Plutarch tells us, that
he took to his subterraneous habitation,
where he would have remained, as I have
said, for two or three months together,
without going abroad or seeing any stran-
ger. And when he came above ground,
and mixed with the world, he would descend at times into his cave, and what
speeches he had heard made, he would recollect and compose better in sentences and
periods. And then, no doubt, he would
study that melody and rhythm which adorned his speeches so much, as the Halicarna-

sian has observed. And it was after this conversation with his friend the player, that I suppose he practised before the glass, and had a sword hung over his shoulders, in order to prevent his raising them too high, which he was in use to do.

In this way was Demosthenes formed to be so great an orator.

CHAP. II.

The Matter *moſt valuable in every good writing.—This holds particularly of the orations of Demoſthenes.—We cannot judge rightly of theſe orations, without knowing the political conduct of Demoſthenes, and the ſtate of Athens at that time.—Of the original government of Athens;—firſt monarchical, then ariſtocratical, and at laſt entirely popular.—The council there did not controul the people, any more than the Senate in Rome.—Of the character of the Athenians:—A noble, magnanimous, diſintereſted people;—in later times the deliverer of Greece from the Perſians;—ſhewed their great temper and moderation, as well as heroic bravery.—The people of Athens corrupted by wealth and luxury:—They deſired to live an eaſy and indolent life at the public expence.—This indulgence firſt given them by Pericles, who introduced the theatrical* money, *which every citizen re-*

ceived.—*After that, under different pretences, the whole money of their treasury was given to the people; and, in the time of Demosthenes, the whole expence of the state was defrayed by the richer citizens. The consequence of this misuse of public money, was to make the people effeminate and indolent;—did not fight themselves, but employed mercenaries, whom they did not pay.—These, therefore, did no good; for which they blamed their commanders:—But still they were a very intelligent and clever people.—Of the state of affairs in Greece,—particularly of the Lacedemonians, Thebans, and Athenians.—In the distracted state of Greece, Philip of Macedon appeared.—A history of his family,—of himself, and his education under Epaminondas.—Of the progress of his arms,—first in Thrace,—then in Thessaly,—then in the war with the Phocians, whom he utterly destroyed,—then with the Locrians; and, last of all, with the Athenians and Thebans, and their allies, whom he utterly defeated in the great battle of*

Chaeronaea.—He was affifted in thofe operations by Perfons whom he had in his pay in the feveral ftates of Greece.—In the beginning of thefe conquefts of Philip, Demofthenes appeared.—The diftracted ftate of Greece then, there being no people among them who were leaders.—In this ftate of Greece, Demofthenes acted the greateft part that ever was acted in the political line.—The wonderful influence of his councils and his eloquence upon the Thebans, when he perfuaded them to join the Athenians againft Philip, which put him to a ftand.—In the decifive battle of Chaeronaea, his behaviour, as a foldier, not fo bad as reprefented by fome authors.—Steady and firm in oppofing the Macedonian power.—Never took money from the Macedonians, as other demagogues did;—formed a great confederacy and great army againft Philip;—In forming this confederacy, he had more difficulties to ftruggle with at home than abroad.—He had three paffions of the Athenians to combat with; their love of pleafure and eafe, their love of money, and their vani-

ty.—Their vanity much flattered by their demagogues.—Demosthenes rather abused them than flattered them:—His Philippics rather an invective against the people of Athens than against Philip, whom he praises for his bravery and contempt of danger.—Nothing but a noble manly spirit, as well as great eloquence, could have persuaded the people of Athens to engage in such a war against Philip.—He encourages the Athenians, by telling them, that if they will yet do what is right, all will be well;—also by shewing them that Philip was not invincible.—What distinguishes chiefly the matter of Demosthenes from that of any other orator, is his insisting so much upon the topic of the pulchrum *and* honestum *:—Examples of this.— Learned this in the school of Plato,—and by imitating Pericles, who had been the scholar of Anaxagoras.—There can be nothing perfect in the arts without philosophy.—Of Demosthenes's skill in mixing together the topic of the* possible, *the* profitable, *and the* honourable.*—The difference betwixt the rhetorical and the di-*

dactic stile in that respect.—One great difference betwixt Demosthenes and Cicero as to the matter.—Demosthenes never speaks of himself in his orations, except when it is absolutely necessary, as in the case of the oration De Corona.—Cicero introduces himself very often into his orations, even in private causes.—Modesty affected by Cicero, a sure sign of the greatest vanity.—A great artist, such as Demosthenes, can never be satisfied with his own performance.

IN all good writing and good speaking, the matter ought to be principal: And this holds with respect to the orations of Demosthenes, in which the matter is of much greater value than the stile, excellent as it is; particularly in his public orations, such as his Philippics, his Olynthiacs, and his orations against Æschines: For in these, besides the sense and argument, there is a spirit and dignity of character, such as are not to be found in any other even of his orations, and which make a great part of

Chap. II. Progress of Language. 341

that δεινοτης, or *weight of matter and force of perfuafion*, as we may paraphrafe the word, by which Demofthenes was diftinguifhed from all other orators.

But however well written or well fpoken thefe orations were, they could not have had the effect, which we know they had, upon his hearers, if his conduct in public affairs had not been fuitable: For otherwife, the fpirit he fhewed, and the dignity he affumed, would have appeared ridiculous. We cannot, therefore, judge truly of the merit of thefe orations, without knowing the political conduct of Demofthenes; nor of that, without being informed of the ftate of Athens at that time, and likewife of the general fituation of the affairs of Greece. This will lead me into a pretty long differtation, but in which I will not lofe fight of Demofthenes; for it is chiefly from his orations that I have collected what I am to fay upon the fubject.

The government of Athens, as well as of every other ftate in Greece, was originally monarchical, the same I believe that was in every country where government was first established by strangers who came from civilized countries, and introduced arts and civility among savages; which was the case of all Greece, and particularly of Athens, originally an Egyptian colony, of which Cecrops the Egyptian was the first king *. But savages, as it is well known, are the freest of all men, and, as those strangers that came into Greece, had not power sufficient to make them submit by force to what they never would submit to of choice, all those antient Grecian monarchies were extremely limited, the kings governing more by persuasion, and superior qualities both of mind and body, than by force or legal authority. This was the case of all those heroic kingdoms of Greece, of which we read in Homer. But their power, such as it was, and their wealth, greater than that of the other

---

* See what I have said upon this subject, in vol. 1st of this work, p. 640, and following.

citizens, did, by degrees, corrupt their manners, and the defire of more power and more wealth made them tyrants, as Thucydides informs us *; the confequence of which, among a people uncorrupted, and whofe minds, at leaft, were ftill free, was a change of government from monarchy to ariftocracy, and from that to democracy. This was the fate of Athens. From monarchy, which was their government at the time of the Trojan war, they changed to a kind of ariftocracy, under, firft perpetual, and then decennial archons. And at laft their government became entirely popular: For though they had a council, which had a confiderable fhare of the government,

---

* Lib. 1. p. 10. edit. Stephani.

† This was called προβυλιυσιν, as appears from a paffage of Demofthenes, περι στεφανυ, p. 168. edit. Morell. where he fays, that upon the news of the taking of Elataea by King Philip, the council affembled, and at the fame time the people, και πριν εκεινην (την βυλην) χρηματισαι και προβυλιυσαι, πας ο δημος ανω καθητο. The fame was the form among the Romans; for among them the authority of the fenate, in antient times, went before the refolutions of the people; but when the peo-

(for by the forms of their conftitution every thing came before the council, before it was propofed to the people †), yet that council itfelf was chofen by lot from among the people; and we do not find, in the hiftory of Athens, that there was ever any great difference of opinion betwixt the council and the affembly of the people, fuch as there was in Rome betwixt the fenate and the people, before the democracy there was perfectly eftablifhed. This was the government of Athens in the days of Demofthenes.

The character of the Athenians, confidered as a people, is, I think, the nobleft to be found in hiftory: For they were not only from the beginning brave and magnanimous, but they were of a nature fo generous and beneficent, that Athens was the refuge and affylum of all the diftreffed in

---

ple there, as in Athens, ingroffed all power to themfelves, they eluded this form by making a law, *ut patres auctores effent in incertum comitiorum eventum;* that is, *fhould autharife* whatever the people fhould determine.

Greece. The Heraclidae, when they were expelled Peloponnesus, they received, and protected, and defended against Eurystheus, whom they killed in battle, and at last, by force of arms, restored them to their country*. Athens, too, was a sanctuary for Œdipus, and those with him, when they were expelled Thebes †; and in the first

---

* That they so far assisted the Heraclidae, as to bring them back to Peloponnesus, is a fact, as far as I remember, only mentioned by Demosthenes; but it is in a decree drawn up by him, in which he certainly would not have mentioned a fact which had no foundation in history. It was the decree upon which the alliance between the Athenians and Thebans was formed against Philip. In this decree he recounts several of the favours which the Athenians had bestowed upon the Thebans: And among others he mentions this; Τυς Ηρακλιυς παιδας, αποστιρυμινυς ‘υπο των Πιλοπονησιων της πατρωας αρχης, κατηγαγον, τοις οπλοις κρατησαντις της αν-τιβαινειν πειρωμινης τοις Ηρακλιυς ’εκγονοις.—(Περι Σιφανυ, p. 171.) As to the fact of their receiving and protecting them, and killing Eurystheus their persecutor, it is related by Thucydides, in the beginning of his history.

† Demost. ubi supra.

Theban war, which followed foon after, they fo far fuccoured the unfortunate Argives, that they obliged the Thebans to give up the bodies of the Argive leaders, whom they had flain: And, to come down to later times, they were not only the firft of the Greeks who durft face the Perfians in the field; but, in the battle of Marathon, they defeated a prodigious army of them with a handful of men; and at Plataeae, when the Lacedemonians declined to be drawn up againft the Perfians, they chearfully undertook it*. In that war they, for the fervice of the common caufe, forfook their city and their country, though they were offered by Xerxes, if they would abandon the common caufe, not only to have the poffeffion of their own country fecured to them, but to have any other country added to it that they themfelves fhould choofe, and to be governed by their own laws. He promif-

* This is related by Herodotus, in his account of that battle.

ed alfo to repair all the mifchief he had done in their country by demolifhing their temples *. And thus, without city or country, they betook themfelves to the fea, and furnifhed twice as many fhips as all Greece befides: So that it was by their means, that the Greeks became mafters at fea; without which it was impoffible that the liberties of Greece could have been preferved. For, if the Perfians had not been defeated at Salamis, they would have fo infefted the coafts of Greece, going round Peloponnefe, and landing wherever they pleafed, that the country would not have been habitable, and the people muft have fubmitted. And, in general, throughout the whole of that moft important and hazardous war, they behaved not only with

---

* See Herodotus, lib. 8. cap. 140. and following, and lib. 9. *in initio;* where we have a moft noble and fpirited anfwer made by the Athenians to thefe offers. One of the council, he tells us, was of opinion, that they fhould accept of them; but the Athenians, he fays, ftoned him, and their wives ftoned his wife. See alfo Demofthenes, *ubi fupra*, p. 174. *Morelli.*—and Ifocrates's *Panegyric*, p. 60. *Stephani.*

the greatest bravery and disinterestedness, but also with so much temper and moderation, yielding in every thing to the Spartans, who, if they had not been allowed to take the lead, would otherwise have abandoned the common cause, that Herodotus very justly gives them the praise of having saved Greece. And in this respect they differed very much from their rivals the Spartans, who were very far from being a generous and disinterested people; but, on the contrary, very selfish and narrow-minded.

But the people of any country, as well as their kings and great men, may be corrupted by wealth and power; and this was the fate of the Athenians: For when, by their conquests and their trade, they had become rich and powerful, they became indolent and luxurious, and were as liable to be flattered by orators and demagogues, as any absolute monarch by his courtiers and favourites; and in this respect I think Aristotle very properly compares a democracy

Chap. II. PROGRESS OF LANGUAGE. 349

to a tyranny *. The first remarkable corruption of their manners began under Pericles, one of the best too of their demagogues, but who, in order to make his court to the more indigent of the citizens, introduced a thing which had very great consequences, and may be said to have been one of the principal causes of the ruin of Athens, and of the loss of the liberty of Greece.

For understanding of this, we are to know that the Athenians, when they were in their glory, had a very great revenue, such as Demosthenes says might be compared with the revenue of all the other states of Greece put together †. And he says, that during the forty-five years that they were the leaders of Greece, they collected a treasure of more than ten thousand talents ‡. This treasure was appropriated

---

* *De Republica*, lib. 4. cap. 4.

† Περι συμμοριων p. 107. in fine. 1st Olynth. p. 7.

‡ Olynth. 3d, p. 25.

for war, and was what they called their χρηματα στρατιωτικα, out of which were paid the citizens, when they went upon any expedition, and likewise such mercenaries as they had occasion to hire. Some time before the Persian invasion, it was proposed to divide among the citizens a great sum which they had then in the treasury; but this was prevented by the wisdom of Themistocles, who, then foreseeing the storm that was coming, persuaded them to employ it in building ships. Nor was this treasure ever employed, as far as we know, for any other purpose than the service of the people, till it was diverted to private uses by Pericles, upon the following occasion. In his time theatrical representations, as well as every other art, were brought to great perfection in Athens, and as the theatre was then only of wood, and put up occasionally, it did not contain all the spectators, so that there was a great crouding to get into it, and great contention about places, which often ended in blows. This produced a regulation, by which every one was to pay for his seat so much, otherwise to have no place; and as the more indigent of the people could but ill afford this, Pericles took the opportunity of making his court to the people, by propoſing that there ſhould be paid out of the military treaſure two *oboli* to every one of the citizens, one of which was to be paid for a ſeat in the theatre, and the other for his maintenance. The bad effects of this appropriation of public money to private uſes were ſoon felt; for one Apollodorus wanted to bring back again the money to the treaſury; to prevent which, Eubulus, a great demagogue in thoſe days, in order to make his court to the people in the ſame way that Pericles had done, propoſed that it ſhould be a capital crime for any man ſo much as to move that the money ſhould be again applied to the uſe of the public *. And thus the χρηματα στρατιωτικα, at leaſt a great part of them, became what they called χρηματα θεωρικα.

* See Ulpian's Comment. upon the beginning of the 1ſt Olynthiac.

Nor did the thing stop here; for the people, having once tasted of the sweets of living in pleasure and ease at the public expence, by degrees laid hold of the whole revenue of the state under various pretences, such as being paid for their attendance in the public assemblies, which they called χρηματα εκκλησιαστικα, and for their trouble in judging causes, which they called χρηματα δικαστικα; so that, in the days of Demosthenes, there was nothing left for defraying any public service, except first, the contributions of the richer citizens called εισφοραι, a very unequal and arbitrary assessment, as it appears, and which gave occasion to great complaints, till Demosthenes got some regulations made which put the thing upon a better foot [*]; and, secondly, what they called the λειτουργιαι, or public services, which was also a burden upon the richer sort, such as the fitting out of ships of war, called τριηραρχια, and the defraying the expence of the choruses for their tragedy and comedy,

---

[*] Περι στεφανε, p. 154.

called χορηγια. For it appears from what the Scholiaſt ſays *, that the *obolus*, which each man paid for his ticket, was given to the architect who put up the theatre and furniſhed the machinery.

Another conſequence of this was, that the people became indolent and effeminate, preferring an eaſy and pleaſureable life, at the public expence, to thoſe toils and dangers for which only they were paid before. They did not therefore chooſe to go upon any expedition themſelves, but employed mercenary troops, which being very ill paid, by reaſon of the miſapplication of the public money, thoſe whom they ſent out as commanders were obliged to employ them in any way in which they could find ſubſiſtence for them, if the ſervice upon which they went was not ſufficient for that purpoſe; and ſometimes, for want of pay, they deſerted to the enemy. This

---

* Ulpian, ubi ſupra.

produced trials and accusations of the commanders, upon whom the people were always willing to lay the blame, rather than upon themselves; and though they were not willing to fight, they were very willing to judge, and were disposed to be remarkably severe in their judgments; and the general opinion that prevailed among them was, that the safety of the state consisted, first, in proper votes or resolutions (ψηφισματα); secondly, in the strict administration of justice. All this appears from the orations of Demosthenes; and, if we can believe Isocrates, they were come to such a degree of degeneracy, that, even when they went abroad upon any expedition, they served as rowers aboard their own vessels, while they employed their barbarous mercenaries to fight for them. But, though they were thus declined in spirit and courage, they continued still to excell in the arts*, and were besides, in the com-

---

* Their taste of pleasure was no doubt very fine, but it was very expensive; for Demosthenes tells us in his fifth Philippic, towards the beginning, that they

Chap. II. PROGRESS OF LANGUAGE. 355

mon affairs of life, people of the quickeſt apprehenſion, and what we would call the cleavereſt people in Greece*.

Such was the character of the people with whom Demoſthenes had to do. We are now to conſider in what ſtate the affairs of Greece were, when Demoſthenes appeared upon the ſtage. The Lacedemonians, after having been for many years the leading people in Greece, had loſt that honour by their defeat at Leuctra, and were now engaged in war with ſome of the neighbouring ſtates of Peloponneſe, who had taken that opportunity to ſhake off their dependence upon them. The Thebans, who, ever ſince their victory at Leuctra, had taken the lead in Grecian affairs, were at this time engaged in an unſucceſsful war with the Phocians, who inhabited

---

ſpent more upon the feaſt of the Παναθηναιαι and of Bacchus, than upon any one of their naval expeditions.

* Demoſthenes, who did not flatter them, gives them this teſtimony, ſυνετοι παντων υμας οξυτατα εγνωκατα. Olynth. 3. p. 23.

a country adjoining to the Straights of Thermopylae. The Athenians, too, were likewise engaged in what they called the social war, which was a war betwixt them and the Chians, the Rhodians, and the Byzantians, who were formerly their allies, or rather their subjects, but now had shaken off the yoke, and formed a confederacy against them *. In this distracted state of the affairs of Greece, a new power appeared on the stage that never was heard of before. This was Philip king of Macedon, a country formerly tributary to the Athenians, and of so little estimation, that, as Demosthenes tells us, a man did not chuse to take a slave from that country. This Philip was the third son of Amyntas, the preceding king. The eldest was assassinated, and the second was killed in a battle with the Illyrians †. By these accidents Philip became king of Macedon. But there was another, which contributed most of all to make him the man he afterwards proved to be, and which may be said to have laid

---

* Libanius in Prolegom. ad Demost.
† Ulpian, ubi supra.

the foundation of the univerfal monarchy of the Macedonians. It was this; Amyntas having had fome difference with the Thebans, who were then the governing people in Greece, and being obliged to fubmit to them, fent his third fon Philip to Thebes, as a hoftage for the performance of the conditions impofed upon him. There he became acquainted with Epamiſondas, the greateſt man, perhaps, that ever Greece produced, who had been inftructed by Lyfis, a Pythagorean philofopher, that happened then to be refiding at Thebes. Befides the inftruction he got from Epaminondas, the care of his education was committed to Naufithous, another Pythagorean philofopher, who was refiding at Thebes while Philip was there *; fo that Philip may be faid to have been a nurfling of philofophy, without which, I think it would have been impoffible that, coming from a barbarous nation, fuch as Macedonia was at that time, he fhould have been fo great a king; as impoffible, as that his

* Diodorus Siculus, lib. 16. fec. 2.

son Alexander should have conquered Asia, and been one of the greatest men we read of in history, if he had not been educated by Aristotle. How sensible Philip was of the benefit of a philosophical education, is evident from a letter of his, still extant, to Aristotle, written upon occasion of the birth of Alexander; wherein he says, That he does not thank the gods so much for having bestowed a son on him, as for giving him the opportunity of having him educated under such a philosopher as Aristotle. Thus instructed, Philip, very soon after his father's death, shewed how much he had profited by these instructions; and first he enlarged himself upon the side of Thrace, where there were many flourishing Greek cities, such as Amphipolis, Pydna, Potidaea *, and, among others, Olynthus, which was a colony from Chalcis in Euboea, and which itself was originally a colony from Athens†. All these cities he subdued; and then he began to extend his power upon the other

* Olynth. 1. p. 5.
† Liban. Argum. ad Olynth. 1.

side, viz. in Thessaly, where taking advantage of the division of that people among themselves, he became likewise master of them. Being thus in the neighbourhood of Greece, he got into it by the means of the war above mentioned, betwixt the Thebans and the Phocians; in which the Thebans being unsuccessful, were prevailed upon by some friends that Philip had there, to call him to their assistance; for Philip, by his money and his intrigues, had procured to himself friends in almost all the cities of Greece, by whose help, as much as by the force of his arms, he subdued that country. Having thus got into Greece, he very soon put an end to the Phocian war, by totally destroying that people, in whose place he was admitted to be of the council of the Amphictyons *. After this, that council having quarrelled with the Locrians, (a contrivance, as Demosthenes says †, of Philip's friend at A-

---

* Liban. Argum. ad Orat. περι ερηνης.

† Περι στεφανυ, p. 164.

thens, Æschines,) on account of some land which the Locrians possessed, but which the Amphictyons said belonged to the Delphic God, and having tried in vain to subdue them by arms, they called to their assistance Philip, and chose him general of the Amphictyons. Upon which he, not minding the sacred ground which was the subject of the controversy, turned his arms against Elataea, a strong town upon the confines of Baeotia, and made himself master of it*. This gave the alarm to the Thebans, and made them join against Philip the Athenians, with whom before they were at variance. Then followed the battle of Cheronaea, which made Philip master of Greece.

It was when this mighty power was yet but in its infancy, and when Philip was beginning to extend himself upon the side of Thrace, by the conquest of the cities above mentioned, that Demosthenes first ap-

---

* Demost. ubi supra.

Chap. II. Progress of Language. 361

peared in the scene of public business. At this time it could not be said that there was any leading people in Greece: For the Thebans, though in war they had prevailed against the Lacedemonians under their philosophical leader Epaminondas, had not wisdom or ability sufficient to fill their place in time of peace. All Greece, therefore, at that time consisted of so many independent states, each contending for the mastery; and, as I have said, Philip had his partizans almost in every city, and particularly in Athens.

In these circumstances, the part that Demosthenes acted was perhaps the greatest that any man ever acted in the political line; and, if Greece could have been saved by counsel and eloquence, it would have been saved by him: And I believe it is true what he says himself*, that, if there had been such another man in each of the cities of Greece, that country never would

* Περι στιφανυ.

have been conquered by Philip. The greatest triumph of his eloquence was in Thebes, whither he was sent ambassador by the Athenian people, after Philip had taken possession of Elataea, in order to persuade the Thebans to join the Athenians against Philip, in defence of the common liberties of Greece. And though he was opposed by Philip's ambassadors, who were there present, and though the Thebans were under great obligations to Philip, and had long been at variance with the Athenians, and though they still felt the loss they had suffered in the unsuccessful war with the Phocians, yet nothing could stand before the force of Demosthenes's eloquence, exciting them to act the noble and generous part, so that with a kind of enthusiasm they ran to arms, and Demosthenes was so great a man among them, that he not only guided their public assemblies as much as he did at Athens, but directed their generals *. By

---

* This is related by Plutarch in the life of Demosthenes, upon the authority of Theopompus, a very diligent and accurate historian, and who lived about that time.

the acceffion of the Thebans, fuch a confederacy was formed againft Philip, as fairly put him to a ftand, and obliged him to fue for peace. But the war going on, the confederates had at firft the advantage in two actions *, till at laft the fatal battle of Chaeronea put an end to the liberties of Greece, an event for which Demofthenes could not be anfwerable, as he fays himfelf, not having the command of the army; for with refpect to his behaviour as a foldier, befides that it could have no influence upon the fate of the day, I fufpect it has been much exaggerated by Plutarch and other writers; for if it had been as bad as they reprefent it, it certainly would have been mentioned, and much infifted on by Æfchines, in his oration againft Ctefiphon, where he throws out all fort of abufe againft Demofthenes.

In his political conduct, too, there was a fteadinefs and a conftancy which is not commonly found in politicians, efpecially

* Demoft. περι στιφανε.

those of modern times: For he opposed, from the beginning, the Macedonian power, and continued to oppose it, while he lived, choosing rather than submit to it, and put himself into the hands of the Macedonians, to go out of life. Whatever truth, therefore, there may be in the story of his taking the Persian money against the Macedonian, or of Alexander's money which Harpalus had run away with *, he was incorruptible by the Macedonian.

---

* As to his taking money from the king of Persia, for stirring up Greece against the Macedonian, Plutarch says, it was proved by writings which Alexander found in Babylon. But with regard to the money which Plutarch says he took from Harpalus, in order that he might not speak against him, and persuade the people to deliver him up to Alexander, I think he is justified by what Pausanias tells *in Corinthiacis;* who relates, that after the death of Harpalus, one of his domestics, who had been his treasurer, was apprehended by a Macedonian commander, to whom he gave an account of all those to whom Harpalus had given money, but Demosthenes was none of them; and when it was laid to his charge, his desiring to have the matter tried by the Areopagus, the most solemn and severe tribunal in Athens, looked as if he had been confident of his innocence.

In forming this grand alliance*, of which it appears he himself was the life and foul, he found more difficulty at home than abroad; for he had two paffions of his countrymen to ftruggle with, both as ftrong as any in human nature, viz. firft the love of pleafure, together with that foftnefs and averfion to toil, and danger and hazardous enterprife, which a life of that kind neceffarily produces. Secondly, the love of money, by which I do not mean the defire of fuperfluous wealth, or what is called avarice; but the defire of money to live upon in the way in which they had been ac-

---

* Plutarch, in the life of Demofthenes, reckons up all the ftates that he confederated againft Philip, viz. the Euboeans, Achaeans, Corinthians, Megarians, Leucadians, Corcyraeans, befides the two great ftates of Athens and Thebes.—(See what Demofthenes himfelf fays of this confederacy *De Corona*, p. 179. edit. Morelii.) —Amongft all thefe, fays Plutarch, he went about as ambaffador, and by his eloquence perfuaded them to join the public caufe; fo that in this way he collected a force againft Philip of no lefs than 15,000 foot and 2000 horfe of mercenaries, befides the national troops belonging to each of thefe ftates. This, perhaps, was the greateft army of Greeks that ever was collected together.

customed to live for many years: For, as I have observed, they were in the use of subsisting upon the spoils of the public, which they divided among themselves, and applied, partly to their living, and partly to their theatrical entertainments *. There was also a third passion of theirs, which Demosthenes had to encounter, equally strong, and as deeply implanted in human nature; I mean their vanity, which was greatly flattered by the demagogues at that time, who, as Demosthenes tells us †, used frequently to ask them, What they would have? What they should move for? What they should do to please them? And in almost every speech made by such orators, they were entertained either with their own praises, or those of their ancestors. This made it very dangerous to speak freely to them, as Demosthenes frequently observes, being very irascible, as all vain men are, and very apt to do severe things in their anger. Nor indeed could Demosthenes have treated them

* P. 351. and following.
† Olynth. 3. p. 24. edit, Morelii.

with the freedom he did, if he had not laid the blame of their ill conduct upon those demagogues: Yet even that way it was by no means safe; and he tells them, that he should not wonder, if he suffered more from them by telling them such things, than those gentlemen suffered by doing them; and he adds, 'For you are not always to be 'spoken to freely; and I am surprised that 'you now hear me *.' And indeed he had reason; for what is called his Philippics, and which, from the name, one should imagine, was an invective against Philip, as the orations of Cicero, bearing the same name, are against Anthony, is rather an invective against the people of Athens, whom he every where reproaches with their indolence, effeminacy, and scandalous abuse

* Olynth. 3. p. 27. & Philipp. 1, *in fine,* where he says, 'That as he knows certainly it is for their advan-
'tage to hear what he told them, so he wished he knew
'as certainly, that it was for his advantage to tell them
'such things; for then (says he) I should have told you
'them with much more pleasure. Uncertain, however,
'as it is, what shall befal me, I venture to tell you what
'I am sure it will be for your good that you should do.'

of public money; whereas Philip he commends for his activity, bravery, and contempt of toil and danger, when set against glory and empire *. And when at any time he mentions the great actions of their ancestors, it is only by way of reproach to them, who had degenerated so much from those ancestors †.

Without this noble spirit of liberty and manly boldness, which feared not the rage of a multitude any more than the frowns of a tyrant, his eloquence could have availed nothing; nor even with it, could any eloquence less than that of Demosthenes, seconded too, and enforced as it was, both

---

* The Olynthiacs, I think, should be rather called the Philippics of Demosthenes; for in them he is very severe upon the vices of Philip, such as his perfidy, his jealousy of superior merit, and his debauchery.—See particularly Olynth. 2. p. 17. It is, however, evident, that he does not do this merely for the pleasure of railing at a man whose power he opposed, without any hatred to his person; but in order to encourage the Athenians, and make them consider his power as not altogether invincible.

† Olynth. 3. p. 25. edit. Morelii.

by his private life and public conduct, have perſuaded a people, ſunk in pleaſure and indolence, to give up their feaſts, their ſhews, and elegant entertainments of the theatre, and what was ſtill more, even their daily bread, to reſume the ſpirit of their forefathers, and to engage in a moſt perilous war againſt a great king, at the head of a mighty army hitherto invincible.

The ſpeeches, by which ſo great things were accompliſhed, are ſuch as might be expected, full of ſenſe, ſpirit, and political prudence. While he reproaches the Athenians for their paſt conduct, he tells them that yet, if they will do what they ought to do, all will be well *. And while he

---

* In the beginning of the firſt Philippic he tells them, that though their affairs had then a very bad aſpect, they muſt not deſpair; ' For,' ſays he, ' what is ' worſt in time paſt, that is beſt with reſpect to the fu' ture:—And what is that? It is this,—that you having ' done nothing of what you ought to have done, your ' affairs are in a bad ſituation; for if they were in ſuch

magnifies the valour and enterprifing fpirit of Philip, he at the fame time fhews his weakneffes; and fays what was certainly true, that it was a fingle man only that they had to deal with, not the ftrength of a ftate *; fo that, if they were to do nothing but gain time, even that would be profitable.

But what chiefly diftinguifhes the rhetoric of Demofthenes, and gives it an air of grandeur which fets it much above that of any other orator, is what Plutarch has obferved, that the topic he infifts moft upon in his public orations is the το καλον, or the fair and the handfome; for it is only from three motives that men are perfuaded to act—the pleafureable, the profitable, and the beautiful or the honourable. Now, of thefe three, the laft is by far the nobleft both for the fpeak-

‘ a fituation, you having done every thing that was pro-
‘ per, there were no hope of their mending.’

* Philipp. 3. p. 73.

er; and the hearers. It was by arguments of this kind, as Plutarch has reported from Theopompus, that he persuaded the Thebans to associate with their enemies the Athenians against their friend Philip, when every motive of interest and safety was upon the other side. It was in this way that in the oration, *about the crown*, he justifies himself for having persuaded his countrymen to act the noble, though unsuccessful part, which they acted, in defence of the liberties of Greece against Philip; and it is this which gives the beauty to that fine passage, so justly celebrated by Longinus, where he swears by the shades of those that fell at Marathon and Plataeae, that the Athenians did not err in preferring what was dangerous and in the event fatal, because it was honourable, to what was easy and safe, but inglorious. And in general we may observe, that the arguments which he uses with the Athenians in his public orations are almost all drawn from this source; and it is particularly in this view that he urges the example of their ancestors, who did so much for the common liberties of Greece, with so generous a neglect of their own interest as is not to be equalled in the history of mankind. He therefore very well deserves the praise which Panaetius the orator, quoted by Plutarch in his life of Demosthenes, gives him, for his insisting so much in these orations upon the το καλον, or what is beautiful and honourable, and which is eligible for his own sake, and preferable to what was pleasant, easy, and even profitable *. And it is certain, that no orator, whose works are extant, insists so much upon this topic in any deliberative or judicial oration.

This elevation of mind, which raised Demosthenes so much above all other orators, and this enthusiasm for the το καλον, it is probable that he acquired in the school of Plato, whose scholar he was. In the same

---

* See Plutarch in the life of Demosthenes, where he gives us the words of Panaetius, which Taylor, in his edition of Demosthenes, vol. 2d. p. 657. has transcribed.

manner Pericles, whom Demosthenes proposed to himself as his model, by hearing Anaxagoras the philosopher, attained to that sublime of eloquence, compared by the writers of his age to the bolt of Jupiter, which nothing could stand before; and it was Cicero's boast that he came forth an orator, not out of the shops of rhetoricians, but from the walks of the academy *. And in general it may be said, that it is philosophy which perfects all the arts; nor is there, without philosophy, any thing truly great in the works of men †.

---

* Cicero, *De Oratore*, lib. 1. where he tells us, that this appeared from a letter of Demosthenes, which it seems was then preserved; and if he had not said so, Cicero thinks that it appears *ex genere et granditate verborum;* I think I may add, that it appears still more from the *matter* of his orations.

† See Quintilian, lib. 12. cap. 2. Of this philosophical rhetoric the Halicarnassian speaks much in sundry places, particularly in his work upon the subject of the antient orators, where he calls it, 'η αρχαια και φι-

And so much for the matter of Demosthenes's orations, upon which the Halicarnassian tells us he intended to write a treatise; but which if he ever executed, it has not come down to us*. In it he no doubt would have explained the order and economy which Demosthenes commonly observes in his orations, and would have

λοιπος ρητοριαν, cap. 1. and says, that it was quite lost in his time, but was beginning to be revived under the patronage of the great men of Rome. He also mentions it in the same volume 2d of his works, p. 203. and 212. of the Oxford edition.

* Who would desire to read more in praise of Demosthenes, may consult Lucian's encomium upon him, which he puts into the mouth of Antipater the Macedonian, upon occasion of Callias, whom he had sent to apprehend Demosthenes, reporting to him the manner of Demosthenes's death. This conversation Lucian pretends was found in the archives of the kingdom of Macedonia; but it is plainly a composition of his own, and, like all his other compositions, very elegant. See another encomium of Lucian upon Demosthenes, which I think still finer. I have quoted it in my Dissertation upon the Composition of the Antients, p. 583. annexed to vol. 2d of this work.

shewn us how artfully he mixes the arguments drawn from several topics, such as the possible, the profitable, and the honourable: For this way of complicating arguments, and so making them more forcible than when single and detached, is noted as a peculiar excellency of Demosthenes. This has been done by the Scholiast upon some of his orations, but in a much less masterly manner than it was done or could have been done by the Halicarnassian.

I shall only further observe upon this head, that the method of teaching and of rhetorical persuasion, that is, persuasion without teaching, are quite different: For in teaching we separate every thing from every thing, and explain things distinctly each by itself; and hence it is that accurate division, as well as definition, is absolutely necessary in matters of science: Whereas in speaking to the people, who are only to be persuaded, not taught, at least not in the space of an hour or two, instead of separating things, we accumulate them, in order to give them more weight; and we follow not the order of science, but such as we think best fitted to influence the opinions and passions of uninstructed men.

The Halicarnassian has given us an admirable treatise upon what he calls the λεκτικη δεινοτης of Demosthenes, that is, the force and energy of his language, of which I shall make much use in the next chapter; and he promises another upon his πρακτικη δεινοτης, that is, the force of conviction which his matter carries. But this work, as I have observed, he either never wrote, or it has not come down to us. This want I have endeavoured to supply, as far as I am able, and I shall only add upon the subject, that both in the invention of arguments, and in the arrangement and disposition of them, there is no orator, that ever I read or heard of, that equals him: And, besides all the force that the rhetorical art gives to his arguments, there is more plain good sense in them than in any oratorial composition I have ever seen: And he excells as much in exciting the paffions of the readers, as in argument: And I think it is true what the Halicarnaffian has obferved *, that if a man has any feeling at all, it is impoffible he can read Demofthenes without being agitated by the different paffions, which the Halicarnaffian mentions. But how much more would he have been agitated, if he had heard Demofthenes fpeak his orations?

As what I have faid of the ftate of Athens and Greece, at the time when Demofthenes was engaged in public bufinefs, is taken almoft altogether from his famous oration *De Corona*, it is proper that the reader fhould be informed upon what occafion this oration was made. Ctefiphon moved in the affembly of the people, that Demofthenes fhould be crowned with a golden crown on account of his virtue, and the good will he had conftantly fhewn to

* De admiranda vi dicendi in Demofthene.—Cap. 22. 50. & 54.

the people of Athens and to all the Greeks, and on account of his firmnefs and refolution, and becaufe he ftill continues faying, and doing every thing for the good of the people of Athens. And accordingly, upon this motion of Ctefiphon, a decree or enactment of the people paffed, and Demofthenes was fo crowned. For this decree Ctefiphon was accufed by Æfchines, as having fet forth to the people what was falfe concerning Demofthenes. He was charged alfo with having acted contrary to law and form, both as to the time and place of the proclamation of the crown*. The trial came on long after the decree was pronounced, after the death of Philip, and when Alexander was mafter of Greece, and engaged in the war againft the Perfians. And as the indictment was fo conceived as to make Demofthenes a party as well as Ctefiphon, he was heard in defence both of Ctefiphon and himfelf. This, as I have obferved, neceffarily led him to

---

* See the whole indictment or γραφη, as they call it, ingroffed in the oration itfelf, p. 143.-edit. Morelli.

speak much of himself, and to set forth what he had done for the service of the Athenians, and for the preservation of the liberty of all Greece. Of all these services you have a short summary account towards the end of the oration *. And the fact undoubtedly was, that he put Philip fairly to a stand, having leagued against him not only the Athenians and Thebans, but almost all the other states of Greece there named; and brought to the field against him an army, as I have said, of no less than 15,000 foot and 2000 horse of hired troops, besides those which were composed of the citizens of each of the states: So that I think it was with reason he says, that he was then at the head of the affairs of the greatest consequence in his time.

There is one thing which distinguishes the stile of history from that of rhetoric more than any thing else, which is, that the orator lays down general abstract propositions of the moral or political kind, from

---

* P. 189. and following.

which he argues. These are called in Greek γνωμαι, and in Latin *sententiae*; and they were reckoned by the antients a great beauty of the rhetorical stile. There may however be too many of them, which will give the oration the appearance of a philosophical discourse, rather than a speech of business: And this is a fault which I have observed in some of Tacitus's speeches, and in those of Sallust; but Demosthenes has used them more moderately, and always arising naturally from the subject. As those he has used are, I think, the finest any where to be found, I will give some examples of them. The first I shall mention is to be found in the third Olynthiac, towards the end, where he tells us, that the Athenians of his time, instead of applying to the great and important affairs of Greece, as their forefathers had done, employed themselves in making high-ways, plastering their ramparts, collecting water in fountains, and such like trifles; and he adds, ' That it is not possible that men, who ap-
' ply to mean and trifling things, should
' be great minded men; for such as the
' studies and applications of men are,

' such of neceſſity will their minds be *.
This is true not only of nations, but of
every individual; for there is no more certain way of diſcovering the ſpirit and genius of any man, than by obſerving his
purſuits, and what he values himſelf for
excelling in.

Another inſtance of the ſame kind is to
be found in the firſt Olynthiac †, ' Where
' a man (ſays he) ſucceeds beyond what he
' deſerves, it diſpoſes him, if he has not a

---

* Εστι δ' ουδέποτ', οιμαι, μεγα και νεανικον φρονημα λαβειν, μικρα και φαυλα πραττοντας· 'οποι' αττα γαρ αν τα επιτηδευματα των ανθρωπων ᾖ, τοιουτον αναγκη και το φρονημα εχειν.

† P. 8. Ed. Monelii.—Το γαρ εν πραττειν παρα την αξιαν, αφορμη του κακως φρονειν τοις ανοητοις γινεται· διοπερ πολλακις δοκει το φυλαξαι ταγαθα, του κτησασθαι χαλεπωτερον ειναι. And here we may obſerve how conciſely, and at the ſame time how clearly this is expreſſed in the Greek. It is expreſſions of this kind, not to be imitated in any other language, which gives that weight of matter to the ſtile of Demoſthenes, not to be found in any other orator, nor any other writer that I know, in which his λεκτικη δεινοτης, as the Halicarnaſſian calls it, conſiſts.

'great deal of prudence, to act very un-
'wisely; and therefore it appears, in ma-
'ny cases, to be more difficult to preserve
'what you have acquired, than to have ac-
'quired it.' This is a maxim, the truth of
which may be verified from many examples,
both of nations and of individuals.

There is a noble sentiment on the subject of the το καλον, and which I am persuaded he brought with him from the school
of Plato. It is in the oration *De Corona* *,
where he says, 'That death is necessarily
'the end of human life, which no man can
'avoid, if he were to shut himself up al-
'together from the commerce of the world.
'But good men it becomes to act the beau-
'tiful and honourable part in life, hoping
'the best, but disposed to bear with forti-
'tude whatever lot it shall please Provi-
'dence to assign them †.'

* P. 153. edit. Morelii.

† The reader who would form a taste of the beauty
of Demosthenes's composition, should read it in the
original, where he will find a very fine period, which

I will only juſt mention another very fine paſſage of the ſame kind upon the ſubject of traitors to their country, ſuch as there were many at that time in Greece. It is to be found in the oration *De Corona* *, where he ſhews that traitors, however happy they may think themſelves by the rewards they get for their treaſon, are truly the moſt miſerable of men, which he proves both by reaſons and facts.

Before I conclude this ſubject of the matter of Demoſthenes, I muſt obſerve one great difference betwixt him and Cicero as to the matter:—Demoſthenes never ſpeaks of himſelf in any of his orations, but where it is abſolutely neceſſary, which it certainly was in the oration *De Corona*; for there, if he had not ſpoken a great deal of himſelf, and enlarged much upon what he had done in defence of the liberty of his country, and of all Greece, muſt have pleaſed the ears of the Athenians, as much as the ſenſe of it their underſtandings.

* P. 142. edit. Morelii.

he could not have defended himself against the charge which Æschines brings against him, that he was unworthy of the honours which had been decreed to him upon the motion of Ctesiphon: But though absolutely necessary, he makes an apology for speaking so much of himself*. How dif-

---

* This apology is so well expressed, and in words so plain and simple, but such as no better could be devised, that I will give them at length as a specimen of his stile, which I admire for nothing more than the plainness of his language, and at the same time the propriety of it, and the weight of matter contained in it. He observes two things in that cause in which Æschines had a great advantage over him. The first was, that upon the issue of the trial with respect to him, depended what he thought of the greatest value, the preserving the good will and esteem of his countrymen, whereas Æschines risked nothing but the losing his suit: And here he uses a figure, called by the Scholiast ἀποσιώπησις, which expresses more by saying nothing, than could have been done by many words. Then follows the other thing: " Ἑτερον δε, ὁ φυσει πασιν ανθρωποις ὑπαρχει, των
" μεν λοιδοριων και των κατηγοριων ακυειν ἡδεως· τοις επαι-
" νουσι δε ἀυτους, αχθεσθαι. Τουτων τοινυν, ὁ μεν εστι προς ἡδο-
" νην, τουτῳ δεδοται· ὁ δε πασιν ὡς επος ειπειν ενοχλει, λοιπον
" εμοι. Καν μεν ευλαβουμενος τουτο, μη λεγω τα πεπραγ-
" μενα εμαυτῳ, ουκ εχειν απολυσασθαι τα κατηγορημενα δοξω·

ferent is Cicero in this respect from Demosthenes? He brings himself into his orations upon every occasion: And not only into his public orations, but also those in private causes, such as that for *Archias the poet*, where he speaks a great deal of himself, and of his application to letters, very near as much as upon the question, which was, Whether Archias was a Roman citizen? beginning the oration with himself, where there is an affected modesty, in these words: *Si quid est in me ingenii, judices, quod, sentio, quam sit exiguum;* which affectation, as I have observed, is always a sign of the greatest vanity: And I think I have shewn that Cicero was perhaps as vain a man as ever lived.

And here it may be observed, that a great artist like Demosthenes, who has most

"ουδ εφ 'οις αξιω τιμασθαι, δακνυμαι. Εαν διαφ' 'α και πε-
"ποιηκα και πεπολιτευμαι βαδιζω, πολλακις λιγων αναγκασθη-
"σομαι περι εμαυτου. Πειρασομαι μεν ουν, 'ως μετριωτατα,
"ταυτα ποιειν. 'Ο'τι δ'αν το πραγμα αυτο αναγκαζη, του-
"του την αιτιαν 'ουτος εστι δικαιος εχειν, 'ο τοιουτον αγωνα
"ενστησαμενος.

Vol. VI.   3 C

diligently studied the art, and by that means discovered the extreme difficulty of excelling in it, can never be perfectly satisfied with his own performance, nor come up to his own idea of perfection in the art. This, I have shewn, was the case of the great painters of old*: And therefore, if a man desires only to please himself, it is better for him not to be so perfect in the art, so that he may rather admire, as Horace says, even his own faults, *quam sapere et ringi.*

---

* P. 276, and 277. of this vol.

CHAP. III.

Stile *divided into the words and the composition of the words.—The words ornamented by* Tropes, *composition by* Figures. *The stile of Demosthenes simple with respect to the words; but the composition artificial.—He excelled in two stiles diametrically opposite to one another, the plain and simple, the artificial and elaborate.— Of his excellence in the first, his speech against Olympiodorus is a proof.—The difficulty of excelling in that composition.— The stile of his public orations perfectly different.—This artificial stile not the stile of conversation, nor of the decrees of the senate and people.—It is made by figures of composition, not by metaphorical or poetical words.—These* Figures *of three kinds, the Figures of the syntax, of the sense, and of the sound.—The Figures of syntax very few in Demosthenes.—His Figures of the sense not such as Cicero uses.—Not so im-*

moderate in his use of *Figures of the sound*
as *Isocrates* is.—*Figures of sound are produced by a certain similarity of sound,
which strikes the ear.*—*The Halicarnassian mentions several of them, among o-
thers* Antithesis, *a figure also of the sense.*
—*Of the peculiarities of Demosthenes's
stile:*—*First, the arrangement of the words.
—That in his public orations very different
from the stile of Lysias, or his own stile
in private causes*—*Examples of the inversion of the natural order.*—*Shewn
that this may be done in some degree in
English.*--*This artificial composition makes
the stile of Demostenes obscure to one who
is not a good Greek scholar*—*Dr. Johnson's judgment of the stile of Demosthenes.
—It could not be obscure to the people of
Athens.*—*Wherein the artifice of this
composition consists.*—*Example of it, with
a correction of the text.*—*The use of accustoming one's self to such a composition.
—Another peculiarity of Demosthenes's
stile is Hyperbatons and Parentheses.*—
This makes the δεινοτης *or* density *of his*

ſtile.—Another peculiarity of his ſtile is the roundneſs or compactneſs of his periods.—A period muſt have a beginning and an end, of which the connection muſt be perceptible, and marked by the voice in reading or ſpeaking.—Of that figure of the ſound which conſiſts of like endings.—This an ornament of the proſe ſtile among the antients, as well as of modern poetry.—Several examples of it from Iſocrates.—The difference betwixt it and what is called the παρονομασια.—Of the ſimilarity of the compoſition or ſtructure of periods.—This figure of ſound alſo much too frequent in Iſocrates.—Iſocrates concludes his periods too frequently with a verb.—This a general practice among the Latin writers.—Some apology to be made for both.—Compariſon of the ſtile of Plato with that of Demoſthenes.—Iſocrates alſo avoided ſtudiouſly the concourſe of vowels gaping upon one another.—Plutarch's account of his ſtile.—Such a ſtile was very ſuitable to the genius and ſpirit of the writer.—Demoſthenes ſtudied the music of his language, and made of it a noble melody and dignified rhythm, with suitable variety.—*The variety of Demosthenes's stile, the most distinguishing characteristic of it.*—*In this he excells all other authors.*—*Demosthenes to be considered not as a writer only of orations, but as a speaker.*—*He studied action and pronunciation very much, and excelled in it more than in any other art.*—*The beauty of his orations pronounced by himself not to be conceived by us.*—*What is come down to us of Demosthenes, only the lifeless carcass of his orations.*—*Those only orators, who speak their orations.*—*It does not appear that Cicero excelled in action.*—*As to the composition of Cicero, it does not deserve the character which Quintilian gives of Demosthenes's composition.*—*He imitated Isocrates more than Demosthenes, particularly in the figures of the sound.*—*Examples of that.*—*Quintilian prefers him to Demosthenes.*—*It became a piece of national vanity among the Romans, to prefer their own writers to the*

Chap. III. Progress of Language.

Greeks.— But this was not the case in the days of Cicero.—The critics of that time disapproved of his stile.

I COME now to speak of the stile of Demosthenes, which, if it be answerable to his matter, must make his orations the finest of all rhetorical compositions. Stile consists of single words, and the composition of these words: And it is either a plain and simple stile, such as is used in common discourse; or it is a stile of art, such as is not commonly used. The words are varied from common use by what are called *tropes*, and the composition by what are called *figures*; of both which I have elsewhere spoken at some length*.

As to the words of Demosthenes, there is nothing remarkable, or what we would call ornamented or *fine:* For they are either the common words of the language, or words of business appropriated to the government in Athens, or to judicial proceedings, which may be called *verba forensia*,

* Vol. 3d. of this work, book 4. chap. 4.

nor is there much of metaphorical language in him, or great ufe of epithets, with which we fo much adorn our profe as well as our poetry. But his ftile, as far as refpects the words, is perfectly fimple*; and it is the compofition only which diftinguifhes it from common language, and, I may fay, from the ftile of every other author: For as to the beauty and variety of compofition, he exceeds all that ever wrote in profe †.

* There is fome part of the oration *about the crown*, which I think is an exception to this rule. It is where he defcribes the education and life of his adverfary Æfchines; for he there ufes words which may be called Dithyrambic, and fome of them, I am perfuaded, were made by him for the occafion; as when he calls Æfchines αντιτραγικος πιθηκος. It was of thofe terms of abufe that Æfchines faid, (as Cicero informs us, *De Oratore Perfecto*), that they were prodigies, not words—θαυματα, η ρηματα. They ferve to fhew, that our orator could have excelled even in that *made* ftile, if he had judged it proper to ufe it upon any other occafion.

† Æfchines, his rival, allowed him the praife of admirable compofition, as well as excellent pronunciation,

And in the firſt place, he is perhaps the only author that has excelled in the two kinds of compoſition I have mentioned, diametrically oppoſite to one another, firſt the ſimple, plain, and unornamented; and, ſecondly, the artificial, elaborate, and ſuch as is as different from common idiom, as the art of compoſition can make proſe. Of the firſt kind are ſome of his orations in private cauſes, ſuch as that againſt Conon, and another againſt Olympiodorus, the ſtile of both which is ſo different from that of his public orations, that I ſhould not believe that they were his, if it was not univerſally ſo reputed. The Halicarnaſſian has ſpoken at ſome length of the oration againſt Conon *, and has told us that it was written in imitation of Lyſias's manner. If ſo, I think we muſt allow that he has outdone his maſter; for there is nothing of Lyſias that

and he appears to have thought that it was by his compoſition chiefly that he got the better of him. See vol. 2d, p. 365.

* Περι της δεινοτητος του Δημοσθενους.

is so perfectly simple. In this kind of composition every appearance of art is avoided, and yet I am not sure, but that the stile of it cost Demosthenes as much pains as that of any of his orations in public causes. For, though it seem very easy, and such as any one might imitate, yet, upon trial, one will be soon convinced that it is of the kind which Horace mentions:

———————————ut sibi quivis
Speret idem; sudet multum, frustraque laboret,
Ausus idem; tantum series juncturaque pollet.

A. P. v. 240.

The other, against Olympiodorus is in the same stile: And as it was spoken by the party, though written by Demosthenes, it is admirably suited to the character of the speaker, who being no orator, but a vulgar illiterate man, in the very beginning declares himself unable to speak, and more than once, in the course of his pleading, puts the judges upon their guard against the artificial arguments of orators, which his adversary had used. It would therefore have been very unnatural if he had spoken in the same artificial manner, and would have entirely taken away that air of truth and ingenuity which runs through the whole oration, and must have had a great effect upon the judges.

The difference of the stile of these orations from that of his public orations, shews that he understood perfectly

Descriptas servare vices, operumque colores *,

and could suit his stile to his subject, than which nothing shews more judgment and taste in a writer.

And here we may observe in passing, that these orations are a proof, among many others which might be produced, that the artificial arrangement of words which we observe in the Greek orators and other elegant writers, was not the common language of the people of Athens, of which the two orations above mentioned were undoubtedly an exact imitation. Neither was it their ordinary stile of business, or of their public acts, as is evident from se-

* Horat. *Ars Poetica.*

veral decrees of the senate and people, which we have in the orations of Demosthenes, and particularly in the oration *about the Crown*. Only there is one decree of the people, drawn up by Demosthenes himself, mentioned in that oration, which I think is an exception to this rule; for, in the first place, it is very much longer than any other decree mentioned in that or any other oration: And, secondly, has a great deal of the rhetorical composition, and also of rhetorical argument *: And it

---

* The sentences in this decree, are almost as long as those in any of his orations. One begins with the words ‘Ελληνιδας πολις, and ends with the word μιγας. The next sentence begins Και 'ως μη, and ends with the word καταδουλουμενους. The sentence containing the decree itself, (for what goes before is only an introduction to it), and immediately following the other two sentences, is almost as long as the other two put together. And it concludes with a period very well composed, containing an argument of the rhetorical kind, drawn from a topic, which, as I have observed, Demosthenes insists much upon, I mean the topic of the το καλον, and to which he has given the rhetorical turn. The words are, Ειδως 'οτι και 'αυτοις μεν προς

is more severe against Philip, than any of the orations we call Philippics, in which he often finds more fault with the Athenians than with Philip.

But we are to consider that this decree was written upon a great occasion, the taking, by Philip, of Elataea, a town of Bœotia, upon the confines of Attica. Upon this occasion it was proper to excite the people of Athens to join with their enemies the Thebans, in a confederacy that was necessary for the preservation of both states, and of the liberties of Greece. And I have no doubt that this decree contained the substance of Demosthenes's speech upon the occasion, in consequence of which the decree was made *.

αλληλους αμφισβητειν περι της ‘ηγιμονιας ουσι ‘Ελλησι, καλον· ‘υπο δι αλλοφυλου ανθρωπου αρχεσθαι, και της ‘ηγιμονιας αποστερεισθαι, αναξιον ειναι, και της των ‘Ελληνων δοξας και της των προγονων αριτης.

* This decree is to be found in Morell's edition, p. 170.

His other kind of ſtile is, as I have ſaid, in reſpect of the compoſition, very artificial. It is the ſtile of his Olynthiacs, his oration about the Crown, and, in general, all his public orations, to which he thought a ſtyle, much more elevated and more raiſed above common ſpeech than that which he uſed in common cauſes, was ſuitable.

But it was not by metaphorical, poetical, and dythyrambic words, as they called them, that he raiſed his ſtile in thoſe orations, (for, as I have obſerved, his words in all his orations are either terms of buſineſs or of common uſe), but it was by figures of compoſition.

Theſe figures of compoſition are of three kinds: For they are either figures of the ſyntax, of the ſenſe, or of the ſound. In theſe three ways language is wonderfully varied, and ſtiles formed exceedingly different from one another. Of the two firſt I have ſpoken pretty fully in anether volume of this work *; and I shall only add here, that with respect to figures of syntax, there are very few of them to be found in Demosthenes, unless we call by that name certain eliptical expressions, which produce a brevity very remarkable in the Attic writers, by which they both express their meaning in fewer words, and arrange these words in a manner different from what is practised by other Greek writers. If to these expressions you give the name of figures, Demosthenes certainly abounds with them. And it is in the use of them, that a great part of the δεινοτης of his style consists; for by them, his matter is more condensed, and makes a greater impression upon the mind of the hearer, or reader, than it could otherwise do. And as to the figures of the sense, Demosthenes has none of those poetical figures which Cicero uses, such as *Exclamation* and *Prosopopoeia*. His figures of that kind consist chiefly of what Cicero calls the *conformatio sententiarum*; by which

---

* Volume 3d.

he arranges his arguments in all the different ways by which he thinks they will have the greatest weight and force. There is one very common figure of this kind, which Demosthenes uses very often, and I think to very good purpose, I mean *Interrogation:* And which is commonly in very short sentences, whereby he not only varies his composition very agreeably, but inforces his arguments. As to the figures of sound, having said very little of them in any other part of this work, I think it is proper to explain them here at some length, more especially as I do not find that done in any antient grammarian or rhetorician. And yet I think they vary the composition very much, and constitute a great part of the florid and ornamented stile in Greek; and which, as I shall shew in the sequel, Isocrates has used very immoderately, but Demosthenes properly and moderately.

These figures are all produced by certain similarities which affect the ear, in the found of the compofition. Under this definition will be comprehended all the different figures of this kind mentioned by the Halicarnaffian *.

To diftinguifh exactly from one another all thefe figures, which the Halicarnaffian mentions, would be a work of fome trouble, and, I think, not worth the pains; and therefore I fhall only obferve, that the figure which he calls Antithefis, is commonly reckoned to belong to the fenfe, as it relates to the meaning of the words which are fet in oppofition to one another: But it is alfo a figure of the found, as it gives the fame form and ftructure to the periods and their feveral members, and fo produces a fimilarity of found.

* It is in his treatife Περι της δεινοτητος του Δημοσθενους. He there mentions the παρισωσις, παρομοιωσις, αντιθεσις, παρονομασϊα, αντιστρεφοντα, and επαναφερομενα: And he adds, και αλλα πολλα; that is to fay, wherever there is a fimilarity of found, fuch as is in the figures he mentions, it is a figure of the kind of which I fpeak, and is reckoned an ornament of ftile.

But, besides these figures of sound, the whole composition of Demosthenes, particularly in his public orations, must have given the greatest pleasure to the ears of his hearers. I have spoken already* of the beauty of his melody, and of his rhythm. This indeed is a beauty, of which we may form an idea, but of which our ear has no perception. But the artificial arrangement of his words is what I think must please the ear of every scholar and man of taste; and it is by this chiefly, that I think his stile is distinguished from that of every other Greek orator.

To be convinced of this, we need only compare his stile in these public orations with the stile of Lysias, or even with his own in the orations above mentioned against Conon and Olympadiorus, where the words are in so simple an order, that they might almost be translated into English in the order in which they stand; or with the stile of other orators of the same age, and particu-

* Chap. 4th. & 5th. of book 2d. of this volume.

larly with the ſtile of an oration, intituled, περι 'Αλοννσυ, which is publiſhed among the orations of Demoſthenes: But we know certainly that it does not belong to him, and by no mark more ſurely than the inartificial ſtructure of the words; and it very probably is the work, as Libanius conjectures, of Hegeſippus, who took the ſame ſide in politics that Demoſthenes did, and particularly in that matter of Halonefus *.

This artificial ſtructure of words, eſpecially if it be diverſified, as it often is, by parentheſes, or by genetives abſolute, which detach that member, where they are uſed, from the reſt of the ſentence, as much as a parentheſis does, makes the ſtile appear very obſcure to a man who is not a good

* See Libanius's argument of that oration. I think it would not be a diſagreeable occupation for a man, who would deſire to know perfectly the peculiar beauties of Demoſthenes's ſtile, to arrange the words, which Hegeſippus uſes in this ſpeech, in the artificial manner of Demoſthenes.

Greek scholar, or has not made a particular study of Demosthenes*. I therefore

---

* Of this artificial structure the Halicarnassian has given us sundry examples in his treatise Περι της λεκτικης Δημοσθενους δεινοτητος, or, as it is rendered by the Latin translators, *De Admiranda vi dicendi in Demosthene*. This, I think, is one of the best of the Halicarnassian's critical works, Demosthenes being an author for whom it appears he had a kind of enthusiastical admiration. But unfortunately the MS. of this piece is more mutilated than that of any other of the Halicarnassian's works: Even where there is no blank in the MS. the text is more incorrect than in any other of his works. This is evident from the passages which he has transcribed from Isocrates, Plato, or Demosthenes himself, which are so ill copied, that if those passages were not to be found in the editions which we have of those authors, they would hardly be intelligible. Many of the errors of Demosthenes's text in this work, Sylburgius and Wolfius have corrected, as many as I believe can be corrected. But incorrect and mutilated as it is, I hold it to be a most valuable piece of criticism, though it may be thought by many, to be trifling, as it relates only to words, and their composition. He was to have written, as mentioned before, a work upon the πραγματικη δεινοτης of Demosthenes, which he says was more wonderful than his λεκτικη δεινοτης; but which is not come down to us. In the

did not wonder when I heard the late Dr Johnson say, That it was impossible that

work that is preserved to us, cap. 9. he has given us two examples of Demosthenes's artificial composition, one of them the famous period with which he begins his third Philippic, and another period in the same Philippic not so long, but I think of more artificial composition. It begins with the words Εἶτ' οὐχὶ, &c. He has taken the trouble to shew us how the words of each of them might have been arranged 'ἁπλῶς καὶ κατ' εὐθεῖαν ἡρμηνίας; but he has arranged them in such a way, that του συνήθους ἐξηλλαγμένην καὶ περιεργον πεποιηκε την λέξιν. Upon both these passages I have commented, in my dissertation upon the composition of the antients, annexed to the second volume of this work, p. 573. and following, where I have ventured to give a translation of the last mentioned passage into English, by which I think I have shewn that the inversion from the natural order of the words is not so great, but that the passage may be translated with the same order of the words preserved, and yet not be obscure, but, in my judgment, (and I am sure Milton would have thought so), more beautiful than if it had been rendered in our common phraseology: For I hold it to be a general rule, that wherever a speaker, upon any great and important subject, can depart from the common arrangement of the words, without making his stile obscure or poetical, he ought to do it, but not constantly, as the Halicar-

the orations of Demosthenes could have been understood by the people of Athens, if they had been spoken as we have them written. But if they should appear obscure to a better Greek scholar than Dr Johnson, it will not from thence follow, that they would not be intelligible to so acute a people as the Athenians, who certainly understood their own language better than any man now living, and who besides were accustomed to that artificial arrangement, and short way of expressing things, more than any other people in Greece, these two qualities of stile, in a greater or less degree, being remarkable in all the Attic writings. For my own part, I have studied Demosthenes's stile so much, and have become so fond of it, that to me it is so far from being obscure, that what appears a disorderly arrangement of the words, conveys the sense to me more

---

nassian has observed: For there must be variety in every work of art, and therefore a great part of the composition should be of words put together in the common and ordinary way.

forcibly, and I think I underſtand it better, than if it were written in plain Engliſh, eſpecially if it be well read to me: For all the compoſitions of Demoſthenes clearly bear the mark of having been written to be ſpoken. There is therefore to me not the leaſt obſcurity in his orations, except what ariſes from our ignorance of particular cuſtoms, laws, and forms of proceeding in judicial matters. But theſe muſt have been all perfectly known to the people of Athens, who were ſo much accuſtomed to hear ſpeeches upon all ſubjects, deliberative and judicial; and were themſelves judges in all cauſes, public and private. And indeed it is impoſſible that they could have praiſed and admired him ſo much, if they had not perfectly underſtood him. At the ſame time they muſt have perceived that he did not ſpeak to them a common language, but a language ſo artificially compoſed, that, at the ſame time that it pleaſed their ears, it conveyed the ſenſe more forcibly to them, than it could otherwiſe have been conveyed; as I think I have shewn in the differtation upon the compofition of the antients, which I have annexed to the fecond volume of this work.

And here it may be obferved, that the ordinary way, in this artificial compofition, is to begin the period with a noun in the genetive, or any other oblique cafe, and then to go on for feveral lines, and at the end of the period to give us the verb or the noun by which the noun in the beginning is governed: And by this means the fenfe is fufpended, and the reader or hearer is obliged to carry on his attention to the end of the period, when the whole fenfe comes upon him at once, and confequently muft make a greater impreffion than if it were frittered down into fmall detached fentences. Of this kind of compofition the public orations of Demofthenes are full of examples. I will give but one, which happens at prefent to be before me. It is in the oration *pro Corona*. The words I give in the note below *. But upon this peculiarity of Demosthenes's stile I will insist no longer here, as I have said a good deal upon the subject, both in the dissertation above quoted, and in the third chapter of the third book of the second volume of this work, where I have shewn, that this artificial composition, however forced and unnatural it may appear to some who pretend to be critics, gives a density and compactness to the composition that otherwise it would not have, and makes the mind exert that faculty, the foundation of all reasoning and science,

---

* Τον μὲν οὖν γράψαι πράττοντα μὶ καὶ λέγοντα τὰ βέλτιστα τῷ δάμῳ διατελεῖν, καὶ πρόθυμον εἶναι ποιεῖν ‘ο, τι ἂν δύνωμαι ἀγαθον, καὶ ἐπαινεῖσθαι ἐπὶ τούτοις, ἐν τοῖς πεπολιτευμένοις τὴν κρίσιν εἶναι νομίζω. p. 144. Ed. Morelli. In this period we see that the word κρίσιν which governs the genetive in the beginning of the period, is thrown to the end of it, by which the sense is brought all at once to the mind of the reader or hearer.

by which it unites several things together, and comprehends them in one view.*

The next peculiarity of his stile that I observe is connected with the former. It is the frequent use of Hyperbatons and Parentheses, by which the period is drawn out to a great length, and the reader obliged to carry on the sense a long way, and to connect words at a great distance from one another. In this respect I know no author that can be compared with him, except Thucydides, whom it appears Demosthenes imitated very much in the stile and composition, as well as in the matter and method of his harangues. But Thucydides carried this farfetched and implicated construction so far as to make his stile obscure; while Demosthenes has used it more temperately, so much only as to raise his stile much above common speech,

---

* Vol. 2d. p. 355.—363. where I have given, from Milton, a fine example of the beauty of this composition, contrasted with the same words, put into what is commonly called the natural order.

and to give to his periods that weight of matter closely compacted together, which makes what is called the πυκνον, or, as it may be not improperly translated, the *density* of his composition.

The third peculiarity I observe is also near a-kin to the last mentioned. It is a roundness and constriction, if I may use the expression, in the form and structure of his periods, which have nothing redundant or deficient, and are equally remote from the loose flow of the historical period, and the pompous and panegyrical periods of Isocrates, and other orators of the epideictic kind. The way in which he commonly gives this roundness to his periods, is, as I have observed, by beginning them with a word, one or more, of which we cannot discover the connection with the other words of the period till we come to the end. In this way we are necessarily obliged to connect the beginning with the end of the period, without which the period is not intelligible; and the great skill in pronouncing such periods, is to mark, by the voice, the connection betwixt the beginning and the end of the period, which, according to Aristotle's definition of a period*, are essential to it. But without being marked by the voice, it may be a period as it is written, though not as it is read or spoken. It is this composition in periods, pronounced as they were by him, which made his stile so fit for business and action, and gave to it the τὸ διαστηριον and παγωνιον, which, the Halicarnassian observes, is a peculiar characteristic of his stile †. And it is so much fitted for speaking, that the words themselves, as they are composed, shew how they are to be pronounced ‡.

* See p. 166. and 168. of this volume, and the references to other volumes of this work in note ‡ of p. 166.

† Dionysius, *De admiranda vi dicendi in Demosthene*, cap. 21.

‡ Cap. 22. ibid.

The next thing I am to obferve in the ftile of Demofthenes, is concerning the figures of found which he has ufed. All thefe figures, as I have obferved, confift of a certain fimilarity of found. Of this fimilarity there is one very common among the moderns; and that is, the fimilarity of like endings in their rhyming poetry. Of this I fhall fpeak at fome length in the next volume, the fubject of which is to be poetry. But at prefent it may be proper to obferve, that there may be rhymes in profe as well as in verfe; when periods, or members of periods, are concluded by words terminated by the fame fyllables, one or more. Of words fo terminated there are very many, both in Greek and Latin: For all the nouns of the fame declenfion muft necefſarily have the fame termination in the feveral cafes: And verbs of the fame conjugation in their feveral tenfes, perfons, and numbers, muft alfo have the fame termination of perhaps two or three fyllables; and likewife the participles of verbs of the same conjugation, in their several numbers and cases.

That these like endings were accounted an ornament of prose as well as of verse, is evident from the practice of Isocrates and others, who have studied the florid and pleasureable stile. The Halicarnassian, in his treatise upon the subject of Isocrates's stile, cap. 20. has given us sundry examples from Isocrates of this ornament of stile: And particularly, he has mentioned one period, where he has used three words rhyming to one another, viz. ἐπιχειροίμην, πράττοιμην, ἀποπλιυσοίμην: And he has given to this ornament the name of παρίσωσις: And then he observes, that there are in this period three members of the same length; and this figure he calls παρομοίωσις: For not only does the ear perceive a similarity of sound, when the periods, or members of periods, terminate with the same syllables; but also, when the periods, or the members of the periods, are of the same length, and of the same form and structure. As

Isocrates has made more use of those figures of sound, of both the kinds I have mentioned, than any other author I know, I will give more examples from him, of this kind of rhyming compofition: And I will take them from his Panegyric, an oration upon which, it is said, he bestowed ten years, and some say fifteen; and where, consequently, every thing he thought ornamental in stile must have been most diligently studied. The first example I give is from p. 132. (Basil edition, anno 1594.) where you have a string of eight sentences, all of which, and their several members, are nearly of the same length, and of the same form and composition, and most of them rhyming to one another. Another example is in p. 170. where you have a string indeed of no more than three short sentences, but all of the same form and structure, and all in rhyme. And in p. 188. you have likewise three short sentences of the same, or nearly the same length, and each of them terminated with the double rhyme of μενης. in the words στρατηγουμενης, αθροιζομενης, and

παρομοίωσις. And here it is to be observed, that it is not the juxta position of words of like endings that makes this rhyming, which is accounted an ornament by such writers as Isocrates; but it is the placing those rhyming words in the same place of a sentence, or a member of a sentence, and where the sense requires that an emphasis should be laid upon them, which makes the above mentioned ornament that they call πάρισωσις; where there is a concourse of such words together, it makes the figure which the Halicarnassian, in the passage above quoted, calls παρισώματα; but it appears to me not to be practised by any good writer in Greek, not even by Isocrates. And indeed it seems to be nothing but an insignificant jingle, which could not please the ears any more than the understanding of such men as the Athenians.

As to the other figure, called by the Halicarnassian παρίσωσις, which makes the sentences, or their members, nearly of equal length, and gives the same structure and form of compofition to the words, there is no doubt a certain concinnity and prettynefs in it, which may pleafe, if not too often repeated; but which I think is ufed much too frequently by Ifocrates, as appears from the examples I have given. And if the reader wants more examples of the fame kind, he may have many more of them in Dionyfius's differtation upon Ifocrates, cap. 14.; where he fhews a moft wonderful fimilarity of ftile, ftudied by Ifocrates, both in the found, and in the antithefis of words to one another. But he obferves, that of thefe pretty little ornaments he abated much in the laft orations he wrote, when he was become old and his judgment more mature.

But in his earlier fpeeches, particularly one περι της ειρηνης, where he has compared the manners of the Athenians of his time with thofe of their anceftors, an oration, upon which he valued himfelf very much, he has fhewn that he abounds in thofe puerile ornaments of the παρισωσις and παρομοιωσις, and particularly the laſt, beginning his periods, or the members of them, with the ſame words; ſuch Εκεινοι μεν γαρ—'ημεις δε,—Τουτο μεν, and τουτο δε. And that he abounds alſo very much in antitheſis, which, as I have already obſerved, though it be a figure relative chiefly to the ſenſe, yet has a great effect likewiſe upon the ſound, if the antithetical words are contraſted with one another in the ſame parts of the period or members of the period *.

There is another ſimilarity in the compoſition of Iſocrates, and which, I think, may be reckoned a ſpecies of the παρομοιωσις ; and that is the too frequent termination of his ſentences with a verb. This is a fault which I have elſewhere obſerved in the Latin compoſition †; and that it applies alſo to the compoſition of Iſocrates, any perſon will be convinced, who will take

---

* Περι της διυοτητος του Δημοσθενους. cap. 20. verſus finem.

† Vol. 4. book 1. chap. 11.

Chap. III. PROGRESS OF LANGUAGE. 419

the trouble to compare accurately his ſtile with that of Demoſthenes, who has much more variety in this, and in every other reſpect, than Iſocrates. It, may however, be obſerved, as an apology for Iſocrates and the Latin writers, that, by terminating the ſentence with the governing verb, the beginning and the end are often connected together, by which the ſenſe of the whole is brought altogether to the mind of the reader or hearer. But though it often ſerve this purpoſe, it ought not to be conſtantly uſed, otherwiſe it gives a tedious uniformity to the compoſition, which to me is offenſive. And yet this is the caſe of almoſt all the compoſition in Latin, both oratorial and hiſtorical. Of the practice of it in their hiſtorical ſtile, I have ſpoken in the paſſage above quoted from vol. 4th of this work. And as to the oratorial, we have but to read one oration of Cicero, to be convinced that he uſes it much too frequently; and from a paſſage in the end of his *Orator*, he very plainly tells us, that the compoſition is defective, if the period is not concluded in this way.

The passage is so remarkable, that I will give it in Cicero's words.

'Quantum autem sit apte dicere, expe-
'riri licet, si aut compositi oratoris bene
'structam collocationem dissolvas permu-
'tatione verborum. corrumpatur enim to-
'ta res, ut et haec nostra in Corneliana, et
'deinceps omnia: ' 'Neque me divitiae mo-
"vent, quibus omnes Africanos et Laelios
"multi venalitii mercatoresque supera-
"runt.' immuta paulum, ut sit, ' multi su-
"perarunt mercatores venalitiique;' pe-
'rierit tota res. et quae sequuntur: ' Ne-
"que vestis, aut caelatum aurum et ar-
"gentum, quo nostros veteres Marcellos
"Maximosque multi eunuchi e Syria Æ-
"gyptoque vicerunt.' Verba permuta sic,
'ut sit, ' vicerunt eunuchi e Syria Ægyp-
"toque.' Adde tertium: ' Neque vero or-
"namenta ista villarum, quibus L. Paulum
"et L. Mummium, qui rebus his urbem
"Italiamque omnem referserunt, ab ali-
"quo video perfacile Deliaco aut Syro
"potuisse superari.' fac ita, ' potuisse su-

Chap. III. PROGRESS OF LANGUAGE. 421

" perari ab aliquo Syro aut Deliaco.' Vi-
' defne, ut ordine verborum paulum com-
' mutato, iifdem verbis ftante fententia, ad
' nihilum omnia recidant cum fint ex ap-
' tis diffoluta * ?"

In this refpect, too, as well as in every other, that variety which characterifes the ftile of Demofthenes, and diftinguifhes it from every other, is preferved: For though he very often terminates his periods with a verb, as in many cafes it is no doubt proper, he likewife often concludes them with a noun, as in that little fhort period which Longinus celebrates fo much, Τουτο το ψηφισμα τον τοτε τη πολη περιστατα κινδυνον, παρελθον εποιησεν ωσπερ νεφος. p. 171. *Morelli.* And the laft fentence of his famous oration *De Corona*, is concluded with the adjective ακραν; and often he concludes with a participle, and fometimes with a pronoun or an adverb. But he always gives that place to a word fignificant of fomething principal in the pe-

---

* *Orator*, cap. 70.

riod, and tending to combine and to give an unity to the several parts of it.

There are two passages, one from Isocrates, and another from Demosthenes, both upon the same subject, and therefore very properly compared together. The subject, too, is very important, and very interesting. It is the comparison of the character and manners of the Athenians in former times, with their character at the time when Isocrates and Demosthenes lived. The passage of Isocrates upon this subject, you have in the 17th chapter of this treatise, and in the three following chapters you have a most accurate criticism upon it, where the author not only shews that the composition of Isocrates is flat and languid, and not sufficiently condensed and rounded; but he shews how it might be made better, which is the most instructive of all criticisms, and indeed it is teaching the reader, as I am persuaded he taught his scholars. And he concludes with saying, that it is full of that puerile figure above-mentioned called παρισωσις, which he says serves to divert the attention of the reader from the subject: And all his periods, he adds, are antitheses to one another, beginning, as I have said, with the words Εκεινοι μεν γαρ—then ἡμεις δε, and with a τουτο μεν, and a τουτο δε.

The passage from Demosthenes, too, upon this subject, is likewise given at length, and both for matter and stile it is wonderfully superior. And indeed I think I never read a finer composition upon any subject. There are very few periods that are figured in the same way: And he enlivens his stile greatly, both in this and his other compositions, by using some short sentences without any period at all: These are commonly interrogations, by which he excites very much the hearer or reader. At the same time he has not avoided altogether those figures of sound which Isocrates appears to have studied chiefly; for he has used them sometimes, but never where it is improper, or where they do not serve to inforce his arguments: As where he sums up what he had said of the noble actions of their ancestors, both in peace and war, he has these words: Ει δη του τα μεν Ελληνικα πιστως, τα προς τους Θεους ευσεβως· τα δ' εν αυτοις ισως διοικει, μεγαλης εικοτως επετυχετε ευδαιμονιας.

Here we have two members of the period concluded, each, with an adverb of the same termination: In the third member there is also an adverb of the same termination, but the member is concluded with the verb διοικει. And the whole period is concluded, not with a verb, as Isocrates's periods almost always are, but with the noun ευδαιμονιας. As to the matter of this composition, it does not belong to my present subject to speak of it: But I think that, in the matter, it exceeds Isocrates still more than in the stile. And I do not wonder at what the Halicarnassian says, that, he could not read the orations of Demosthenes, without feeling most sensibly all the several passions which he wants to inspire, such as fear, contempt, hatred, anger, envy, pity, and the rest. And that

Chap. III. PROGRESS OF LANGUAGE. 425

he was agitated by a kind of enthusiasm, like those who were initiated into the mysteries of the great Goddess. And if we, he adds, so far removed from those times, and having no concern or interest in them, are so much moved by his speeches, how must the Athenians and other Greeks, living at that time, and so much interested in the affairs which are the subject of those orations, have been affected by them, when spoken by him who is allowed by every body to have excelled so much in Action, the first quality of an orator*. It was his excellence in that art, which made Æschines observe to those who so much admired his oration *De Corona*, when it was read to them, that they would have admired it very much more if they had heard him pronounce it †.

* Ibid. cap. 22.

† See p. 321. of this volume, and Cicero, *De Oratore*, lib. 3. cap. 56. where the story is told at some length.

VOL. VI.   3 H

He next compares two orations of Plato and of Demosthenes, both on the same subject, namely, the praise of the Athenians. The oration of Plato is a λογος επιταφιος, that is, a speech in praise of those who had fallen in battle, fighting for their country. It is contained in that dialogue of Plato called *Menexenus*. See chapter 25th and following of the Halicarnassian, where we have a very severe criticism of the stile of Plato, shewing that he is full of those pretty little ornaments first used by Georgias, as he tells us, of *antithesis* and *parisosis*, for the sake of which he has made his stile much too diffuse, and enervated the sense of it: And he gives an example in this period: Εργων γαρ ευ πραχθεντων, λογω καλως ρηθεντι μνημη και κοσμος τοις πραξασι γινεται παρα των ακουσαντων; where he observes, that in this short period there are three words that are παρισα to other three, that is, of the same form and structure, each to each. Then he says that the words in the end, viz. παρα των ακουσαντων, add nothing to the sense, but serve only to give a termina-

Chap. III. PROGRESS OF LANGUAGE. 427

tion to the period which pleased the ear of Plato*. In another passage of this panegyric he observes these words, τυχικαμενε δι και ναυπηγησαμενη, κεδιξαμενη τον πολεμον; where we have three words with a triple rhyme to one another. Such rhymes, as I have observed, are not uncommon in Greek; but in good composition the words should be separated from one another, and should not be put in any remarkable place, such as the beginning or end of a period, or member of a period, so that they may appear to answer to one another. And he has given us another flower of Plato in these words: Ως ενεκα και πρωτον, και υστατον, και δια παντος, πασαν παντος προθυμιαν, πειρασθε εχειν; where there is a strange gingle of words. But, in order to do all justice to Plato, he has given us the conclusion of this speech at full length †, which, he says, is very justly admired: And indeed, for the matter it is much better than the

---

* Cap. 25. and 26.
† Cap. 30.

rest of this oration; for there is a great deal of excellent morality in it, and much said in praise of a virtuous and a noble death, such as that of those men. But Dionysius says that it is more political than rhetorical; I would add, more philosophical: And his stile favours more of the Socratic dialogue than of public speaking. And, upon the whole, I am of opinion, that it is only in philosophy and dialogue-writing that Plato excels; and I think Dionysius very properly applies to him what Jupiter in Homer says to Venus:

Ου σοι, τεκνον εμοι, δεδοται πολεμηια εργα·
Αλλα συ γ' ιμεροεντα μετερχευ εργα γαμοιο.

As the professed purpose of this work is to shew the excellency of Demosthenes's stile, by comparing him with other famous orators, (for, says he, every thing is best known by comparison with other things of the same kind*), he gives us a long passage from Demosthenes's oration περι

* Cap. 30.

Chap. III. Progress of Language. 429

στιφανοι, upon a very fine subject, and not unlike the subject treated of by Plato in his λογος ιπιταφιος, I mean the praise of the Athenians*. It is a most wonderful composition, and I cannot praise it higher, than by saying that I think it the finest to be found in Demosthenes. It is, both for the matter and stile, very much superior to the passage from Plato, which he sets against it, and which, he says, is the best thing in that funeral oration. There is none of those puerile ornaments in it which I have observed in Plato, but a great variety in the structure of the periods, which are now and then intermixed with short interrogations; and sometimes a single word makes a sentence by itself. And, in the whole of the composition, there is a tone of public speaking and of contention (for he was pleading against Æschines) which distinguishes it from all other kinds of stile, even from the stile of a panegyrical oration; I say the tone of public speaking,

* Cap. 31.

which is felt by every body when the orator speaks his orations: But I think it is to be perceived even in the written compofition of Demofthenes*.

But to return from Plato to Ifocrates.— This author has taken another way, befides thofe I have mentioned, to fmooth and polifh his ftile; and that is, by avoiding moft anxioufly the gaping of vowels upon one another. And, in general, I think Plutarch gives a very good account of the eloquence of Ifocrates in the end of what he has written *De Gloria Athenienfium*, where he fays that he fpent his time in contriving Αντιθεσις, παρισωσις, and what he calls ὁμοιοτητα that is, words of like flection, joining and foldering words together, and fmoothing his periods as it were with a chiffel and a plane.

From what I have faid, it is evident that Ifocrates ftudied very much the fimilarity

---

* See the Halicarnaffian upon the fubject of Demofthenes, cap. 22.

of found in his compoſition. And I am perſuaded he was a man of ſuch a genius, that he ſpent a great part of the many years which he employed in writing his famous oration, the Panegyric, in ſtudying ornaments of that kind. And I think it was natural enough that a little minded man, ſuch as Iſocrates appears to have been, ſhould employ himſelf in ſtudying thoſe puerile ornaments, more than the matter, or the real beauties of compoſition: For that he was ſuch a man, we muſt believe, if the ſtory be true which Plutarch tells of him in the paſſage above quoted, that being aſked, when he was very old, How he lived? As well, ſays he, as a man can do, that is above ninety years of age, and thinks death the greateſt of all evils.

But Demoſthenes had a genius above thoſe puerile ornaments, which can only pleaſe boys or vulgar men. There is therefore very little of the ſimilarity of ſound, of either of the two kinds I have mentioned, to be found in Demoſthenes.

But, in place of those gingling ornaments, and that uniformity of composition so frequent in Isocrates, he studied what was of much greater value, the music of his language, and laboured to grace his composition with *a noble melody and dignified rhythm*, to use an expression of the Halicarnassian, giving it also that variety which, as the same author observes, must be studied in the melody and rhythm, as well as in every other part of the composition*.

The Halicarnassian, in his treatise *De Admiranda vi dicendi in Demosthene*, has told us, what I think must certainly be true, of a musical language, such as the Greek, that with respect to the sound of the composition, nothing has such a power to affect the ears as the rhythm †:

* See vol. 2d. p. 382.

† Ου γαρ δη φαυλον τι πραγμα ρυθμος εν λογοις, ουδε προσθηκης τινος μοιρας εχον ουκ αναγκαιας. αλλ' ει δει τ'αληθες, 'ως εμη δοξα, ειπειν, 'απαντων κυριωτατον των γοητευειν δυναμενων, καλων τας ακοας.—Cap. 39.

Chap. III. PROGRESS OF LANGUAGE. 433

For in all mufic, whether it be the diaftematic mufic, that is, what we commonly call mufic, or the mufic of language, the rhythm is moft powerful, and is what affects very much, not only the ears, but the mind ; for, according to the antient faying, ' Rhythm is all in mufic *.'

I have faid a great deal of both the melody and the rhythm of the Greek language, in the fourth chapter of the fecond book of this volume, where I have endeavoured to fhew, that though we have no practice of them in our language, nor indeed hardly an idea how they fhould be applied to language and make it fo beautiful, yet we ought not for that to deny that they exifted in the Greek language, and made a great part of the beauty of compofition in Greek. And I will only add here, that the admirers of modern times, or rather of themfelves, ought to confider, that the antients were men much fuperior

---

* Παν παρα τοις μουσικοις 'ο ρυθμος.

VOL. VI.   3 I

to us in all the arts, and particularly in the great art of language, the greateſt, in my opinion, as well as the moſt uſeful of all the human arts. If it were not ſo, we ſhould be much to blame in paſſing ſo many of the moſt docile years of our life in the ſtudy of their language and arts: and a claſſical education, for promoting of which ſo many foundations have been made by our anceſtors of ſchools and colleges and univerſities, would be a great abſurdity. Now, if this ſuperiority be admitted, we ought not to be ſurpriſed that the antient languages are not only ſuperior to any modern in the grammatical part, which is ſo much more perfect in them than in the modern languages, that we could not have had an idea of its perfection, if their grammatical art had not come down to us exemplified by their writings, but alſo in the ſound, which could not be tranſmitted to us as their grammar has been, and of which, therefore, we never can have the practice, though we may learn a little of the ſcience of it, by what ſome of their authors have told us; as much, at leaſt, as may ſatisfy us of the poſſibility of its exiſtence. For my own part, the more I ſtudy antient books, and the more I live in the antient world, where I live as much, or rather more, than in the modern, the more I am convinced of the benefit of a claſſical education, without which, I think, no man can excel in any art or ſcience of any value, nor can act a great or noble part in life *.

Every work of art, though in every other reſpect perfect, yet if it want variety, can never pleaſe. Now Demoſthenes has made his compoſition ſo various, that by variety itſelf he has diſtinguiſhed it more from the compoſition of other authors, than by any other mark; for in moſt authors there is ſome word, or phraſe, or particular turn of expreſſion, which marks their ſtile, in the ſame manner as any ſtrong feature diſtinguiſhes a face. But

---

* See farther upon this ſubject, p. 147. and following of this volume; alſo p. 165. and 166.

there is nothing of this kind in Demosthenes; for there are no such words or phrases in him. There is nothing like the *esse videatur* of Cicero, with which he concludes so many of his periods *: And the general colour and complexion of his stile is as various as possible; for sometimes he composes in long periods of many members, and sometimes in short periods; the members of his periods are also of different lengths, and variously joined together; and though it be true, what Cicero says of him, that he has hardly said any thing without some particular turn or figure of one kind or another †, yet these are so varied, that he has no figure recurring so often as to distinguish his stile from that of any other author; and you will hardly find in him two periods together of the same form and structure. And there is a considerable part

---

* See what I have said of this clausule of Cicero's periods, p. 273. .

† Nullus fere ab eo locus sine quadam conformatione sententiae dicitur. *De perfecto Oratore.*

of his compofition that is not in periods; for though there can be no good rhetorical compofition without periods, more or fewer, yet it would be a fault if the whole compofition was in periods; for it would be too uniform, wanting that variety, without which no work of art, as I have often had occafion to obferve, can be beautiful. And this is a fault which I obferve in Ifocrates, in whofe orations you have hardly any compofition without a period. Such a ftile I call declamatory; for there may be declamation in the found of the compofition, as well as in the words and the figure. Now Demofthenes has avoided that, by throwing in, among his periods, fhort fentences, commonly in the form of an interrogation, by which he excites the attention of his hearers, and brings home to them the argument more forcibly. The fhort fentence πολλου γε και δει, he ufes very frequently; and he fometimes makes the fingle word μηδαμως ftand for a fentence*. At o-

* P. 156. *Ed. Morelli.*

ther times he throws the single word, disjoined from all the rest, into the middle of a sentence, as in the word ὅρος, in the oration *De Corona* *. And, in the same oration, he throws into the middle of a period these two words, ἀκούεις, Αἰσχίνη? unconnected with the rest †. In this way he not only varies his composition agreeably; but he takes from it altogether the air of declamation, inforcing his arguments as if he were in private conversation with his hearers; which makes his orations much more persuasive than any declamation can be.

The reader ought not to be surprised that I have dwelt so long upon the sound of the language in Demosthenes's orations; which he has varied not only by melody and rhythm most agreeably, as the Halicarnassian thinks, nor by composition

---

* P. 179. *Ed. Morelli.*
† Ibid. p. 156.

only in periods, but by that variety of arrangement of his words, which so perfect a language as the Greek admitted, but which in him is more remarkable than in any other Greek author; and which, I am perfuaded, muſt have very much pleaſed the ears of his hearers. Now, to pleaſe the ears of thoſe he ſpeaks to, is a great part of the art of an orator: For, as I have obſerved elſewhere*, through the ear the mind is not a little affected, even of the beſt judges: And as to the people, they may be ſaid to be *led by the ears:* And accordingly the ſtatue of the Gallic Hercules, who, it ſeems, was their God of eloquence, was repreſented, as Lucian deſcribes him, drawing the multitude after him by a chain, which reached from his mouth to their ears †. How much the order and arrangement of words was ſtudied among the Romans, I have proved from a paſſage of Cicero quoted a-

---

* Vol. 3d. p. 63.

† Lucian's treatiſe of the *Gallic Hercules.*

bove*: Nor can we suppose that it was less studied by Demosthenes, though I think I have shewn, in what I have written upon the composition of the antients, that he did not study it for the pleasure of the ear merely, but likewise for the sense, which is more forcibly conveyed by one arrangement of the words than by another †.

The pleasure which an oration gives to the ear, must depend upon the pronunciation of it: And therefore I consider Demosthenes, not as a writer only of orations, but as a speaker of them. It was in this that he excelled more, I believe, than in any other quality of an orator. Such was the opinion of his enemy Æschines, who certainly was a very good speaker himself; and yet he acknowledged the superiority

---

* P. 420.

† See the Dissertation on the Composition of the Antients, annexed to volume 2d. of this work, particularly p. 572.

Chap. III. Progress of Language. 441

of Demosthenes in that branch of the art *. Nor would Demosthenes have said that Action, of which pronunciation is the chief part, was the first, the second, and the third quality of an orator †, if he had not himself excelled in it. He learned by his own experience, as well as by the advice of his friend the player ‡, that the best composition, if not well pronounced, could not have the effect it ought to have upon the hearers: And I have no doubt but that, in his subterraneous retreat, his chief application was to form his voice and gesture §. There must have been a beauty in the pronunciation of such compositions as his, with all the various changes of voice, of countenance, and of gesture, that the subject required, and, joined to all these, the melody and rhythm of the

---

* See p. 425. of this volume.
† Ibid. p. 206.
‡ Ibid. p. 333.
§ Ibid. p. 329.

Greek language, (with the agreeable variety, too, which we are told he gave them *), such as we can hardly form an idea of, but which we are sure, from the effects it produced, must have pleased and moved his audience exceedingly. The written orations of his, that have come down to us, we may consider as only the carcases of his orations, without that life and animation which his Action must have given them. And it is only the authors who spoke their orations, as Demosthenes did, not those who, like Isocrates, did no more than write what others spoke, that I dignify with the name of orators: For the speaking orator may be compared to Daedalus, who, it is said, gave life and motion to his statues; whereas, those who only write speeches, are like our statuaries, who make statues without life or animation.

Whether Cicero excelled or not in this principal quality of an orator, we do not know with any certainty; but I should

---

* See p. 161. and 162. of this vol. and p. 382. of vol. 2.

rather think that he did not: For none of the cotemporary writers speak of his being eminent in action, not even he himself, who is never deficient in his own praise; nor does Quintilian, who praises him so much, speak of his eminence in that way; and Cicero himself tells us, that it was quite neglected by the orators of his time*. When this was the case, I do not think that it is probable that it was much attended to by Cicero.

As to composition, I think there is no comparison betwixt him and Demosthenes: Nor do I think that he deserves at all the character which Quintilian gives of Demosthenes: ' Tanta vis in eo, tam densa ' omnia et quibusdam nervis intenta sunt, ' tam nihil otiosum is decendi modus, ut

---

* Lib. 3. *De Oratore*, cap. 56. where, after saying a good deal of the beauty of action in an orator, and the effect it had upon the hearers, he adds, ' Haec eo ' dico pluribus, quod genus hoc totum oratores, qui ' sunt veritatis ipsius actores, reliquerunt; imitatores ' autem veritatis histriones occupaverunt.' Where the reader may observe, that the distinction is very well laid down betwixt an orator and a player.

'nec quid redundet, invenias *.' Now, this denfity or conftriction, if I may ufe the expreffion, in the form and ftructure of the periods of Demofthenes, which have nothing in them redundant or diffluent, and are equally remote from the loofe flow of the hiftorical ftile, and the pompous and panegyrical periods of Ifocrates, is wanting in Cicero. He is copious, indeed, but he is too much fo. He has a great deal of the *opimum* and *adipatum genus dicendi*†: For he has much flefh, but it is loofe, not firm, nor of a good colour. And though he ftudied Demofthenes much, and even tranflated fome orations of his; yet he appears to me to have formed himfelf more upon the model of Ifocrates, and to have imitated him particularly in the figures of found, and even to have exceeded him, as I think I have fhewn. And indeed there is a rhyming, or rather a gingling of founds, not fet at

---

* Quintilian, lib. 10. cap. 1.

† Lib. *De Oratore perfecto.*

Chap. III. PROGRESS OF LANGUAGE. 445

some distance from one another, as in Isocrates, but joined together *, such as I am persuaded would not have been endured in Athens, not even by the boys there, though it is likely that in Rome he was admired for them, and clapped in the manner that we applaud our players. And there is in his oration for Milo, (one of the most laboured, I believe, he ever wrote) a string of *antitheses* and *parisoses*, upon the subject of self-defence, such as is not to be found in Isocrates.

It is evident, however, that Quintilian prefers him to Demosthenes, and to every other orator of Greece. But it appears to me, that it had become a piece of national vanity among the Romans, as I have elsewhere observed †, to prefer their own writers to the Greek. This began as early as the days of Cicero, who has not scrupled to say, that his own countrymen had made greater discoveries than the Greeks;

* P. 304 of this volume.

† Vol. 5th. p. 225.

and what they had taken from the Greeks, they had improved *. But, at the time when Quintilian wrote, the study and imitation of the Greek writers appears to have been, in a great measure, laid aside among them; and their own authors were set up as standards of perfection in every kind of writing; Cicero in oratory, Virgil in poetry, and Livy in history.

But matters had not gone so far in the days of Cicero; nor do I believe that there was then in Rome a man of any taste or genius, who preferred Cicero to Demosthenes: Nor was Cicero's stile approved of by the critics of that age. His friend Brutus, and likewise Calvus, used the freedom to find fault with his composition, even to himself; and both the Asiniuses did the same †. Cornelius Nepos, likewise, who is

---

* Tuscal. Quaest. lib. 1. *in principio*. See what I have further said of the national vanity of the Romans, p. 281. of this volume.

† Quint. lib. 12. cap. 1.

himself a correct and chaste writer, differed so much from him in judgment of stile, as Cicero himself tells us, that he disapproved very much even of what Cicero thought best in his own writings. These critics thought that his stile had not the true Attic colour, and was not suited to please a people, to whose taste Cicero himself bears this testimony, that, ' eorum
' semper fuit prudens sincerumque judi-
' cium, nihil ut possent nisi incorruptum
' audire et elegans *.' They thought his stile had the Asiatic tumor, and was florid but not pure, nor what they call *sincere*. In short it was of that taste which, as Cicero himself tells us, prevailed in Caria, Phrygia, and Mysia, but which the Rhodians, though separated from these people only by a narrow sea, disapproved of, and which the Greeks, particularly the Athenians, utterly rejected †.

But I have said enough, and perhaps more than enough, in another part of this

* *De perfecto Oratore.*
† Ibid.

volume, to shew that Cicero, as an orator, cannot be compared with Demosthenes, who, I agree with the Halicarnassian, was the greatest of all the antient orators, and therefore the greatest orator that ever has been. and the greatest that ever will be: For, as I have observed elsewhere *, we have not materials in the modern languages, of which it would be possible to compose such orations as those of sthenes, any more than it would be possible of such rough stones as we have in this country, to build temples such as those of Athens were, built of Penthelic marble. As, therefore, he is the perfection of the rhetorical art, it was proper that I should explain, as well as I was able, all the virtues of an orator which he possesses. I have for him an enthusiastical admiration, such as the Halicarnassian seems to have had †; for I have studied him more than any other Greek or Latin author; and he has been

---

* P. 320. and following of this volume.

† Ibid. p. 424. & 425.

my companion in my journies for many years. I have alfo tranflated a great deal from him, and in fhort have formed my ftile upon him, and have made it as like to his as a didactic ftile, fuch as mine, fhould be to a rhetorical. This, I know, makes my ftile very unlike the fafhionable ftile of this age; but I flatter myfelf that it is not unlike the ftile of Milton, the beft Englifh writer, in my opinion, both in verfe and profe, and who, I have no doubt, formed his ftile, particularly in his fpeeches, by the imitation of Demofthenes.

I will conclude this chapter, with recommending to the reader, if he defires perfectly to underftand the beauty of Demofthenes's compofition, to ftudy what the Halicarnaffian has written upon the antient orators, and particularly his treatife *De admiranda vi dicendi in Demofthene*, which, both for the matter and ftile, I think, is the beft of his critical works. He is, of all the writers upon criticifm, the best teacher I ever read; for he not only shews you what is ill written, and gives you the reasons why it is so, but he likewise shows you how it may be better written, than which nothing can be more instructive. I know no author of any reputation, of whose works the manuscripts are more incorrect; and in several of his works, particularly his treatise upon Demosthenes, as I have observed *, they are, in many places, mutilated and imperfect. But there is one use the Greek scholar may make, even of the defects of the manuscripts or of the printed editions; and that is to exercise his talents of criticism, by trying to anticipate the corrections made from the Vatican manuscript, or by such excellent scholars, as Henry Stephen, Sylburgius, and Wolfius, before he looks to their conjectures at the bottom of the page. It will be for a scholar, an agreeable, and I think not an illiberal amusement.

* P. 404.

I will only add one observation more upon the ſtile of Demoſthenes, which I do not think has been made by the Halicarnaſſian, and it is this: That of the three kinds of eloquence, the Deliberative, the Judicial, and the Epideictic, he appears only to have practiſed the two firſt. This made him perfectly maſter of the ſtile of theſe two, which he has practiſed without any mixture of the Epideictic, and of thoſe figures with which the Epideictic abounds, ſuch as the *pariſoſis, paronomaſia, antitheſis,* and *like endings,* by which the ear may be agreeably entertained; but the ſtile will want entirely the nerves and the force which we have both in the matter and ſtile of the deliberative and judicial orations of Demoſthenes. And this makes the ſtile of Demoſthenes more the ſtile of buſineſs than that of any other orator I know; for buſineſs muſt be treated in the ſtile of buſineſs, not in the pompous ſtile of declamation. When ſuch is the ſtile, we are more apt to admire the orator, and to be pleaſed and entertained than convinced by his arguments; and in narrative, that ſtile is ſo far from being convincing, that it rather diſpoſes us to believe that the ſtory told by the orator, is a work of fancy and imagination.

CHAP.

CHAP. IV.

Of Lord Mansfield's oration pronounced at Oxford upon the subject of Demosthenes speech, De Corona.—*The greater part of it lost by the fire which burnt his house some years ago.*—*The whole of what remains not translated from the Latin, but only some observations made upon it.*—*First observation is, That Demosthenes insists more upon the topic of the* Pulchrum *and* Honestum, *than any other orator.*—*This observation made also by Panetius the philosopher.*—*Demosthenes learned this in the groves of the academy.*—*It was particularly necessary that he should insist upon it in this oration, and it was the only way he could reconcile the Athenians to the measures he had advised.*—*He swears, that they did not err, that famous oath, by the manes of thofe that fell at Marathon, Salamis and Plataeae.—The people to be admired who liftened to fuch a topic of perfuafion, as well as the orator who ufed it.—The character of the people of Athens at that time, compared with their character in later times.—What Livy fays of them then.—2d Obfervation of Lord Mansfield, That Demofthenes has neceffarily introduced the praife of himfelf, and with it connected the praife of the Athenians, fo that he could not have made a defence, that muft have been better received by the people.—3d Obfervation of Lord Mansfield, That Demofthenes has concealed the orator under the form of a hiftory in which he has given us an account of the lofs of the liberties of Greece, by the corruption of the Daemagogues, fuch as Æfchines, in the feveral ftates of Greece.— This hiftory otherwife very curious and inftructive.—Lord Mansfield's obfervation upon the ftile of Demofthenes.—That it is as excellent as the matter, but appears not at all elaborate, and draws the attention of the reader, not to the words,* but to the matter.—This the greatest praise of stile.—He excels in concealing the art which he bestows upon his words.—This art, as he practised it, was wonderful.—But the generality of readers so carried away by the importance of the matter, as not to perceive it;— but it is perceived by the learned critic. —Æschines acknowledged his excellence in composition.—He abounds with Parentheses, which are a great beauty in a stile that is to be spoken: But the pronunciation of Parentheses must be good;— if so, they convey the meaning more forcibly than if they were connected with the rest of the sentence.—Lord Mansfield prefers the stile of Demosthenes to Cicero's.—If his discourse had been continued, he would have given examples of the puerilis fucus *of the stile of Cicero.—One given by the author, where two passages from Demosthenes and Cicero, containing the same thought, are compared.—The words both of Cicero and Demosthenes given.—Of the use my Lord Mansfield has made of his eloquence, formed upon *the model of Demosthenes ;—has made one use of it very suitable to the office of a judge.—Conclusion of the volume, with an address to my Lord Mansfield, exhorting him to bear with patience the infirmities of old age, comforting himself with the thoughts of a life so well spent.*

I should be ungrateful to a man to whom I owe many other obligations, if I did not acknowledge how much I am indebted to him for the observations I have made upon the oratory of Demosthenes. The man I mean is the Earl of Mansfield, who, before he left Oxford, made an oration upon the subject of Demosthenes speech *De Corona*, (the finest of all his speeches, in the judgment of the Halicarnassian,) in very elegant Latin, where he has shown, in a most masterly way, the great talents of an orator exhibited by Demosthenes in that speech. A great part of the manuscript, (for it is not printed, which I think it should have been), was consumed in the fire which burnt my Lord

Mansfield's house in London some years ago. With a copy of what remains of it I was favoured by my Lord Stormont, whose love and knowledge of Greek learning I have taken occasion elsewhere to mention *.

All that my Lord Mansfield has written upon this famous oration, I will not here set down; for what he has said in so good Latin, I do not chuse to say over again in worse English. I will, therefore, only take notice of some few things which he has observed on this oration.

There is one thing which he has observed and dwelt upon a good deal, as it is what distinguishes Demosthenes, more perhaps than any thing else, from every other orator; and that is, his insisting so much upon the topic of the *pulchrum* and *honestum*, the *beautiful* and *praise-worthy* in sentiments and actions. There is a good deal of this in almost all his public

* Vol. 4th, p. 336.

orations, but particularly in the one at present under our consideration, that *De Corona*. It is the noblest topic of oratory, being the noblest passion of the human mind, and furnishes arguments more persuasive to a great-minded man, than any that can be brought from what is pleasant, profitable, or even safe. This peculiarity of the oratory of Demosthenes, Panetius, the philosopher, observed, as Plutarch has informed us in his life of Demosthenes: And I have no doubt that Demosthenes, as my Lord has told us, learned from Plato this philosophy in the groves of the Academy, which we know he frequented, and where Horace learned his philosophy *. And it was a very necessary topic in this oration, where he was to defend the measures he had advised,

---

* Horace, after relating the education he got in Rome, which I think was little better than our education, adds,

'. Adjecere bonae paulo plus artis Athenae,
' Scilicet ut possem curvo dignoscere rectum,
' Atque inter sylvas Academi quaerere verum.

Epiff. 2. lib. 2. v. 43.

which had succeeded so ill; and which indeed could not be defended upon any other principle, than that the part, he advised the Athenians to act, was most honourable, and worthy of them and their ancestors; and that they would have disgraced themselves and their country, if they had acted otherwise. He has carried this so far as to say, ' That if they had
' all known what was to happen, and you
' Æschines, instead of being silent as you
' then were, had foretold every thing that
' happened, yet the Athenians ought to
' have done what they did, if they had
' any regard to their own reputation, to
' the fame of their ancestors, and to the
' testimony of posterity.' So strong an assertion as this needed some preface, and preparation of the minds of the people for it: And accordingly, he conjures them, in the name of the Gods, not to be surprised at the paradox he was to advance, but to hear him with patience and good will *.

* See the whole passage transcribed by the Halicarnassian, cap. 31. Περι της δεινοτητος του Δημοσθενους, and his excellent observations upon it, cap. 32.

And he carries it so far, as to affirm upon oath, that they did not err, when they followed his counsel, though with such ill success, swearing that famous oath, which the antient critics celebrate so much *, ' By ' the Manes of those, who perished at ' Marathon, Salamis, and Plataeae, defend- ' ing the liberties of Greece.'

Who can read this without admiring not only the orator, but the people who had suffered so much by his counsel, and yet could hear him speak thus, not only with indulgence, but even with applause. They were not then indeed such a people as when they conquered at Marathon, Salamis, and Plataeae: But they were still a noble-minded people, and much better than they were some generations after that, when Livy the Roman historian, speaking of what they did in the war betwixt the Romans and Philip of Macedon, says, ' Athenienses literis verbisque,

---

* See Taylor's notes upon the passage, p. 656. of vol. 2.

' quibus folis valent, bellum adverfus Phi-
' lippum gerebant *;' words, that I can
never read without feeling compaffion,
and fome indignation againft the author,
who makes this reflection upon a people,
to whom the Romans owed, not only all
their arts and learning, but all the virtue
they had in later times, and to whom the
inhabitants of Europe, at this day, may be
faid to be indebted for all the arts and
fciences they poffefs: For if Xerxes had
fucceeded in his enterprife upon Greece,
which muft have happened but for the
Athenians, it appears to me that we fhould
have been little better than favages at this
day.—But to return to Demofthenes's o-
ration.

Another obfervation of Lord Manf-
field's is, That Demofthenes has introduced into this oration, with great propriety,
not only the praife of his own conduct in
public affairs, without which he never
could have defended Ctefiphon, who was

*Livii, lib. 31. cap. 44.

accused for having bestowed upon him a crown which he did not deserve; but also the praise of the Athenians, without which he never could have reconciled them to the measures he had advised them to follow, and which in the end proved so fatal. And, besides, nothing could make his cause more favourable than to connect his defence with the praise of his judges; and in such a way, as not to appear to be mere flattery, but belonging to the cause.

Another excellent observation of Lord Mansfield's as to the matter of this oration is, That Demosthenes under the historian conceals the orator: For he has given us what may be called a history of Greece at that period, where he shows that the liberties of Greece were lost by the corruption of the Demagogues in the several states, who acted a part very different from what he acted in Athens, and were truly the mercenaries of Philip, such as he says Æschines was. Besides its importance in the cause, I think it is a very curious and instructive piece of history, showing us from what small beginnings great changes in human affairs may be brought about: For the loss of the liberties of Greece took its rise from a trifling quarrel betwixt the Amphyctions, and a tribe of the Locrians about some acres of ground, which the Locrians took possession of and cultivated, but which, the Amphyctions said, were consecrated to Apollo. This quarrel, Demosthenes says, was instigated by Æschines for the purpose of bringing Philip into Greece; and which accordingly happened, the Amphyctions having called him to assist them against the Locrians.—And so much for my Lord Mansfield's observations upon the matter of this oration of Demosthenes; about which, what is preserved of Lord Mansfield's discourse is chiefly employed.

As to the stile, he has said what is certainly true, That it is as excellent as the matter, being most chaste and correct, having nothing wanting in it, nor any thing superfluous or redundant; and without those *pigmenta*, or that *puerilis fucus*, as he very well expresses it, of which I have given so many examples from the stile of Isocrates. He farther says of the stile, that, ' Demostheni, rerum magnitudine ' occupato, non vacabat esse diserto.' And it is certainly true, that, even reading him, we are so much carried away by the weight of the matter, that we give but little attention to the words; and this must have been much more the case of those who heard him pronounce his orations. Now I hold it to be one of the greatest praises of stile, not to draw the attention of the reader or hearer from the matter to the words. At the same time, from what the Halicarnassian has told us, we are sure that he studied his words very much, not only the arrangement of them, and the composition in periods, but even their rhythm and melody [*]. But, as my Lord has observed, he excelled, more than

---

[*] See p. 300. of this volume, and several other passages where I have spoken of the melody and rhythm of the Greek language.

any orator ever did, in that greatest art of a speaker or writer, the concealing of art. And therefore, though he laboured his words very much, the weight of his matter and the force of his arguments were such, that he seemed to the generality of his hearers or readers to be so much taken up with the great affairs, which were the subject of his orations, that he gave no attention at all to the words, further than to convey his meaning. But the learned critic will perceive a worderful art in the order and arrangement of these words, by which not only the ear is much pleased, but the sense more forcibly conveyed, than it could otherwise have been, as I think I have elsewhere shown *. His excellence in composition, his rival Æschines acknowledged. But so artificial a composition must have been very well pronounced, otherwise it would have been hardly intelligible; for it abounds with parentheses,

---

* Dissertation on the composition of Demosthenes, annexed to vol. 2d of this work.

some of them very long, and with parentheses within parentheses, as the Halicarnassian has observed. Now a parenthesis, properly introduced and well pronounced, I hold to be one of the greatest beauties of stile, and particularly of what is written to be spoken. For it not only gives a density and compactness to the matter, but, by being detached from the rest of the sentence, it draws the attention of the hearers the more. It should therefore contain some thing worthy of that attention; and, if it be also pronounced with a proper variation of the voice, suitable to the subject matter, will give great force and weight to the meaning of the whole sentence.

My Lord Mansfield agrees perfectly with me in preferring Demosthenes to Cicero. And if the rest of his discourse had been preserved, I am persuaded, we should have had many proofs of that preference. I will supply this want, as well as I can, by giving one example from Cicero of the *pigmenta*, and the *puerilis fucus* of his stile, compared with the simplicity and solidity

of the ſtile of Demoſthenes upon the same subject. The passage in Cicero is taken from his famous oration *pro Milone*; and I have no doubt, that it was imitated from a similar passage in Demoſthenes, but made very much worſe in my judgment, and really *puerile*, though there are, I know, who will think it much amplified and adorned. The passage of Demoſthenes is in this oration *De Corona*, where he complains of the injuſtice that Æſchines did him, by imputing to him the ill ſucceſs of the war againſt Philip: ' If a man,' ſays he, ' commit injuſtice willingly, he is a
' proper object of anger and puniſhment.
' If he err unwillingly, he is to be forgi-
' ven and not puniſhed. But if, neither
' committing injuſtice nor erring, he en-
' gage in public affairs, manage them in
' the way that ſeems beſt to all, but do not
' ſucceed, and be with the reſt of the citi-
' zens involved in the general calamity of
' the ſtate, him it is unjuſt to reproach
' or abuſe, inſtead of grieving with him
' for the common misfortune.' Then follows the passage which Cicero has imitat-

ed. 'This,' says he, 'must appear not
'only to be the law of Athens, but of Na-
'ture herself, which she has established by
'laws unwritten and by the manners of
'men*.'

* The words are, 'Φανησεται τοινυν ταυτα παντα
'ουτως, ου μονον εν τοις νομοις, αλλα και 'η φυσις αυτη τοις
'αγραφοις νομιμοις, και τοις ανθρωπινοις ηθεσι, διοριζειν.'
p. 573. of volume 2. of Taylor's edition. I recommend to the reader to study the whole passage in the
original, beginning at the preceding page with the
words, 'Βουλομαι δε των ιδιων απαλλαγεις, &c. and going on to about the middle of the following page;
and he will there see two examples of long parentheses, very properly, I think, thrown in; which
I find marked in Taylor's translation, but not in the o-
riginal, as I think they should have been: So that,
unless the reader be a good Greek scholar, and well
acquainted with the stile of Demosthenes, he will be o-
bliged to cast his eye down to the translation, which I
always very unwillingly do. And in general it may
be observed, that if a composition, so artificial as that
of Demosthenes, be not carefully pointed, it is hardly
intelligible to a modern reader; though, as points were
not used in the antient manuscripts, and not even the
division of the words in some of the most antient, the
readers of those times would by custom learn easily to
make sense of what we cannot understand without
much difficulty.

Chap. IV. Progress of Language. 469

I will now give the words of Cicero, which I have given elsewhere*, but will here repeat. They are upon the subject of self-defence, a law as common as that which Demosthenes has mentioned, but which Cicero has expressed in a manner very different. His words are, ' *Est e-*
'*nim, judices, hæc non scripta sed nata lex:*
'*Quam non didicimus, accepimus, legimus;*
'*verum ex Natura ipsa arripuimus, hausi-*
'*mus, expressimus: Ad quam non docti sed*
'*facti, non instituti sed imbuti sumus.*' Here the artifice of the composition is such, that it must draw the attention of the hearer or reader as much or more to the words than to the matter: For there is a string of antitheses, in which the words are made to answer exactly to one another both by their position and in the forms of the case or tense, but also in the sound: For they rhyme to one another, and we not only have single rhymes but double, of two syllables; and with all this vain ostentation of art, this *puerilis fucus*,

* Vol. 3. p. 88. see also p. 303. of this volume.

there is no more meaning expreſſed than what Demoſthenes has given in a few plain words, put together in the moſt ſimple manner.

Upon this ſo perfect model of eloquence, my Lord Mansfield formed a chaſte and correct ſtile of ſpeaking, ſuitable to buſineſs, and particularly the buſineſs of a judge; to whoſe office it belongs, not only to determine controverſies betwixt man and man, but to ſatisfy the parties that they have got juſtice, and thereby give eaſe and contentment to their minds, which I hold to be one of the great uſes of law. In this my Lord Mansfield, as it is well known, was ſo ſucceſsful, that even the loſing party commonly acknowledged the juſtice of his decrees: And I knew myſelf one example of a man, who had loſt more than one half of his fortune by a judgment of his Lordſhip's, which neverthelefs he acknowledged to be juſt.

' Having ſpent ſo many years of your
' life, more I believe than any man of

' this age, in the adminiftration of juf-
' tice, with fo much applaufe and public
' fatisfaction, I hope, my Lord, you will
' bear with patience and refignation, the
' infirmities of old age, enjoying the
' pleafure of reflecting, that you have
' employed fo long a life fo profitably
' in the fervice of your country. With
' fuch reflections, and a mind fo entire
' as your's ftill is, you may be faid to live,
' over again, your worthy life, accord-
' ing to the old faying,

' ⸻⸻⸻hoc eft
' Vivere bis, vita poffe priori frui.

' That you may live this life as long as
' you retain a mind capable of enjoying
' it, and without pain of body, fuch as
' would difturb that enjoyment, is the ear-
' neft wifh of all your friends, and of none
' more than the author of this work: For
' in the midft of all your great public oc-

' cupations, you have always found time
' to cultivate private friendship; and I
' believe no man living has enjoyed more
' the two greatest pleasures of human
' life, that of loving and being loved.'

Here I conclude, and I hope the reader will think not improperly, this volume upon the subject of Rhetoric. The next volume, with which I propose to conclude this work, will treat of Poetry, the finest of all the fine arts, if the poet be not a mere versifier, or servile copier of history or nature, but be what his name imports, a *maker*, or what may be called a *creator*, which I hold to be the greatest effort of the genius of man, showing more than any other art he practises, the *particle of divinity* that is in him. For this work I have collected a great many materials,

———————— quae———
Multa dies et multa litura coercuit;———

and, if I shall live to put these materials in order, and to finish this great work upon

Language and Stile, I think I may venture to fay, that it will be the greateft work of the kind, (whether well or ill executed, does not belong to me to determine), that has been publifhed in later times.

END OF VOLUME SIXTH.

www.ingramcontent.com/pod-product-compliance
Lightning Source LLC
Chambersburg PA
CBHW031948290426
44108CB00011B/720